Praise for *Come Home to Yourself*

"Sadhvi Bhagawati Saraswati is a great teacher of spirituality and consciousness. Her inspiring wisdom illuminates the path to healing, happiness, and inner peace."

—Deepak Chopra

"We often search for happiness outside of ourselves, but at some point, hopefully, we discover that what we've been looking for is here and now. Sadhvi Bhagawati Saraswati's Come Home to Yourself *is a masterful blend of wisdom and practicality, showing the way toward a life of inner peace, boundless joy, and spiritual freedom."*

—Prince EA

"Sadhvi Bhagawati Saraswati has crafted a beautiful, soul-stirring guide in Come Home to Yourself. *This book is a reminder that no matter where you are on your journey, you have the power to rise, to heal, and to thrive."*

—Lisa Nichols, CEO of Motivating the Masses and
featured teacher of *The Secret*

*"*In Come Home to Yourself, *Sadhvi Bhagawati Saraswati shares profound spiritual insights with clarity and compassion. This book is a gift for anyone seeking to deepen their connection with their True Self."*

—Michael Bernard Beckwith, founder and CEO of Agape International
Spiritual Center, author of *Life Visioning* and *Spiritual Liberation*,
and host of the *Take Back Your Mind* podcast

*"*Come Home to Yourself *is a treasure chest of spiritual wisdom. Sadhvi Bhagawati Saraswati's insights are keys that unlock the doors to our deepest potential and provide a profound roadmap to inner peace and self-discovery. Her words resonate with the wisdom of the ages, guiding us gently yet powerfully toward our highest selves."*

—Jack Canfield, coauthor of the *Chicken Soup for the Soul* series

"Come Home to Yourself *is a luminous guide to living a life where happiness is the foundation and miracles unfold naturally. Sadhvi Bhagawati Saraswati's profound understanding of the human heart and spirit shines through, offering readers the tools to create a life of joy and boundless possibility."*

—Marci Shimoff, *New York Times* bestselling author of
Happy for No Reason and *Chicken Soup for the Woman's Soul*

"Come Home to Yourself *is a powerful exploration of the mind-body connection and a transformative guide that aligns with the science of epigenetics and consciousness. Sadhvi Bhagawati Saraswati masterfully weaves spiritual wisdom with the science of consciousness, bridging the gap between spirituality and science. She empowers us to harness the full potential of our minds and spirits."*

—Bruce H. Lipton, PhD, stem cell biologist, epigenetic science pioneer,
and bestselling author of *The Biology of Belief, Spontaneous Evolution*
(with Steve Bhaerman), and *The Honeymoon Effect*

"Come Home to Yourself *by Sadhvi Bhagawati Saraswati is a profound invitation to rediscover the depths of our inner world. Through her compassionate teachings, she illuminates a path where mindfulness, love, and spiritual wisdom converge. This book serves as a powerful guide for those seeking healing, purpose, and the courage to live authentically, reminding us that true peace is found within."*

—James R. Doty, MD, professor and author of
Into the Magic Shop and *Mind Magic*

"Come Home to Yourself *is a profound exploration of the human experience. Sadhvi Bhagawati Saraswati offers wisdom that helps us navigate relationships and life with greater understanding and love."*

—John Gray, author of *Men are from Mars, Women are from Venus*

"Come Home to Yourself *is a profound and beautiful guide to discovering the love and divinity within. Sadhvi Bhagawati Saraswati's wisdom is truly extraordinary—her ability to bridge the sacred teachings of the East with the needs and hearts of the West is unparalleled. Her words resonate like a sacred invitation to come back to the essence of who we truly are."*

—Arielle Ford, author of *The Soulmate Secret*

"Come Home to Yourself *is a deeply nourishing and insightful guide for the soul, filled with Sadhvi Bhagawati Saraswati's profound wisdom, sincerity, and compassion. Her teachings are both inspiring and grounding, offering a clear and direct path toward inner peace and self-realization. This book is an essential companion for anyone seeking to reconnect with their true self and live a life of purpose, grace, and spiritual fulfillment."*

—Seane Corn, author of *Revolution of the Soul*

"Come Home to Yourself *offers a gentle yet profound guide to understanding the purpose of life and discovering our true, infinite selves. Through personal insights and spiritual wisdom, Sadhvi shows how meditation and spiritual practices can help us overcome the obstacles of the mind, body, and emotions, allowing the divine flow of universal intelligence to transform our lives. An inspiring and practical book for both novice and advanced spiritual seekers."*

—Dawson Church, bestselling author of *Spiritual Intelligence*

"Sadhvi Bhagawati Saraswati's Come Home to Yourself *is a beacon of light in the journey toward self-realization. Her teachings gently guide us to discover the divine within, leading to a life of joy and fulfillment."*

—Deva Premal & Miten, Grammy Award-nominated musicians

"Come Home to Yourself *is a sacred dance of wisdom and grace. Sadhvi Bhagawati Saraswati's teachings are like a flowing river, guiding us back to the ocean of our true selves.*"

—Shiva Rea, founder of Samudra Global School of Living Yoga

"Come Home to Yourself *by Sadhvi Bhagawati Saraswati is a must-read book for every woman committed to living in alignment with her highest truth. Sadhvi's compassionate insights and timeless teachings speak directly to the heart of every woman seeking inner peace, self-realization, and the courage to live authentically. Whether you're navigating relationships or personal challenges, or searching for your highest purpose, this book offers the answers that will inspire you to awaken to the fullness of who you truly are.*"

—Claire Zammit, PhD, founder of WomanCenteredCoaching.com

"*Sadhviji was born in Los Angeles and has lived for almost thirty years in India as a devotee of Truth. If you let her sit with you and share stories from her evening gatherings, I firmly believe you will gain profound insight into your own life. This book is an entertaining and divine gift that helped me feel oneness with all.*"

—Gurmukh Kaur Khalsa, cofounder and director of the
Golden Bridge Yoga Center and author of *Eight Human
Talents* and *Bountiful, Beautiful, Blissful*

COME
HOME
to Yourself

TO HIS HOLINESS *Pujya Swami Chidanand Saraswatiji,*
who showed me the path to my true self and through whose
blessings I am now able to show the path to so many others.
It is not easy for a world-renowned Hindu monk to create
the space for a white, American woman to step into spiritual
leadership in India. Not only have you created the path for
me, but through me you have also lit the way for countless
other women of all races and religions to break stained-glass
ceilings and walls and step into their highest purpose.

COME
HOME
to Yourself

SIMPLE ANSWERS TO LIFE'S
ESSENTIAL QUESTIONS

SADHVI BHAGAWATI SARASWATI

MANDALA

San Rafael Los Angeles London

CONTENTS

INTRODUCTION   11

FROM HOLLYWOOD TO THE HIMALAYAS   17

Part 1: The Purpose of Life   25

Connecting to the Divine   28

Knowing and Finding the Purpose of Human Life   37

Success and Spiritual Development   44

The Path of Spirituality   50

Looking for Something Versus Running Away   56

Part 2: Our Minds   61

Calming and Understanding the Wandering Mind   63

Helpful Tools for Our Spiritual Journey   68

Breaking Out of Negative Patterns   76

The Mind and Conditioning   83

Withdrawing the Senses   86

Part 3: Our Emotions   91

Using Anger as a Positive Tool for Action   93

How to Deal with Disappointment   101

Overcoming Fear and Anxiety   104

Overcoming Temptations   116

Nonjudgment   122

Compassion   125

Love   132

How to Deal with Loss   141

Desires and Attachment to the Fruit of Our Actions   152

Part 4: Spiritual Practices   163

Meditation   165

Renunciation   176

Part 5: Our World   181

Living Human Values in Our Daily Lives   183

Appreciating Human Diversity   187

Living as Mindfully and Harmlessly as Possible   189

Privilege and Responsibility   203

Part 6: Spirituality Throughout Our Lives   213

Creating Change   215

Dharmic Relationships   222

Raising Spiritual Children   227

Parents   237

Living Through the Golden Years   240

CONCLUSION   247

ACKNOWLEDGMENTS   251

ABOUT THE AUTHOR   255

INTRODUCTION

I vividly remember the first *satsang* (spiritual question-and-answer session) I gave. It was almost twenty years ago. I had been in India for ten or eleven years by that point, living, doing sadhana and *seva* at Parmarth Niketan ashram in Rishikesh under the guidance and blessings of my guru, Pujya Swami Chidanand Saraswatiji. One evening, we were gathered in Swamiji's *jyopri*, the bamboo and cow dung hut in his garden, following the evening Ganga *arti* (sacred sunset lighting ceremony) on the banks of the sacred Ganga River. Gathering together after the arti was a near daily ritual. Swamiji's garden door was open to anyone seeking blessings, guidance, wisdom, or our involvement and assistance in a charitable project. It was also a time for people to ask spiritual questions.

That evening, sometime in the mid-2000s, there was a group visiting from the United States, and one of them asked a question about anger and forgiveness. Swamiji turned to me and said, "Sadhviji." I waited to hear the rest of the sentence. I expected him to give me some instruction, for example: "Sadhviji, please bring books for this group," or, "Sadhviji, please tell the cook that these people will all have dinner before they leave." So I waited. But no further instruction came. It was just "Sadhviji." Sadhviji period, not Sadhviji comma. I turned to look at my guru. His eyes were now closed, and his hands were in *dhyan mudra*, the traditional pose for meditation, upon his knees. Suddenly I realized he wanted me to answer the question. I panicked.

I had already been doing a lot of public speaking, particularly about Indian culture, on tours for the *Encyclopedia of Hinduism* project and at Hindu temples and events. However, those were situations when I knew in advance that I was going to have to give a lecture. I had some time to prepare myself, even if it was just ten minutes on the stage when Swamiji would signal to me, "You will also speak." But here, there was no time to even gather my thoughts.

I closed my eyes and tried to recollect all the knowledge I had about anger and forgiveness. I regularly wrote articles for Swamiji and had written several on the subject of emotions and the importance of forgiving, forgetting, and moving forward. So the topic wasn't new, but I still needed some time to organize my ideas and thoughts. I tried to sift through the index cards in my mind. Growing up, when I had written papers for school or studied for exams, my parents had taught me to use three-by-five-inch index cards to arrange topics, ideas, and points in systematic order. It worked beautifully. However, in the stress of the moment, I could not arrange the cards in my brain quickly enough.

I squeezed my eyes tightly closed, praying the way children do, to somehow make this group of people just disappear. Maybe if I kept my eyes squeezed shut and prayed very hard, this whole embarrassing situation would turn out to be an illusion. Finally, I opened my eyes. The group was still sitting there, staring at me expectantly. I looked again at Swamiji. His eyes remained closed, and he was deep in meditation. He was not going to rescue me from the deep ocean into which he had just thrown me.

I closed my eyes once more, this time not to try to make the people disappear but in full, humble surrender. I spoke to my guru silently in my mind. I told him, "I'm so sorry. I don't have it in me. I don't know what to tell these people. I don't know the answer. I am so sorry to disappoint you. I just don't have it in me."

As I gently opened my eyes, fully prepared to face my own shame in the eyes of the eagerly waiting group, my mouth also opened slowly and, from somewhere other than my own brain, the answer flowed. I spoke and spoke to them, and tears filled their eyes and rolled down their cheeks.

Satsang literally means in the presence of truth. It is a time of delving deep into the truth of who we are and who we are not. The ignorance of our false identification with our body, our stories and dramas, our history, our roles and identities, is what leads to our suffering. If we can free ourselves from this ignorance by diving deep into the truth, we can learn to live in joy, peace, truth, and love. We can even, if our practice is deep and dedicated enough, attain that coveted state of self-realization, enlightenment, or moksha, meaning liberation, which is ultimately the goal of our lives.

From that first satsang until today, the truth is the same. I don't know the answer. It is not *in* me. However, if I can get my small self, my ego-self, out of the way, if I can create space within me, the answers come through. What each person needs to hear at a given time and in a particular way simply flows through me, due to no merit of my own. To be used as a vessel, as a channel for this flow of grace-filled wisdom, is the greatest blessing in my life.

For nearly twenty years now, each evening, following the sacred Ganga arti, I give satsang. It began in a casual way sitting in Pujya Swamiji's hut. Sometimes he would answer the question, but with more and more frequency he told *me* to answer it. Then, after a few years, we shifted satsang to its own garden—the satsang garden—where I sit with the audience from around the world and together we dive into truth.

People ask questions in person or send them in advance by email or via social media. I am humbled every evening by the gratitude in the eyes of the audience, and I am deeply aware that, as they are grateful to me for being the vehicle of wisdom, so am I grateful for the opportunity to be this vehicle and for the cosmic source of the answers that flow through me.

The pages of this book are filled with direct transcriptions of answers from the satsangs I've been blessed to give over the years.

This book is divided into different sections. We open as I look back at my own life, my choices and decisions, and the lessons that nearly three decades in spiritual India have taught me. From my personal life, we expand into *your* lives. What is the purpose? Why are we all here on earth, and how can we find and fulfill our dharma or highest purpose? We then examine the tendencies of our mind—how to understand it, to calm it, to work with it—as the mind can be the greatest obstacle or the greatest asset to living our highest purpose and greatest joy. From the depths of the mind we move into our emotions, which are, of course, part of the mind, but this section delves more deeply into individual emotional states and how to overcome them (like anger) or open our hearts to them (like love). Then comes a section on specific spiritual tools and techniques, like meditation, and how they can be helpful for us to access a place of inner joy, calm, and fulfillment as well as take us beyond the body, beyond this individual karmic journey, into a true experience of the very infinite nature of the self. From the meditation cushion we move into the manifest world. What does spirituality look like in action? What does it demand of us? What do spiritual relationships look like, and how do we foster them with ourselves, our families, and our communities? The book concludes with a look at how our spirituality manifests throughout the different phases, roles, and relationships of our lives.

As you read these pages, do not peruse them as you would a textbook. These are not just teachings that we read and then have dinner, fight with our family, watch TV, go to sleep, and forget all about them. These are teachings on how we should live each moment of our lives.

Let the words carry you to the source of truth within yourself. The truth of which I speak in my satsangs is the truth within all of us.

FROM HOLLYWOOD TO
THE HIMALAYAS

How did you end up in India, taking sanyas? What has living in India taught you?

Most people go to India seeking enlightenment, or at least advanced yoga studies. I went because I liked the food. Nearly thirty years ago, I had graduated from Stanford University and was in the midst of my PhD in psychology, preparing for my research and dissertation. But I was an avid traveler, and it was time for a travel break. I agreed to go to India, a place I knew nothing about, only because I was a staunch vegetarian. In India, I knew I wouldn't have to grill waiters in languages I didn't speak about whether there was chicken broth in their vegetable soup.

I was not religious. I was not even one of those people who says, "Well, I'm not religious, but I'm spiritual." I was an academic and a hippie. If anyone ever said you couldn't dance all night on Saturday at a Grateful Dead show and still ace a neuropsychology exam on Monday morning, I would have proven them wrong. I was not consciously seeking or yearning for God's grace, and yet, thirty-six months after being one of the very few students to ever get an A+ in Dr. Phil Zimbardo's Psychology of Mind Control class at Stanford, I was sitting on the banks of the Ganga River in Rishikesh, India, with tears of ecstasy streaming down my face.

The transformation happened suddenly. "I'm going to put my feet in the river," I said, after we dropped off our bags at the hotel. I wasn't looking for spiritual awakening. I didn't even know it was something to be yearned for, but it happened, even before my toes touched the water.

It felt as though a veil had been torn off not only my eyes but off of every way I had of knowing myself and the world. Suddenly I could see, and I still don't have words to describe what I saw. It was a visual experience, but it wasn't only visual. It was an experience of being in the presence of the Divine. It wasn't an experience of separation, though, that the Divine was over there and I was over here. It was an experience of the Divine permeating everything around me and permeating *me*. For the first time in my life I realized that I was one with the universe, one with the Divine.

Prior to that moment I had always felt like I was lacking in some way. I wasn't pretty enough or smart enough or popular enough. I wasn't fulfilled enough or motivated enough. I wasn't pure enough or good enough. Some of this stemmed from the general tragic cultural conditioning that most of us soak up in our early years, and some stemmed from the personal challenges and trauma I had experienced in early childhood and from the depression, anxiety, and eating disorder I later struggled with in my adolescence and early twenties.

Suddenly in that moment on the banks of a river I didn't even know was holy, everything was exactly right. Not only right but exquisite. Whole. Full. Infinite. Divine. All I could say was, "Oh my God, it's so beautiful! Oh my God, it's so beautiful," with tears streaming down my face. They were not sad tears, of course, but they weren't happy tears either. They were tears of the truth. Tears of coming home. Home to my self.

That which was given to me as I stood on the banks of the Ganga was more real than anything I had experienced in my twenty-five years of life. There was no way to turn back. Even though it wasn't the package that I had ever anticipated happiness would come in, it was undeniable that I had been given something extraordinarily precious.

I spent the next several days in Rishikesh in meditative bliss. I thought, "Okay, this is where I belong, but where? How? Doing what?"

My connection with Parmarth Niketan, the ashram where I now live, began simply as a pathway for me to go from our hotel to the river. I was walking through the ashram one day, and I heard a voice say, "You must stay here." I looked around to see who had spoken. If there was a voice, someone must have spoken. There was no one. In my entire sphere of reference and experience, the only people who heard voices when no one had spoken were schizophrenics and Joan of Arc. But since I was not Joan of Arc and I hoped I was not schizophrenic, I did what any self-respecting scientist would do: I ignored the voice. If no one had spoken, I must not have heard anything.

About thirty seconds later, I heard it again: "You must stay here." Again I looked around and again there was no one. I was just about to ignore the voice for the second time when I remembered a vow I had made on the airplane from San Francisco to Delhi. As I had no idea why I was traveling to a country I knew nothing about and had no specific interest in visiting, I realized there must be a reason that I just didn't know. I had never believed in a randomness of existence. Although I wasn't spiritual or religious, I definitely believed there was a capital-P Plan and therefore also a capital-P Planner, as the scientist in me wasn't convinced that all this perfection in creation had unfolded randomly. So on the plane I made a vow that I would keep my heart open in order to hopefully realize what it was that drew me to India, as surely it wasn't just good vegetarian food!

So as I heard that voice again, I looked up and saw a sign that said OFFICE. I went in and told them I wanted to stay. At that time, spiritual India was not very open to foreign women. They were perfectly polite, but they said I needed to get special permission from the president of the ashram, and unfortunately he was out of town.

"Okay, so when is he due back?" I asked. "Maybe tomorrow," they said.

Being American, and not yet attuned to the bendable nature of truth in India, I assumed that the president would, in fact, return the next day. Every day, I went back and asked if the president had returned, and every day they'd say, "Maybe tomorrow," which I only later learned could also mean "I have no idea but I want to be polite." Finally he did return, and he turned out to be not only the administrative head of the ashram, but His Holiness Pujya Swami Chidanand Saraswatiji, one of the most revered spiritual leaders of India.

"Welcome home," Swamiji said when I finally met him.

Although my physical life's journey has been truly and quite literally from Hollywood to the Himalayas (also the title of my full memoir), you do not

COME HOME TO YOURSELF

have to make that physical journey in order to benefit from the powerful lessons that India has taught me. The key piece of wisdom I've learned is that the Hollywood way of thinking, which tragically is pervasive not only in Hollywood but also across much of the modern world, indoctrinates us to believe that we *are* our bodies. We are the size, shape, color, history, relationships, success, talent, and more. Thus we suffer. We suffer competition, jealousy, greed, not-enoughness, resentment, grudges, and more. And we bring suffering onto others. The Himalayan way of thinking, on the other hand, teaches us that we *have* a body, but we are not the body. We are soul, spirit, consciousness, love, divinity. We are the full, whole, eternal, infinite nature of the universe. Core fundamental teachings such as *Aham Brahmasmi* (I am the Divine), *tat tvam asi* (thou art That), or even the meditation mantra of *so hum* (I am That) remind us that we are not separate from the very boundless presence of eternal and infinite reality. When we make that mindset shift, wherever our bodies may be, that is the beginning of the end of suffering.

So what else has living in India taught me? First, stay open. The universe has a plan for you. Yes, of course, we have to choose a path and walk it, but we only do that until we get a sign that says, "Turn right now." Look at the caterpillar. It spends most of its life crawling on the ground, and then one day it hears a voice or it gets a sign that says, "Climb the tree." Now, it's never seen anyone go up that tree and come back. Mom's gone up, Dad's gone up, but no one has come back. That tree is the Bermuda Triangle for caterpillars. But when it receives the instruction to climb, it does. It gets a signal to go out on the branch, weave itself into a cocoon, and sometime later burst forth, jump, and fly away. It has no idea how to fly! It's never flown before, but when it is time to jump, it does.

A caterpillar never misses a chance to become a butterfly because it is too scared to climb a tree, or because it doesn't know how to weave a cocoon, or because it jumps out of the cocoon too soon and plummets to the ground. Butterflies never climb back down the tree instead of flying because they don't believe they can really fly. It never happens.

There is an intelligence in the universe that pervades all of creation, including us. But we have to trust it, and we have to be quiet and still enough to hear it. If the caterpillar spent its entire life bemoaning the fact that the millipede got hundreds of legs while it got only six, it might miss the call to climb the tree.

Also, I've learned that your self is much more important than your shelf. Most of us spend a lot of time and energy focused on filling our shelves with possessions, and we spend very little time thinking about the fullness of our self. But it is in that fullness that real abundance lies. No matter how much we have, most of us want more. We think, "If I could just have that, or achieve this, then I'd be happy." But if our happiness is contingent upon filling shelves, then happiness and abundance will always be an arm's length away.

When I first came to India, the local people would implore me, "Please, please come home for a meal, come for a cup of tea, come for a cold drink." These were people who could not even afford to properly feed their families, but they would ask until I agreed. I learned that abundance was not building mansions while others lived in shacks, or eating caviar while others starved. Abundance is connecting deeply with the fullness of our self, recognizing that our cup runneth over, and eagerly sharing with others.

Lastly, and most importantly, in service to others I have discovered the fullness within myself. Not from the perspective of one who has, serving those who don't, nor a humanitarian serving the masses, but service of self to self.

If you trip and injure your right leg, your left leg will pick up the extra weight. We call this limping. There is no need for anyone to say, "Oh great humanitarian left leg, would you mind picking up a little bit of extra weight?" The left leg does not anticipate an award or a gold star. It does it because it understands that the right leg is self. That is the goal of service— to serve myself in you.

In serving children, I found myself. We build schools, orphanages, and women's empowerment programs; we run medical care programs and install toilets, hand-washing stations, and water filters in schools, colleges, and across communities.

It's a fundamental tenet of a deep, real, true spiritual path to be of service to others, to provide for them as we provide for ourselves. When I open my eyes from my meditation, if my meditation is real and deep, I should experience oneness not only with a formless Creator but also with creation—our sisters and brothers with whom we share this planet. Thus, we serve.

Pujya Swamiji explains that now, seeing the global crisis around the dearth of clean water, sanitation, and hygiene, which is the cause for thousands of deaths occurring each day, we need to shift our focus from building temples to building toilets. So we started constructing toilets and hand-washing stations and teaching proper sanitation. We formed the Divine Shakti Foundation and Global Interfaith WASH Alliance, with leaders of many different religions coming together and agreeing that it is time to expand our definition of peace. It is no longer enough to simply say, "Thou shalt not kill." Today, true peace can only exist when our sisters and brothers of all races, religions, and species have access to safe, sufficient water, sanitation, hygiene, education, and primary health care. Children across the world are suffering and dying. They are our responsibility.

A spiritual awakening does not take us farther from the world, it brings us closer. Spiritual awakening does not separate us, it connects us. Spiritual awakening is not about my bliss in the midst of your misery. Spiritual awakening is awakening from the illusion that who we are is based on what we earn, acquire, or achieve. It is an awakening into the reality that each of us is an embodiment of the Divine. It is awakening out of the illusion of our separateness into the reality of our oneness, a reality in which there is no place that I end and you begin. It is awakening from a life that is in pieces into a life of peace.

PART 1

The Purpose of Life

At some point in most of our lives, we wonder, "Why am I here? What is the point? Is this it?" First, we tend to strive toward success—academically and professionally. Then we tend to strive toward fulfillment in our relationships—spouses, children, friends. Maybe we dive into the beauty of culture—music, art, poetry, literature. Yet, despite our achievements—or lack of achievements—in all of these areas, there tends to be a nagging question that arises from time to time: Is there anything else?

One of my favorite psychology studies occurred when researchers took a group of students and gave them a simple short video to watch. The video was of a basketball game between a red team and a white team. The students were simply asked to count how many baskets the red team made and how many the white team made. At the end of the video, they were given a quiz to fill out with three questions: 1) How many baskets did the red team make? 2) How many baskets did the white team make? 3) Did you notice anything else? The students all counted the baskets correctly, but more than half of them wrote "no" to the third question. As it turned out, the true experiment here was not at all about basketball. It was about attention and intention. Halfway through the game, a large gorilla came onto the court and danced for about thirty seconds, center court, and then exited. A gorilla in the middle of a basketball game! And more than half of the students missed it. How? They were clearly watching the game. They didn't nap or look away or zone out. They were attentive enough to count all of the baskets. So how did they miss a dancing gorilla? Simple. It wasn't what they'd been instructed to look for. That's it. What were they looking for? What instructions were they following? If the students were told in advance, "By the way, don't miss the dancing gorilla," they didn't miss it. Even if they were told, "By the way, make sure you see the surprise," they still didn't miss it. They only missed it when the instructions were simply to count baskets.

I love this study because it is such a great metaphor for our lives. We are given instructions—get a good education, get a good job, make a lot of money, get married, have kids, have a nice big home. So we do those things. But, like the students watching the basketball game, most of us don't realize that that is not actually the whole point. The point is something else entirely, and most of us miss it. Usually not until very late in life or when faced with a terminal illness do we ask, "Did I miss something?" Don't wait. Realize now that there is something else. This doesn't mean you shouldn't try to get a good education, a good career, a great salary, and a beautiful family. By all means, do those things. But realize that you must keep your eyes open—not just your physical eyes, but also your inner eye—for that "something else." In the midst of fulfilling these duties and roles, make sure to stop periodically and check in with yourself. Who are you? What are you here for? Are you anchored deeply in full awareness, so that every moment you are open to the very presence of the Divine?

This first section dives into the "Why are we here and what is our purpose?" question. I will give you the bottom line at the very beginning: Each of us is here to wake up to the truth of our selves. In Vedanta, the example is frequently given that when you dream, everything in the dream seems so real. Maybe you go to Paris in your dream. The airport, the airplane, the Louvre, the cute coffee shop where you had a cappuccino on the banks of the Seine, the nice proprietor at your hotel—it all feels real. You can taste the croissant, smell the coffee, see the artists along the river banks. Then you wake up. There is nothing but you in the bed. What happened to it all? Where did it go? Nothing happened. It didn't go anywhere because there was nowhere to go. It was a creation of your mind and it existed only in your mind. When your mind shifted to a wakeful state, the dream automatically faded away. Similarly, we are told, this drama here seems so real, but it, too, is a dream. When we awaken into truth—through meditation, prayer, and spiritual practice—all of the ways in which we are suffering, all of the ignorance and illusion, will fade away.

Connecting to the Divine

What is God, and what is our relationship with God?

No metaphor is perfect when you're speaking about God. Words, which are finite, are incapable of aptly describing that which is infinite. Words are two-dimensional and cannot do justice to something that defies dimension. By using words, we are able to simply run circles around the truth, inching closer to it bit by bit but never actually getting to the bull's-eye.

One way of thinking about God is akin to the way we perceive the sun. Though the sun is not infinite, it is a useful analogy here. If you place a large number of vessels on the ground and fill them with water, each will reflect the sun's light differently depending on the size, shape, and color of the vessel.

A blue container shaped like a bowl will reflect it differently from the way a glass container that is vertical and translucent will. It's the same sun, but there are different images of it because the containers are different.

You will get as many different reflections of the same sun as the number of different vessels you place on the ground. But the sun is always only one.

So, too, God is one infinite, divine presence, reflected by the myriad containers here on earth—all of us! Each of us, all of nature, all of creation, is a different vessel, reflecting and manifesting the light of God in different ways. As the containers differ, it may appear that there are different gods. But truly there is nothing but God.

There is a beautiful teaching in the Upanishads: "*Isavasyamidam sarvam yatkinca jagatyam jagat.*" It means that everything in the universe is pervaded by the Divine. There is nothing and no one that is not pervaded by the Divine.

If there is nothing but God, that doesn't mean that God is everything *but* your boss, or God is present in everyone *except* your mother-in-law, or everything is God *except* you. If everything is God, then everything is God.

In our lives, we tend to identify with the container. We see the bowl instead of the sun. When people ask, "Who are you?" I say, "I'm a woman, I'm white, I'm fifty-three, I'm American, I'm a *sanyasi*, I'm a PhD, these are my parents, this is my life, this is how much I weigh, this is how tall I am, this is what I'm allergic to, this is what I like and don't like." But that is just describing the vessel, not the sun! Our bodies and brains, our different life stories, are just different vessels. They are form, not content! Just as the bowl is a vessel for the sun, all we are and all we have is a vessel for the presence of God. The content of us is God.

We can't see the sun's reflection until and unless we have a vessel. But we must not mistake the vessel for that which it's reflecting. We must not mistake the form for the content! However, just because your truest, highest, deepest nature is God, that doesn't mean that, without deep spiritual practice, you should just start assuming you are God! There's a great story of what happens to so many of us when we embark on the spiritual path and gain some of this knowledge without the deepest level of understanding.

A guru was teaching his disciples that everything is Brahman the ultimate, divine reality, and there is nothing but Brahman. One day, two of his disciples went into the city and heard a loud shout that there was an elephant coming their way. The man who was atop the elephant shouted, "Get out of the way!" But the disciple thought, "Well, my guru says everything is God, so I'm going to stay here because this elephant is just an illusion. It's really Brahman, it's God, and I'm really Brahman, I'm not this weak guy, so why do I have to get out of the way?"

The elephant handler was screaming at this point, "Get out of the way, get out of the way!" But the disciple said to himself, "No, no, it's all good, it's all God, no problem!" The elephant, of course, scooped him up with his trunk and tossed him hundreds of yards away. He lay there, broken. Finally, his fellow disciples came to where he lay bleeding and in pain. He cried out to them, "I hate our guru! He gave us this false piece of information. That was a horrible elephant; that was not God. I'm never going back to the ashram!"

29

The disciples went back and relayed everything to the guru. The guru went to the man and asked him what had happened. The disciple, in a fit of ego, replied, "I was just trying to implement your teaching; you are the one who said everything is God. Look what the elephant did to me."

And the guru replied, "Ah, but you really didn't implement the teaching."

Perturbed, the man said that he saw the elephant as Brahman.

The guru explained, "But what about the elephant handler who told you to get out of the way? What about all of the people who tried to grab you and pull you out of the way? I told you everything is Brahman, but in your ego, you decided it was just going to be you and the elephant. You left out the elephant handler, all the people, and all your fellow disciples who tried to help you."

Sadly, this is what happens to us. When we gain just a bit of knowledge, but it's not very deep or we haven't delved fully into the personal practices such as meditation, we tend to develop very narrow views about what being God means. We say things like, "I am God, therefore you should do the dishes tonight." No. If I am God, then so are you, and so is everyone and so are the dishes! When there is nothing but God, *there is nothing but God.*

How can we implement, practically, the idea that there is nothing but God?

It is not easy to move through the world remembering there is nothing but God. There are errands to run, bills to pay, meetings to attend, people who annoy us, food we like! How can we keep remembering that it is all God? It gives us a very beautiful spiritual opportunity to live in a "Yes, and . . ." experience of life. Yes—everything is God. There is nothing but God. All separation is an illusion. All forms are transitory, ephemeral, therefore illusory. Only the Divine is unchanging, eternal, and therefore real. And—there is this divine *leela*, a beautiful divine drama that God has created in which we've been given these roles in human bodies with our own karmic journeys. We've been given hearts that love and minds that think. We have been given the ability to have compassion and to lend a helping hand. We have these beautiful bodies with our five senses that interact with the creation and enable us to experience the creation. We are not meant to ignore or deny the *leela*. Rather we are meant to live it fully, sincerely, deeply! Yet, we must remember not to identify as it, to remember—even as we are playing our roles to the fullest and best that we can—that ultimately we are nothing but God. So we have to live with this "Yes, and . . ." awareness rather than "Either . . . or . . . ."

One of the tragic pitfalls of a superficial understanding of these truths is that we tend to blindly use them to our benefit. We tell ourselves, "Well, everything is God, so why do I have to do my homework? Everything is God, so why give charity? Why pay my taxes? Why help others? Why do anything? If it's all perfect, if there's nothing but God, why do I have to wake up in the morning and meditate?"

Such limited thinking lends itself to very challenging games of the ego. So, what I have found, personally, is that it's beautiful to hold that truth of there being nothing but God, to remember it, to know it as the highest truth, but to simultaneously realize that although I can't live that truth every moment of every day, I can at least live my humanity, rather than push my humanity away.

One way to think about existence is to imagine the old TV sets with dials to switch from one channel to another. On the highest channel is the all-encompassing truth in which it's all God. But on another channel, we're here in this human form, wherein we have the ability to smile at each other, hug each other, help each other, feed each other, and use our talents and abilities to serve each other.

We don't want to dismiss that, because it is a critical aspect of our core humanity. If God had wanted us to just disconnect entirely from the world, to be indifferent and disconnected, I do not believe we would've been born with the ability to experience empathy and compassion, and to cry at the plight of one another. If someone falls down in front of us, we don't intellectually process in our brains: Is it God? Is it not God? We just reach out and help that person because the core humanity within us connects to the core humanity within them. If we refuse to embrace our humanity, then we would be throwing away a gift that God has given us. If we are simply supposed to ignore the human experience then why were we given a human birth with the capacity for consciousness, love, and intuition?

Imagine if you give a gift to someone you love. Then a few years later they tell you, "Guess what? I've totally forgotten about the gift you gave me. I have ignored it completely and left it hidden in the back of my dark closet. I never think about it or use it!" Would you be happy? Of course not! When you give someone a gift you want them to use it, to enjoy it. In the same way, when God gave us this gift of a human birth, this gift of a heart that loves, eyes that cry, hands that help and touch, a brain that can think, plan, initiate, and create, do you think God wants us to just ignore these things? I don't believe so. I don't believe that the Divine would gift us something so exquisite just so we can ignore it, or dismiss it, or deny it.

So, we use those very human gifts with an awareness that the perfect, all-knowing Divine gave them to us for a reason. We hold in our awareness that the highest, deepest, truest truth is that it's all perfect, *and* we reach out and help the person who tripped in front of us, because that channel of love and compassion also exists, connecting us to one another, as long as we are tapping into the best of being human.

How do we connect with our divine self, and then stay connected?

First, I'm going to change the phrase to *true self,* because if we say, "divine self," it implies that there is a nondivine self; that is to say, part of me is my divine self, and part of me is my nondivine self. What we have is a true self and a nontrue self. The nontrue self is the stuff that most of us actually identify as: our name, our age, where we're from, the size and shape of our body, the color of our skin, our bank account, our career, our titles, all the labels we identify as, but which actually aren't us. The way we know all that isn't truly self is because it keeps changing. Truth can't possibly be that which is constantly changing! My size and shape, my title, my wealth—all of it is in constant flux. Truth is that which is stable, constant, eternal.

If you're driving down the freeway and someone calls you on the phone and asks, "Who are you?" and you say, "I'm exit thirty," they will say, "No, I didn't ask *where* you are, I asked *who* are you." Then if you say, "I told you, I'm exit thirty, but actually now I'm almost exit thirty-one," they would think that either you couldn't hear them or that you had gone crazy. We understand that exit thirty or thirty-one is simply the intersection of time and space that our vehicle has reached. That's *where* we are, but it's not *who* we are.

If I say to you that I am fifty-three, a woman, white, American, and a sanyasi, all of that is true, none of it is a lie, and yet, it's what we'll call the lowercase-t truth. It's true at this exact intersection of time and space. It's my *where*, not my *who*. It's not the capital-T Truth; it's just telling you the story of my vehicle and where it happens to be at this exact intersection of time and space. My vehicle is a 1971 American female model. But that's not *who* I am. That's just the container, the form I am currently in. Our true self is the Divine, the essence. When we connect with our true self, what we have to do is drop deeper than the container. If we remain stuck to the container, we won't get to the essence.

If I pick up a glass of water and spend all my time marveling at how beautiful or ugly or solid or soft the glass is, the water is not going to quench my thirst. In order to do that, I actually have to drink what's inside. There's nothing wrong with admiring the beauty of the glass; it just doesn't do anything for my thirst. Similarly, there's nothing wrong with paying attention to our body vehicle—we've only got one, and it's a temple. In Hindi we say, "*Sharir ek mandir hai*," which means "The body is a temple." We have to take as much care of it as we take care of our temples, our churches, our synagogues, our mosques, and wherever the Divine resides. However, we shouldn't confuse form for content, packaging for essence.

Our true self is the essence, the spirit. There are so many ways to connect with it. One simple and easy way is through a meditation practice called *neti, neti*, which means "not this, not this." We begin by saying, "I am not my orange sari, I am not my skin, I am not my bones . ..." Should anyone doubt this, we know it is true because the skin keeps sloughing off but *I* am still here. My bones break, but I'm still here. Similarly, I'm not my blood. I could get a blood transfusion or donate blood, but I'd still be here. I'm not my organs. I could get an organ transplant, but I'd still be here. I am not more or less me based on whether I'm receiving or giving blood, receiving or giving organs, or peeling off my sunburned skin. We then go deeper, recognizing that all of the cells of our body actually regenerate over a period of time. Every eight or nine years, I am brand new! If there is any anger or pain that I am holding on to about something that happened eight or nine years ago, it did not happen to me. It did not happen to the me who exists today!

Then we go a little bit deeper, and we say, "Well, I'm also not my thoughts, emotions, feeling states, or my memories." The reason I know this is because I'm not always angry. I may be angry too frequently but I'm not *always* angry. When I'm not angry, I don't cease to exist. If I *am* my anger, I would cease to exist when I'm not angry. Then we drop deeper. I'm not my thoughts. There's a space in between my thoughts, and in that space, I don't evaporate. If I did, if I were my thoughts and I ceased to exist even momentarily between my thoughts, who would think the next thought?

Another way to understand that we are not our thoughts is to say, "I am not the chemical and electrical patterns of activity in my brain." I am not serotonin or dopamine or norepinephrine. I am not the gray matter and white matter inside my skull. I am not my limbic system! I am not an electrical impulse traveling down an axon. This is obvious and clear. But if I am not the chemicals or the electrical signals or the different parts of my brain, then by logical extension I am not my thoughts or emotions or feeling states or memories. All of those are simply patterns of chemical and electrical behavior in certain pathways of my brain. So we realize, deeply, that we are not our thoughts.

As we do this meditation, after a while maybe some other aspect of self-identity will arise. "I'm the child of an alcoholic," a voice in our head says. And again we realize *neti, neti*. Not this, not this. That child is not who I am anymore. Every single cell in my body has literally regenerated since I was that child. There is no part of my body today I can show you and say, "This was abused. This was abandoned. This was harmed." Every cell has died and new ones have taken their place. Of course, if you believe in past lives, then none of these identities was true in your past birth so it can't be who *you* are.

This way we slowly go as deep as we can until there's no layer of identification left to remove. If we do this in a quiet, meditative place and we allow ourselves to just sit there, peeling away layer after layer, what we find is a beautiful stillness, a beautiful openness into which the experience of the true self can emerge.

When we discard identification with everything that is not self, we ultimately reach the experience that the Buddhists speak of as nothingness and the Hindus speak of as everythingness, but which is the same experience of infinity. Imagine I have a glass jar full of air and the jar breaks. What do I have? On one hand you could say I have nothing, as I no longer have my jar of air. It broke, so I have nothing now. On the other hand you could say that the only thing that happened was I lost that dividing line between *my* jar of air and *all* of the air, so now actually I have *all* of the air instead of just one jar of the air. Neither is right, neither is wrong; they are just two ways of looking at it, but you'll recognize that they actually take us to exactly the same place. We all agree that we're left with just air. When the border and boundary dissolve, when the walls of the container shatter, you realize you have always been the infinite, you have always been consciousness, you have always been divine.

The last aspect of how we can stay connected to that divine is just in remembrance. There's no magic formula, unfortunately. It would be convenient if every time we forgot, we received an electric jolt of remembrance and awakening. But that isn't part of the package deal of human life. What we have is just practice.

When you start meditating, you will find that your mind wanders more than it's still, and your meditation can feel like simply a process of trying to bring your mind back. But then, slowly, the spaces in between having to bring the mind back lengthen, and the mind stays. You're able to catch it faster and bring it back faster, and slowly you're able to accumulate lots of consecutive moments of just being in that spaciousness. This is what it's like living within our true self. It's about remembrance, about coming back. A mantra can serve as a great life raft to bring us back when we are drowning in the ocean of thoughts, distraction, stress, and illusion. Our breath is also a great life raft to bring us back. These are techniques to bring us out of where we've gone, out of the swirling whirlpools in the ocean, and back into who we are. And gradually we keep living as that.

You can also plan specific ways to remember. For example, every time you are going to eat or drink anything, just take a moment and reconnect. Close your eyes for thirty or forty-five or sixty seconds. Drop in. Remember who you really are. You can link this remembering to almost anything you do frequently during the day, then slowly it will become automatic. I no longer need to remind myself to reconnect before drinking or eating. It just happens. If you drive a lot, take a moment before each time you turn the engine on. Or you could tie it to checking your inbox or your Instagram account! Just a moment of remembering. Before you hit refresh, take a moment to close your eyes and remember. Ah, I am not the story I am projecting. I am not the role I'm playing. I'm not the mask I'm wearing. I am not the body I'm inhabiting. I am divine. I am one with all. I am infinite consciousness.

An integral aspect of staying connected is to remember not to berate ourselves whenever we lose the connection. Many of us are very comfortable with a practice of compassion, love, forgiveness, and seeing the Divine in all as long as it relates to everyone other than ourselves. It becomes very difficult when we have to turn it inward. Ironically, our practices of compassion and loving-kindness can become anything but compassionate and loving. We so frequently berate ourselves for forgetting: "Oh my God, you are so stupid! You forgot to be compassionate again. You'll never be spiritual!" Here I am, criticizing myself for not being compassionate to another. But where's my compassion for myself? As we work on staying connected to the Divine, it's not just about God outside of us and in those around us, but it's about God within us. When we lose that inner connection, we have to have the same compassion, love, and understanding for our self that wandered off that we have for the world around us.

Knowing and Finding the Purpose
of Human Life

What is the purpose of human life?

The purpose of human life, the whole reason we're here on earth in these human bodies, is to experience the true divinity of our self. This can be called self-realization, God-realization, enlightenment, liberation, or nirvana. The key is that we are here to remember. To remember who we really are, which is divine. We have been granted a human birth in order to wake up and realize the Divine within ourselves. The purpose of life is to understand who we are and accept wholeheartedly the incredible invitation the universe has given us to fully embrace the sacred, divine spirit in ourselves and the world around us. It's believed that only humans have the ability to achieve that consciousness, to transcend the identification with the body and conditioned mind.

This is why human birth is seen as the pinnacle of not only physical evolution but also spiritual evolution. It's believed that humans are the only species who can see the self, be conscious of the self and witness the self.

However, judging by our actions, we cannot say that humans are the highest stage of evolution. Animals harm others only for two reasons—either because they are hungry or because they feel immediately threatened. If you are hiking and inadvertently come upon a mother bear with her cubs, she will attack if she feels threatened. Or if you come upon a hungry tiger, chances are you will become its lunch. But these actions are for survival. Humans are the only species that harm others for reasons other than food or self-defense.

So while we are definitely not the pinnacle of evolution where ethical instincts are concerned, we are said to be the pinnacle spiritually due to our unique ability to be conscious of ourselves, of being able to step back, witness, and say: "I am not my body. I am soul." There is a beautiful mantra that says:

āhāra-nidrā-bhaya-maithunaṃ cha;
samānam etat pashubhir narāṇām

dharmo hi teṣhāmadhiko visheṣho;
dharmeṇa hīnāḥ pashubhiḥ samānāḥ

This mantra reminds us that both humans and animals eat, sleep, and experience sensual pleasure and fear. The only difference is that as humans we can wake up, see the truth of who we really are, and fulfill our true dharma.

The human ability to witness ourselves and be conscious of our own consciousness is a crucial component of enlightenment. If I'm unable to look beyond my body and personality, I'm not going to experience enlightenment. I have to be able to connect with the one within me who's aware of my actions, who's aware of the drama, who says, "Oh yes, now there's anger coming." I have to be able to connect with that awareness, that consciousness that is always present. The object of which we are aware keeps changing. But the one who is aware does not. If I only identify as "I'm angry," or "I'm a rich CEO," I'll never get there. That is identifying as the *object* of my awareness when I need to identify, instead, as the *subject*, as the one who is aware, not *what* I am aware of!

So to make the best use of our human birth, we need to learn to step out of the role of the actor and be the one witnessing the drama but unaffected by it. That's why we're here, to have that experiential awareness.

So if we are not the body or our dramas or our identities, then what is the guiding principle we are supposed to live by? What are we supposed to do?

Once we know who we are, what to do comes naturally. Our problem is we don't know who we are, so we don't know what to do. We look at the people around us, our friends, the people we see on TV, on social media, and we judge and identify ourselves accordingly. We think, "Oh, I want to do what he's doing; that looks really good. My brother did this, my neighbor did that." We judge ourselves based on what other people do: "Oh, I should also do this; oh, I'm also like that." We flop around from thing to thing, like a fish out of water, doing what others are doing, because we have no idea who we are.

The minute we know who we are, living comes very naturally. A dog or cat may chase a bird to the top of the building, but when the bird flies off, the dog or cat never follows. They understand they're not a bird. They know that it's not who they are, that they do not have wings. We don't even have that same level of self-awareness. We do things based simply on copying what others are doing, or trying to live up to others' expectations of us, or to fulfill some arbitrary societal goal around success.

Through our meditation, spiritual practice, sadhana, and purification of the mind, we start to see the truth of who we are. It is like cleaning the dirt off our windows so that we can see the light that's always been shining. Everything in life then becomes an opportunity to fulfill our dharma.

Many people justify their inaction by saying, "I'm just waiting until I figure out what my dharma is and then I can fulfill it. In the meantime I can just sit back and relax." But all scriptures and teachings tell us the exact opposite—that our dharma is about every minute and every moment of how we live. It's not about that one amazing feat we accomplish, that remarkable, unprecedented, extraordinary thing we do. It's about every minute and every moment, finding that integrity, that sincerity, that connection, that truth. It's about being so present and so conscious with each moment that we are able to bring our full being and our full dharma to each moment.

I was recently in Kolkata for an event, and on the morning we were leaving, we found that we had some extra time, so we went to the Dakshineswar Temple dedicated to Maha Kali, which is where the famous mystic Paramhansa Ramakrishna lived. Ramakrishna is world renowned as an extraordinary seer and teacher, who experienced the Divine Mother in each moment. As we toured the temple, the priest said, "You know, it's amazing. Ramakrishnaji was just like one of us, a priest in the temple, doing what we're doing. But in doing it, he was so in love with the Mother, so in love with the Goddess, that divine magic happened. Magic that now, a hundred years later, is still drawing people." And you can feel it; the magic is still there.

That's what the purpose of life is about—how you are doing what you're doing. Paramhansa Ramakrishna was so there, so present, so connected that the Goddess was always tangibly present for him. That's where magic happens. Your dharma is right here in every minute and every moment. Make sure that, in whatever you do, you live with the conscious awareness of divinity, so that everything becomes sacred and a means to your own unfolding, to your own awakening.

How do we gain direction in life when we feel lost? How do we harness our intuition and know that the voices we hear are pointing us in the right direction?

According to science, we have five senses. Science tells us that the only way we can really know the world is through that which we see, hear, smell, touch, and taste. But we have another sense, and that's our intuition. It's not something that some people have and some others don't. We all have it. Most of us don't tap into it, though, and sadly don't learn how to use it.

Our intuition is always available, but if we haven't developed it, we don't know what to make of it. We can't make sense of the inner voice we hear, or a calling or a signal we may receive. This is why it's so important to cultivate the power of intuition through listening and trusting.

When it's hot, you can feel the sun's rays. You never doubt your brain. If you hear a tune, you know you're listening to music. If you're standing in a shower or a river or a swimming pool, you feel wet and you know that you are, in fact, wet! You trust those five senses, because they're what you've become habituated to. They have become a source of truth that you trust.

You won't trust your intuition if you haven't become attuned to it. You have to develop a relationship with it the same way that you have a relationship with your eyes, ears, tongue, nose, and hands, so that you can learn to trust it.

To use it, you have to give it your attention and your intention. You have to consciously listen for it, and when you hear it you have to follow it. In that way the voice gets stronger, clearer, and more readily accessible. As you develop a relationship with your intuition, slowly you'll be able to distinguish the difference between the voices in your head—the voices of judgment, criticism, fear, ego, and the voice of deep intuition.

Of course, intuition doesn't always present as a voice. Many times it's actually just a feeling or instinct or knowing. Tuning in to your intuition can be simply discovering places that feel really right or maybe not right at all, people who feel right or who feel energetically off, projects or programs or pathways we embark on that feel expansive or ones that feel contracting. That ability to notice subtle differences is intuition. We have to nurture and trust it just as we develop our sight, smell, hearing, taste, and touch.

But I hear so many voices in my head. How do I know which one is intuition?

This is a common problem. It is the reason why learning to distinguish the voice of intuition is so important! Our minds are filled with near constant cacophony, and when we need to tap in to intuition, sadly all many people hear is chaotic noise and competing voices. Our fears, our desires, the voice of society, the voice of our parents, teachers, and so many others shout loudly inside of us, drowning out the voice of intuition. So for example you may feel the intuition, the deep yearning of your spirit, to be a musician, or to be an artist, or a gardener, or a kindergarten teacher, or to live a life of spiritual renunciation in an ashram, but the voice of society shouts in your head, "Oh, no, no, that's wrong. You've got too good of an education to waste it. You've got to make something real of yourself." The voice of fear tells us, "How will I feed myself? Artists and musicians and teachers don't make any money. I have to do something sensible." We get distracted from our true dharma by the voice of desire for material wealth and the acceptance of society, and so we choose to follow the voices of desire, fear, and societal conditioning rather than the inner voice of our true intuition. We may end up with a good job and an abundant bank account, but having suppressed our intuition and hence having *not* fulfilled our life's path, we likely won't feel deeply content or satisfied.

My guru, His Holiness Pujya Swami Chidanand Saraswatiji, often says that when you enter a destination address into your GPS device, there's always one more step. There's a button that says, ACCEPT or START. You have to push that button in order for guidance to start. Most of us just haven't pushed that button in our life. We've keyed in an address, a destination we want to go to, but we haven't actually accepted the voice of our own intuition to guide us on the path to reach there.

So how do I focus and make decisions in my life?

Focus on discovering who you are. What to do will follow easily and naturally. And when a path isn't immediately clear, you'll make a decision anyway, and either way will be right. Wisdom very frequently comes not so much in the decision itself but in how we live with the decisions that we've made.

When you visit an ice cream shop for the very first time, you have no idea what strawberry, vanilla, or chocolate tastes like, but you have to make a choice. In life, very frequently we have to make decisions without having sampled all the options. Life's opportunities lie in correctly utilizing the decisions we've made. In many cases, wisdom comes *after* we make the decision, not before. Wisdom comes from learning how to turn your decision into the *right* decision. If it turns out that you made an incorrect decision and your intuitive wisdom guides you to change paths, then courageously accept that you made a wrong turn and quickly reroute. Sometimes even the voice in our digital GPS provides us with rerouting directions and shows us how to get back on track. There is nothing to be ashamed about if you need to make a U-turn in life or if you need to ask for directions along the way.

The best way to make conscious decisions that are in alignment with your highest self is to meditate upon them. When you're in a state of meditative awareness, calmness, and spaciousness, simply picture yourself having made each of the different options. If you're trying to choose, for example, between moving to Paris or New York. Picture yourself living in each city. What does it look like? What does it feel like in your body, in your heart? Picture yourself five years from now having made each of the different decisions. Then picture yourself ten years from now. How does each decision feel inside of you? Allow yourself to drop into the body, into the breath, into your heart. How does it *feel*? Use that feeling sense within the body to access your intuitive knowing. If one option feels spacious and you expand into it, and the other one makes you contract or tense up, chances are the first option is the right one. This is where we sometimes use the term *gut instinct*. When something makes our abdomen contract and tighten, it can be a strong signal to stop and assess if we are really making the right choice. Our gut is literally yelling for our attention. That's another way our intuitive voice speaks to us.

However, one thing to be aware of is that sometimes the tightening in the gut is due not to the decision being wrong but due to our fear of taking the risk. That butterflies-in-the-stomach feeling as you're about to walk on stage doesn't mean you shouldn't go on stage. You most definitely should! But it's a risk and when we take risks, we frequently experience a tightening and discomfort in the gut. Don't mistake that for a signal that you're making the wrong decision. It is simply a signal of a courageous and uncomfortable decision.

Success and Spiritual Development

Can success and spiritual development go together?

Absolutely! If you look at the Hindu epics, the stories of the incarnations of the Divine on earth in the form of Krishna and Rama, you'll see in both cases that they were kings. Krishna was king of a city called Dwarka, which was a city made of gold! There is no teaching that says in order to be spiritual one must relinquish success or wealth. Spiritual problems around success come not from the success itself, but from two main sources: 1) our definition of success, and 2) our single-pointed focus on material prosperity to the exclusion of our spiritual development.

Most people tend to see their success and their spiritual development as separate pursuits and separate goals: success over here, spiritual development over there. But let's look at what success really means—what sort of success do we want, and why do we want it?

If you ask anyone what their definition of success is, most people will tell you that success means being wealthy and powerful. But let's look at that deeper and really examine it. The CEO of a large corporation is certainly a wealthy and powerful position, so imagine then that you're a rich and powerful CEO. Then what? Then most people say, "Well, then I would have financial abundance, and therefore financial freedom." Okay. But then what? What does that get you? Then they'll say something like, "Then I wouldn't have to worry so much about making money." Okay. Great. So success becomes that which leads to a stress-free life. See how the definition has changed already in just a few questions diving deep? Then what after that? What after having enough money not to worry about money? Then people say, "Oh, then I would have time for my family. I'd have time for my spiritual pursuits. Then, ultimately, I would be happy."

Even people whose definition of success is material and financial are actually ultimately looking to have time for their spiritual practice, time to be with their family, time to take a walk in the park, time to watch the sun set. They know these are the things that will make them truly happy. They just think the pathway to those things is through money.

If we recognize that our core desire is happiness and peace, we can actually strive toward those goals right away without running through the circles of trying to achieve one thing (money) with the belief it will give us something else (happiness). If we can start immediately, directly working to bring happiness into our lives, it can free us from decades of stress and unnecessary tension.

There's a great parable about the investment banker who goes on vacation to a beautiful seaside village. One morning he's sitting under a tree near the ocean and sees a fishing boat come in, dock, and the fisherman get off the boat. The fisherman comes to sit near the banker. This investment banker asks him, "So, what do you do?"

The man says, "I'm a fisherman."

The banker says, "Oh, but you've only got two or three fish."

"Yes, that's enough. That's all my family needs."

"But there're so many hours left in the day. It's still early. You could've stayed out. You could've kept catching more and more fish."

The fisherman asks the banker, "Well, why would I have done that, since this is all my family needs?"

The banker replies, "You could sell the extra fish, get a bigger boat, and make more money. Then you won't even have to go out. You could start a company of fishermen. Hire people who will go out for you."

"And then?" the fisherman asks. "These days I sleep until late in the morning. The reason I only go out for a few hours is because I sleep longer, take a beautiful walk, and spend time with my family. I spend time with my friends and go to our local church."

The banker exclaims, "No, no. See, you've got to spend time in the ocean and catch the fish. Then you can start a company, hire other people, and they'll keep fishing and bringing in the money. Then, of course, you'll have to move to the city, but you'll be the one in charge of the biggest fishing company that the country has ever seen."

"And then what?"

"Well, that's the great part. You'll have so much money in just a couple of years that you'll be able to retire, move to the beach, sleep in the mornings, spend time with your family, take a walk, only be out in your boat as much as you like, and enjoy your life!"

"But that's what I already do!" exclaimed the fisherman.

We laugh when we hear this story because we see the ridiculousness of it, and yet that is the very trajectory most of our lives take. That's why when we talk about success and spiritual goals, we realize that they're actually the same. The ultimate goal of both is joy, peace, fulfillment, and freedom.

The straightest path to success is to ask yourself: What matters to me? What is it that I ultimately want most of all? There isn't a right answer. Ask yourself deeply. What most people are looking for—through money, careers, achievement, fancy houses, name, and fame—is happiness in life. We're yearning to have time to take a walk and watch the sunset, to have time to spend with our families, to meditate. That's success, and it goes hand in hand with our spiritual goals.

There's a beautiful teaching by a revered saint, Swami Dayanand Saraswatiji, who used to live in Rishikesh, just opposite from Parmarth Niketan, where I live. He said that the only definition of success that matters is how we respond to the inevitable times when the universe does not act the way we think it should. Can we be peaceful, stable, grounded, wise, compassionate, and joyful in both the ups and the downs of life? That's our spiritual goal, our spiritual practice. The only way for us to respond with peace, calm, love, and understanding in challenging times is when we are spiritually grounded and anchored, when we are not looking to other people or situations for our happiness.

If my happiness depends on my bank balance or whether you give me a raise, vote for me, or buy my product, then every time the stock market goes up or down, every time my company's ratings fluctuate, every time my bank balance or my relationships change, I'm going to lose my connection to joy and peace. I'm going to react in an unconscious way.

Real success is the connection that only comes from spiritual practice. Success and spiritual development go hand in hand. Spiritual awakening is actually the highest level of success. We can't eat money, we can't sit across the dining room table from it and have a nice romantic dinner, we can't come home to it and cry to it about the trials and tribulations of our day, we can't put our arm around it in bed, we can't use it to wipe our tears, or get a hug when we're feeling down, and it doesn't laugh at our jokes. All the real joy and real connection that we're looking for in life doesn't come from money. The great tragic fallacy is our belief that through money, through a very circuitous route, we will find joy and connection. We think, "If I have money, people will respect me. If they respect me, they will love me, they'll pay attention to me. If they love me and pay attention to me, I'll feel worthy, I'll feel like I matter. I'll feel loved and loveable." For all that we do under the guise of achieving success, ultimately we are looking for love and connection.

So why not go straight there? There is nothing wrong, of course, with being the president or the CEO, or with having money and big houses, as long as we're not looking to these things to give us that inner experience of peace, joy, and happiness.

There is a wonderful story of a woman who is on her hands and knees on the road at night, searching for something under a bright street light. A wise man walks up to her and asks her, "Mother, what are you looking for?"

She says, "I've lost my key."

The man feels bad for her, so he also gets down on his hands and knees to search. After some time, he asks her, "Mother, where exactly did you lose your key?"

"Oh, I lost it in the house."

Baffled, he says, "Then why in the world are you looking for it on the road?"

"It is dark in my house," she answers matter-of-factly. "I have no light to see. Here there is this bright streetlight. So I figured I would look where there is light rather than in the dark where I cannot see."

"Go back to your house, Mother," he tells her gently. "Even an army cannot find your key here. It may take some time, but you will find it in the house."

I love this story because this is how so many of us live. We search outside for that which we've lost inside. For that lady maybe it was a key to a cupboard, and for us it's the key to happiness and peace in our life. We also look outside where it's light, rather than inside where the key actually is. It is very bright in shopping centers, in stores, on the screens of our devices, in the world around us, and of course all the marketing gimmicks shout

COME HOME TO YOURSELF

at us, "Buy this and you'll be happy." But no matter how hard we look, no matter how much we buy or achieve or attain financially or professionally, we never find that key because it just doesn't exist there.

It's important to mention, of course, that happiness, peace, and professional success or wealth are not mutually exclusive. It's not that having expensive things or a successful job or a big house steals our peace and happiness. The problem arises only when I am looking *in* those things for my peace and happiness. If the woman in the road had answered the wise man's question with, "Oh, I'm just taking a walk and enjoying the moonlight," there wouldn't even be a story. She would have been enjoying the outdoors for what it can offer—fresh air, moonlight, a nice walk. This story is significant only because she was searching for what was not there. Similarly, we face a problem when we think that by achieving something or buying something we will get happiness. It just isn't there. We can buy comfort, convenience, luxury, and entertainment, but we cannot buy happiness.

I did a personal study on this once. After I had been in India for about a year or two, I felt that I had some very deep life lessons around what really brings happiness. I could feel it, experience it, and know it within myself. But, remember, I am still a scientist at heart even though I'm in an ashram instead of a university! So, I wanted to conduct a study to see if my instincts were actually true. I spoke with about ten people I knew, each of whom was a great success in a different field. There was a CEO of a billion-dollar company, a tenured professor at Stanford, a well-known Hollywood actress, a singer with songs in the Top 10 chart, and an athlete who played professional basketball. Some of them I spoke to on the phone and others I met in person. In the midst of our conversation, I discreetly asked them all one question: "Are you happy?" That was the real point of my study.

The answers I got fell into two categories. About half of them said, "I will be happy when _____," and they filled in the blank with different accomplishments or life changes, including "the kids finally going off to college" or "I finally get this raise, this promotion" or "I finally lose weight." The other half replied, "I would be happy if _____," and they filled in the blank with varied wishes, including "the kids would only clean up their room," "my husband would work less," "there wasn't so much traffic." Every single one of them had reached the absolute pinnacle of what the rest of the world is striving to achieve, yet they were all still one thing away from happiness. This is the key about happiness. When we go down an external, circuitous route to reach happiness, there will always something between us and the goal. I have to get this degree, then that job, then this promotion, this much acclaim. I have to reach that level and then I'll be happy. But when we keep going at it that way, there's always one more thing between us and real happiness, which, remember, is our true goal, and is real success.

Try to shift your definition of success to: What's the shortest route to get where I want to go? Mathematics teaches that the shortest distance between two points is a straight line. Let us walk the straightest line to our ultimate goal.

It's important also to realize that there's a big difference between the deep, true, lasting happiness I'm talking about and the fleeting pleasure of eat, drink, and be merry. The shortest distance to a very temporary happiness for some people may be a couple of shots of alcohol or a scrumptious meal. But that's not what I'm talking about because that isn't deep or lasting. You have to keep doing it over and over in what we call the *hedonic treadmill.* Like hamsters on a wheel, we keep running to get another hit of this fleeting happiness.

Real happiness is that which actually takes you *out of* your individual self, not *into* your isolated self. If happiness to you is just a few hours of drinking or eating or shopping or binge-watching a TV show to escape your pain or boredom or loneliness or frustration, that's not real happiness. That's escapism, denial, and numbness. Do it too frequently and it becomes addiction.

There is, of course, nothing wrong with a movie or a great meal or even spending some time resting on the couch enjoying a TV show. The problem again arises when we look to those momentary pleasures for meaningful or lasting joy.

True happiness is the state in which we are able to experience deep joy. We don't need a funny movie, a drink, approval, or promotions. The happiness our spiritual path brings is a sustained level of happiness that doesn't fluctuate with traffic or weather or stock market patterns. We don't become indifferent to the world around us, but our inner peace remains consistent even in the world's inevitable ups and downs.

The shortest route to that is spiritual practice. When that becomes our focus, we turn onto the path of true success.

The Path of Spirituality

What is the purpose of spirituality? Why do I have to be spiritual? When there's so much to do in the world, so much to achieve, why should I be spiritual? Why bother?

First, we must understand what spirituality truly is! Spirituality does not say you must chant a certain mantra, perform a certain ritual, or pray in a certain way to a certain manifestation of the Divine. Spirituality simply means that you have consciously chosen to live your life focused on spirit and attentive to spirit. There are two ways to see the world—materially or spiritually. The materialist viewpoint sees matter and objects. This is my body over here, in this shape and size. Then there is empty space. That is you over there, with your size and shape. Then there is more empty space. Someone else, then, is over there on the other side of the empty space. Spirituality says: You have a body, but you're not the body. You are spirit not matter. There is no place I end and you begin. There is no empty space between us. We are inextricably connected as spirit. Even these days advanced science is telling us something similar. With our naked eye, the body looks very separate. Our boundary is at our skin and bones. We know where we end and the rest of the world begins. But if you look at us under an electron microscope, you won't see borders and boundaries. You'll see whirling and twirling electrons spinning around. Quantum physics tells us that we are all connected. Slowly science is getting closer to telling us what spirituality has been saying since the dawn of time. So spirituality is important because it connects us to the very truth of who we are and what our relationship is to the rest of the universe. Spirituality simply says that as I go about my day, instead of focusing on matter, I will focus on spirit. Instead of seeing myself and others as objects with various characteristics of gender, appearance, size, shape, color, and age, I will try to see all as spirit, as a reflection of divinity.

In that conscious intention toward spirit, we find that we become free of much of what ails us today—stress, depression, anxiety, addiction, anger, frustration, and conflicted relationships.

Let's say one morning you wake up and check your temperature, and your thermometer shows 101 degrees Fahrenheit. You ask others what their temperature is and they say 98.6 degrees Fahrenheit. What does that mean? It means you have a fever. It means something is not right. In order to regain your health, you'll rest, drink fluids, visit a doctor, take medicine or herbs. You'll understand that the systems in your body are running awry. But now imagine that when you ask around, everyone says their temperature is 101 degrees Fahrenheit. Do you still have a fever? Yes, of course you do.

In the first case, you know that something is off and look for a solution. But when everyone's temperature is 101 degrees Fahrenheit, what happens? You assume that it's normal and so you don't rest or drink extra fluids or go to the doctor. The fever is still ravaging your body, but because everyone else has it too, you don't look for a solution. Hence it gets worse. You just get sicker. This is what is happening with depression, anxiety, and misery today.

A huge percentage of people are living in a regular state of stress, worry, anxiety, and depression. But when we talk to our friends, we find that they're also stressed, worried, anxious, and depressed. This has become the new normal. Tragically we've started to accept this way of being and have stopped trying to become free of it. But remember: The fact that others are also sick does not mean you are not! Just because so many people are also depressed and anxious does not mean that it's okay for you to be! Spirituality helps bring our metaphoric temperature back to normal. It's what helps us get grounded, centered, balanced, healthy. It helps us stay afloat while the waves of life go up and down.

What is on the surface of the ocean? Waves. And what do waves do? They go up and down, up and down. If I live only on the surface of the ocean, I'm going to go up and down with the waves. If my emotional state is based on other people's actions or words, my emotions will go up and down. If my happiness and peace are based on interest rates or the stock market or my weight or my followers on Instagram, I'm going to go up and down, because these things keep changing. When they're moving in the right direction, we feel really good. But what does physics tell us? Everything that goes up has to come down. This is the very nature of nature. If I'm attached to something on the superficial level, I may love the ups, but those downs will cause stress and depression.

This is what happens in our lives. If I am living only on the surface level of life, in the waves on the surface of the ocean, then when I'm rising I may be temporarily satisfied, but I will always worry about falling. When I'm falling, I'm stressed and depressed. The answer to this up-and-down existence lies in spiritual practice. Spirituality doesn't say, "Get out of the ocean. Don't live, don't enjoy, don't get wet." Instead, it says, "Anchor yourself in the depths of the ocean rather than only on the surface." The depths of the ocean are always very still, very calm. There is no high tide or low tide in the depths of the ocean and no stormy seas.

Also, there's more life and beauty in the depths. When you look at the surface of the ocean, it looks just like water with a few patches of darker or lighter hues. But when you put on a snorkeling mask, you start to see all the beautiful colors, the coral, the fish. If you go scuba diving, even deeper in the ocean, you really experience the full exquisiteness of life underwater. The deeper you go, the more beautiful it is. The deeper you go, the more powerfully fulfilling it is.

The same is true about life. We stay on the surface because we think that's all there is, but we must dive deep. The deeper you go, the more stillness, calmness, and peace you will find. The deeper you go, the more beauty, the more life, the more color. That's where the real excitement is. It's not a shallow excitement of going up and down with waves. It's a deeper, consistent exuberance found in the depths of your very self.

I want to devote some time of my life every day to moving ahead on the spiritual path, but how do I know that this path actually leads anywhere? How do I know that there is actually a self beyond the physical body? If I'm going to dedicate some of my time to something, I want to make sure that there are going to be some returns.

Here's the dilemma you face: Your tool of knowing is the mind. That's how you know things, how you process information. You are going to try to justify the presence of the self and the value of searching for it with your thinking, analytical mind. Therein lies the problem. The mind cannot know about something unknowable by the mind. And so a question like this puts us in this very interesting position. You need to convince a part of yourself that—by its very nature—cannot understand.

When I'm sitting in satsang with you all, I know that there are people sitting in front of me. How do I know that? My eyes can see them. If I had a mask over my eyes and I couldn't see them, they would still be there. Maybe one of them would speak, and with my ears I would know they're there. But if I were wearing earplugs along with my eye mask, I wouldn't be able to see or hear them. Maybe then I'd reach out and identify them by touch. Or maybe someone is wearing perfume that I can smell, or maybe the ground shakes ever so slightly when someone heavy walks by and I can feel that slight shift in the ground. In all circumstances, I know that there are people in front of me through my senses. If I were blind, or my eyes were closed and none of these people spoke or moved, if none of them had any scent at all, and if they were too far away for me to reach out my arms and touch them, I would have no way of knowing they are there. But that doesn't make them disappear. It just means that I don't have any way of knowing them.

This brings us to our dilemma, because we cannot see, hear, smell, taste, or feel the Divine or our true self. Most people demand proof of God. But when they say, "Prove it to me," what they mean is, "Prove it to me through the methods that I have deemed acceptable. Prove it through my five senses, with the tools of science. What does God look like? What color is God? How big is God? Where exactly is my true self located in terms of latitude and longitude so I may locate it?" But of course neither God nor our true self, not our soul, our spirit, nor our consciousness has a size, shape, weight, color, or form that can be detected through any of the five senses or through any tool developed by science. So we find ourselves skeptical because God's existence is not provable in the same way as a tangible object or a mathematical calculation.

Interestingly, neither is love. If I ask you, "Do you love your husband or wife, or your mother or father?" you'll say yes. Of course you do. But if I say, "Prove it. Show it to me," you cannot. There is no weight or size or shape or color or any tangible qualities of love through which you can prove it. But your inability to prove that you love them does not diminish your awareness that you do, in fact, love them. The fact that you cannot adequately convince me of your love through scientific means does not make you doubt your love. You know it. You feel it. You experience it as deep truth.

Once you've experienced love, the fact that you can't see, hear, or smell it is irrelevant. Nobody can convince you that love doesn't exist if you've ever been in love. If I say, "How much does your love weigh? What's its size and shape? Put it here in this crucible or beaker," what will you do? You'll laugh at the sadness of me not understanding what love really is. But you won't start disbelieving in love because you've actually experienced it! It is the same with God and the same with the presence of the Divine within our own selves. It cannot be proven in a mathematical or scientific way. But it can be experienced deeply and profoundly through spiritual practice. As long as we relegate our knowing to five physical senses, we limit our entire lives.

This is why the practices of meditation, prayer, and selfless service are so important. These practices bring you closer to God and put you in touch with what you can call a sixth sense, or another way of knowing. You cannot use the same way of knowing that you are used to.

Our religious libraries are filled with accounts from sages and mystics of all lineages and traditions sharing their deep spiritual experiences. Another way of knowing is through believing those whom you trust. Surely, if God didn't exist and there was no true benefit to a spiritual path, there would not be thousands and thousands of books by and about the world's greatest seers. Choose one. It could be Paramhansa Ramakrishna or Kabir or Mirabai or St. Francis of Assisi or Rumi or Tagore. Find one who touches you and allow yourself to believe the words they are sharing about their own lives and experiences.

Lastly, although we cannot use our five senses and science to know God, we can certainly use science to study the benefits of faith and spirituality. There are many studies that have been done at reputed institutions such as Johns Hopkins, Duke, Dartmouth, and more, which demonstrate quite robustly that people who are spiritual are not only happier, less stressed, and more joyful, but they are also actually physically healthier!

So the benefits of walking this path are not only spiritual benefits of awakening and divine connection but are also beneficial to your life as a human being in a body with a brain.

Looking for Something
Versus Running Away

What is the difference between looking for something and running away from something?

There are two ways of getting somewhere. One is to move toward the destination, and the other is to move away from the opposite direction.

For example, in order to get to Rishikesh from Delhi, I can focus on Rishikesh and find a vehicle to get me there. Or if I hate Delhi, I do my best to get away from it. If I happen to be pushing against Delhi in the northern direction and I do it for long enough, I'll end up in Rishikesh. The result is the same, but they are two very distinct paths. One path was focused on getting to Rishikesh. The other was focused on getting away from Delhi.

This is the difference between being pulled toward something versus running away from something. Some people embark on a spiritual path because they are yearning to experience the Divine. Life may be great but they want something more; they want to expand their consciousness and connect with their deeper, truer, higher self. They are moving toward something deep, looking for it, embracing it. Another way to come onto the spiritual path, though, is by pushing away from the life we are living. Sometimes people push against life—against the pain or struggle or difficulty of their relationships, their jobs, or other life circumstances. They move to an ashram or isolated retreat center, start meditating, take up yoga, and embrace spirituality as a way of escaping the trials and tribulations of their former life.

If you find yourself on a spiritual path only because you're running away from something, it's not going to go very deep. It'll last only as long as your pain is unbearable. Maybe someone broke your heart, maybe you lost a loved one or you were fired from your job. Maybe you hate your mother-in-law or your partner. It stings, and in order to get away from that sting, you might move to an ashram and join a spiritual community for some time. If your agenda is only being free of the pain that broke your heart, then the minute that pain heals, which it inevitably will, you discover, "Oh, I don't really like living in an ashram," or, "Oh, I'm actually way too busy to keep up my meditation practice." Or if you move away just to escape a difficult family member, what you find is that there are difficult people in ashrams also! Wherever you go in life, you will find different types of people. Inevitably some of them will rub you the wrong way. If your spiritual path was just a way to avoid that, it won't be satisfying for very long. In these situations spirituality was simply an escape. Yes, it is better than alcohol or drugs or binge-watching TV serials, but this way of adopting a spiritual life doesn't go deep and isn't lasting.

There is also another possibility. You might get on a spiritual path in response to something that's happened; perhaps you are pushing things away, but if—once you are on the spiritual path—you actually allow it to touch and expand your heart, and if you allow yourself to truly dive deep, then it doesn't matter why you got on it.

If you allow yourself to be really open to that, it's going to transform you, regardless of how or why you got into it.

Sometimes, spirituality is also used as a Band-Aid for our brokenness: "I don't want to think about something that's hurting me, so I will just do my mantra instead." In some ways, that's a great practice. One of the great benefits of having a mantra is that when you find your mind going off in dysfunctional, nonhelpful, pain-inducing directions, you can chant a mantra instead. But if there's something important in your life you need to look at or work through or heal, the answer is not to ignore it and just chant your mantra. The answer is to actually do the work to move through the pain. Spiritual bypass is never a beneficial solution.

Whether you run toward it or come to it by running away from something behind you, don't worry. The question now is: Once you're on the spiritual path, how do you open yourself fully to the power, the possibility of where you are, and enable your life to be fuller, richer, and deeper through your spiritual practice?

Why is a spiritual life sometimes painful? Isn't it supposed to be only joyful?

There are no mistakes in the universe. This doesn't mean, however, that everything feels good. We were never promised a life without pain. There's no scripture I know of in which God says, "Come to Me and I'll make sure you never get fired from your job," or "Come to Me and I'll make sure everyone always does exactly what you want, when you want it," or "Come to Me and I promise you'll never get sick or lose a loved one." We were never promised anything like this. A spiritual life is not an inoculation against poverty, failure, loss, or challenges. Look at Bhagawan Krishna and Bhagawan Rama. They are worshipped as the Divine here on earth in human form. And yet, their lives are full of trouble, pain, and loss—full of far more challenging circumstances than most of us face. If even God on earth faces struggles, it shows us clearly that being spiritual does not exempt us.

What a spiritual life promises us is the opportunity to discover who we are, and through that understanding we stay anchored, grounded, and connected regardless of what happens in the world around us. And yes, along the way there are going to be moments of pain as our way of knowing and understanding gets rearranged and as we let go of the death grip with which we've been grasping at the world.

When we've identified deeply and fully with the ego-self, with our physical body, with our history, with our relationships and roles, with our patterns of thinking, it can be quite painful to set ourselves free! It's like the metaphoric Band-Aid getting ripped off our skin. We know it needs to come off. We know it has served its purpose and now is not only useless but actually detrimental. Nonetheless, to rip it off causes a moment of pain. Similarly, as we embark on a spiritual path and peel back layers and layers of the not-self so that the true self can emerge, some of those layers of ignorance don't peel away easily.

I remember saying to Pujya Swamiji in the beginning, through streams of tears, "Nobody ever told me that when you annihilate my ego you take my heart with it!" We talk so frequently about the annihilation of the ego on the spiritual path, and that sounds really good in theory. But we don't realize how the arms of the ego, like an octopus, have wrapped themselves around so much of how we identify ourselves, including our emotions and our hearts. It doesn't always feel good, just as having a tumor removed does not feel good. But no one with cancer would ever say, "Forget it, Doctor, the surgery is going to be too painful. I don't like being in a hospital." We understand that removing the tumor is critical to survival.

I've also learned that much of what I identified as my heart, giving it semantically the great importance of my intuitive center, is *not* actually my deep, intuitive heart but rather is simply mental patterns of thinking and identifying that have become tightly interwoven with my emotions. So, for example, to realize that certain ways we have always behaved, thought, and identified ourselves are fundamentally not true is painful. It can feel like a very stuck Band-Aid getting ripped off our minds and emotional hearts. But the emotional heart that reacts to insult, criticism, rejection, and loss is not the deep intuitive heart our spiritual traditions speak of. That is why emotional pain can actually be such a great catalyst for spiritual growth, because it sends us looking deeper than the emotional feeling states we've always identified as our heart and into the actual expansive, spacious, nonattached source of true love!

When we're on the spiritual path and it doesn't feel good, when in meditation we find ourselves face-to-face with our own darkness and shadows, it can be tempting to run from that. We need to understand, though, that we're here on earth in this body, with this incarnation, for a reason, and we must allow ourselves to really open up to the fullness of this particular incarnation and what its unique dharma may be. Underneath it all, it's beautiful. It is nothing but grace.

PART 2

Our Minds

Our minds are the steering wheel for our lives. You would never buy a new car—no matter how beautiful, sleek, and fast it was—if there was no steering wheel, or if the steering wheel had a fundamental defect. You would instinctively realize that being able to go from zero to one hundred in a few seconds flat is not only useless but seriously dangerous if you cannot control the car's direction. Mahatma Gandhi said beautifully, "What is the point of that fast speed which has no direction?" Our minds give the direction to our lives. They are literally the steering wheel. What we think tends to become what we do. From our actions unfolds our destiny. Our minds determine our inner state. Am I happy, sad, fulfilled, dejected, envious, satisfied? These are states of the mind. So, it determines our inner experience and our outer experience. The way we interact in the world, the choices we make, the preconceptions with which we arrive at each moment, each interaction—this is all determined by the mind.

In the Bhagavad Gita, Krishna—the embodiment of the Divine—tells us that our life is like a horse-drawn chariot. The chariot is our physical body. Our senses are the horses—eager to run here and there, getting constantly diverted and distracted by every nice smell or taste. When they have the run of the show, we find ourselves directionless and astray. The reins are the mind, and the intellect (an aspect of the mind) is the charioteer.

Only a mind that is anchored deep in intelligence and wisdom can keep the horses from running astray. And the most important part is that our true self, soul, *atman* is the passenger. It means that the ultimate success of your soul's journey here on earth—in a body with a karmic package to work out—is dependent upon the functioning of your mind. If the mind gets lost, the horses run off, carrying not only your body but also your soul's journey off the path.

In order to walk a path in life that is going to bring you the greatest sense of joy, meaning, and fulfillment—and which will give you the sacred opportunity to realize the very truth of yourself and step into that experience of oneness with the Divine—you need your mind to be on your side. It must be attentive. Its intentions must be in alignment with high spiritual goals, rather than focused on the next quick fix. Think back to the example I gave at the beginning about the students counting baskets and the gorilla who came and danced on the court in the middle of the basketball game. Their eyes saw the gorilla. They couldn't have missed it. Why did the sensory experience not register in the mind for them to notice? Because they were not being attentive to gorillas. They were being attentive only to baskets. It was the instruction they'd given their minds. The mind's intention was only to count baskets. So we work with the mind in order to a) bring peace to the mind and free us from negative patterns that cause suffering, b) enable our attention to align with what we *know* we are looking for rather than get distracted every moment, and c) set our intentions to attainment of the highest and deepest wisdom and experience of our true self rather than simply mimic whatever the influencers on social media are doing or whatever our next-door neighbor is doing.

But how do we get our mind to work *with* us instead of *against* us? This section dives into the *why* of the wandering mind and how to bring it back as well as how to work with the different patterns and tendencies of the mind without getting stuck in them. Remember: The mind is not the enemy. It can be your best friend if you approach it with love, awareness, patience, and diligence.

Calming and Understanding the Wandering Mind

Where is the mind? Why, whenever I try to meditate, does it wander so much?

Where is the mind? The mind is nowhere. We can't pinpoint and say, "This is where the mind is." But what we do know is that we experience the mind through the brain.

We know this because things that happen to our brain affect our mind. If you drink alcohol, a physical substance that has a chemical reaction on your brain, your experience of your mind changes. Maybe you were feeling stressed, so you had a drink and now you're not so stressed. Maybe you were feeling shy, so you drank alcohol and now you're ready to dance with the world. We know that physical changes in the brain impact the mind, whether the physical change is from alcohol and drugs or brain injuries or neurodegenerative illnesses. Each of these very physical things taking place in the neurons of our physical brain has a profound impact on our experience of our mind. So we know that the brain is the medium through which we experience the mind and all its qualities like thought, emotion, and memory.

Several years ago someone very close to us passed away of Alzheimer's. I know from my personal background in neurology a little bit about the way Alzheimer's changes the brain. We watched her brain disintegrate. Here was a woman who used to be loving, kind, and generous, who had suddenly become angry and violent, hitting people around her, not recognizing her own family members. It made me wonder about love. Love feels so deep; it runs deep in my heart and soul. Yet, with a little bit of degeneration of the dendrites and glial cells in the brain, where does that which we identify as the deepest love go? How does that love disappear in the face of disruption to brain cells?

I thought a lot about this at that time. Love lives in the heart, not in the dendrites. Are we so shallow that our deepest love is rendered obsolete as the proteins in our brain run amok?

This made me start to think, as she was the first person I knew so closely to have this sort of illness, and having studied about it, I was fascinated by what was happening.

Here's what I realized: Of course love doesn't live in our dendrites or glial cells. Of course it is much deeper than that. Yet, the brain is the medium for the experience of thought and feeling, the same way that the eyes are the medium for the experience of sight. Sight does not exist in my eyes, but if you pull out my eyes, I will no longer be able to see. In the same way, when the brain is changed—chemically or electrically or physically—our experience of our mind changes. There is a vast literature on this in the field of neurology. My favorite is a book by Oliver Sacks called *The Man Who Mistook His Wife for a Hat*. Obviously, his wife had not become a hat, but due to an injury in his brain, he was unable to utilize his thinking and feeling mind to recognize her and distinguish the face of the woman he loved from a hat! So his mind became troubled due to a very physical issue in his brain. It was not a problem of the mind, but a problem of the brain. However, the brain is the medium through which we experience the mind and interact with the world.

Since that time, I have had another opportunity to witness the intersection of brain and mind as I've watched my own mother suffer from severe dementia due to a massive cerebral hemorrhage. She doesn't know who she is or who anyone else is. Much of the things she says don't make any sense at all, and when they do make sense they don't relate to anything happening in the present moment. She has lost most of her long-term memory and the ability to form new short-term memories. She is, by God's grace, mostly happy and content but she hates being bathed, hates having to stand and walk to exercise. Now, nothing happened to her as a woman, as my mother, other than some blood that leaked from a blood vessel into her brain, causing widespread damage. A purely physical assault on the gray and white matter of her brain. And yet in the wake of it, she no longer likes what she used to like (bathing, exercise, healthy food) and now she likes things she never liked before (junk food and sitting around all day on a couch listening to music on an iPad). She doesn't recognize her family members or friends, and doesn't remember most of her own life: a 180-degree change in personality due simply to damage in the physical brain.

And yet, even though her brain doesn't know who I am, her deeper self does. The part of her that is neither brain nor mind absolutely recognizes me (as evidenced by all the kisses she plants all over me and the way her eyes light up whenever I visit). It's been an incredible experience to connect on a level beyond the brain, beyond the mind, deep in the actual intuitive spiritual heart, which wasn't damaged at all.

Why doesn't that mind let me sit still? Why is it negative?

The mind tends to be negative because we have become habituated to negativity. Children's minds are not negative. They're usually happy and smiling. They're only negative when they're hungry, tired, or have a full diaper—when their physical bodies and survival are at risk. Feed them, clean them, and they're happy again. Hold them, love them, and they're extra happy. In adults, the thinking mind, the ego-identifying mind, starts to steal that happiness.

We are raised to identify as our body, what it looks like and what it can do. We are praised for being good-looking and successful. Thus, even as young children we start to identify our self-worth by our beauty and achievements. We learn to compare ourselves with others—our siblings or other students in school.

Along with this we are also indoctrinated into a mindset of scarcity: There isn't enough success or praise or love to go around and we have to compete with others for it. That means every time someone else is beautiful or a fantastic athlete or super intelligent or achieves something wonderful or even gets married and has a baby, we find ourselves feeling badly rather than happy for them. It's as though their success has taken a piece out of the finite pie of goodness in the universe and now there is less available for us. So the mind gets primed to be negative. Either we judge others negatively, allowing ourselves to feel better about ourselves, or we judge ourselves negatively! Either way the mind is negative.

As we grow older, we frequently end up with one of two pathologies: Either, "I'm the worst. I don't deserve anything. I'm useless and worthless," or, "I deserve everything but the world isn't giving it to me. The world is at fault." In both situations, we are mired in negativity.

The judging mind is always negative. It's how we are raised: "This is pretty, this is ugly, this is good, this is bad. This is what good girls do, this is what bad girls do." We're constantly labeling, constantly judging: "Mommy's pretty little girl," "Mommy's good girl," or "You're a bad girl." So we develop a mental habit, this *sanskara,* of labeling things, and carry it into our world: "I'm beautiful, I'm ugly. I'm successful, I'm a failure. I'm worthy, I'm not worthy."

This is what occupies the mind, and it is never-ending. With more than eight billion people on the planet, there is no end to the number of those with whom you can compare yourself, or to the judgments you can pass. With all these games of the mind, you find that you are everywhere except here in the present moment.

The truth is that right here, in this breath, in this moment, you're okay. You're enough. It's enough. This breath is enough. This presence is enough. This moment is enough. But the habits and games of the mind do not let you be in the present and so you are spiraling around in the drama of not-enoughness.

When you start meditating, the mind actually amps up its patterns of negativity. Love, surrender, acceptance, and enoughness are enemies of the conditioned mind that indulges in competition, judgment, and negativity.

When you begin to touch the truer, deeper layer of the self, negative thoughts will frequently appear at the beginning. This is the ego's way of trying to prevent you from breaking free of the ego. But don't let this deter you. Just keep going, deeper and deeper, because as you go farther on your spiritual path, every time you surrender more, every time you experience your own fullness, every time you connect deeper and deeper, these negative thoughts will recede and eventually disappear almost entirely.

Interestingly, you may not even notice your wandering, judging, negative mind so much until you sit to meditate. Meditation shows us what is really going on in our own minds. It is the mirror of the mind. Once we see the pattern, we can work to overcome it.

Remember, though: It's not the mind that's the enemy, and it's not even the negative thoughts. Your conscious mind must ensure that you don't give the reins of your life to the conditioned, unconscious ego mind. As has been beautifully said, the mind is a great tool, but not a good master. If you want to solve a math problem, you need your mind. If you want to balance a checkbook, or enter data into a spreadsheet, or compare and contrast different route options for your trip, you need your mind. Your intuitive heart has no idea how to make a spreadsheet or how to read a map or follow instructions for a recipe; your mind knows how to do that.

We need the mind, but it's not supposed to be running the show. It's supposed to be a tool in our hands. This is where meditation becomes so important. It enables us to extricate ourselves from the clutches of the mind, and to experience a freedom of spaciousness and connection to our intuitive hearts. Eventually, as you practice meditation more and more, you become able to string more and more of those moments together.

Helpful Tools for Our Spiritual Journey

Why do some people react so inappropriately or hurtfully to various situations in life? Why does it seem like some people are not even capable of love or compassion?

We move through the world with our own toolbox, and that toolbox is how we respond to the world. Each of us comes into this world with our own karmic journey, our own karmic package. Part of that karmic package is our toolbox.

Suppose you find yourself in a situation where compassion, resilience, patience, or understanding is required. If, in your personal toolbox, you don't have these qualities, you're not going to be able to respond to that situation appropriately. Usually what happens in our world is people hurt us because they are not able to respond to situations skillfully.

Let's say I'm walking down the road and I see a nail sticking out of a wall and I realize that nail might hurt someone. What am I going to do? I'm going to pull out a hammer and try to hammer it back into the wall so it stops sticking out. I'm going to try to take care of the situation skillfully. But if I open up my toolbox and there is no hammer, and all I've got in there is a paintbrush or a toothbrush or a fork, I'm not going to be able to hammer the nail back into the wall effectively. I'll do the best I can with the tools I have, but inevitably I will make a mess of the situation. If the nail were a living being, it would yell, "Who the hell are you? What are you doing? Don't you understand that I'm a nail? Don't you realize I need a hammer right now, not a whacking from a toothbrush? Why are you whacking me?" The nail doesn't understand that we'd love a hammer, but we just don't have access to one right now.

This is a metaphor to answer the question of why people hurt us in life. There are so many times when what we need from someone is understanding, patience, and compassion, but people react with impatience, anger, and criticism. So we get hurt. But we blame the person for that, without understanding that they didn't wake up in the morning planning to hurt us, or intending to make a mess of that situation. They're just moving through the world with a not-very-well-stocked toolbox, and when the situation requires love or generosity or openness or understanding, they find that they don't have any of those things. What they have is fear, anger, confusion, violence, and resentment, so that's how they respond to the world.

Our toolbox is built up throughout our lives. It begins in our childhood. Our parents give us the first tools. If we are raised with patience, understanding, and generosity, we develop the tools for these qualities. But the opposite happens if we're raised with impatience and abuse.

However, if you were raised without adequate tools, don't despair. You can develop a very full, healthy toolbox on your own with clear intention and attention. Practices of meditation, yoga, mindfulness, prayer, spiritual study, selfless service, introspection, contemplation, and even therapy build up our toolbox. These are the sources from which we acquire tools for handling what life throws at us. So if you know that your personal toolbox is insufficient for the way you would like to see yourself moving through the world, allow yourself to dedicate some time and attention to building it.

What have been the most beneficial tools on your spiritual journey?

On a personal level, I think the tool that has been most beneficial for me throughout my life has been the knowledge, the deep awareness, that I deserve and am entitled to a happy life and good things in life, and that the world by nature is good. It's the way my parents raised me. They taught me, "You can do anything, be anyone, have anything, achieve anything."

When I was very young, my mother used to take me to the small amusement park on the Santa Monica pier at the beach near our house. The pier has a huge slide that is maybe as tall as a three- or four-story building. I loved the slide, but my mom was too scared to go down it with me. So she would grab any random man going up the stairs and ask, "Would you take my daughter down the slide?" I was maybe four or five years old. Today, people would call her crazy to casually hand off her toddler girl to some unknown male passerby! But my mother had a deep belief in the innate goodness of people, and it never occurred to her that anything could happen to me. She used to teach me, "Strangers are just friends we haven't met yet." That was the motto I was raised with. And with all that combined—faith in the goodness of people, faith in the universe, awareness that I was entitled to good things—I was secure in my belief that there would always be enough. I was not raised with fear or scarcity. I was raised with a sense of plenty.

What that did for me was it enabled me on my spiritual journey. If I didn't have faith in the universe, in its fundamental goodness or rightness, I think it would have been very difficult at the age of twenty-five to leave the world that I came from, to leave a path that I knew was going to take me toward financial and career success, to leave all that for a spiritual life. To walk out of a world in which everything is set for you, on a physical, tangible level, and walk into a place where you don't speak the language, you don't know anybody, you don't know anything about the culture, you have no idea what tomorrow is going to bring or how long they are going to let you stay—that's quite a risk. When I first moved to the ashram, Parmarth Niketan had a policy wherein each guest could stay for a maximum of fifteen days, and beyond that you needed special permission to continue living there.

If I had been raised to fear what's going to happen to me, where my next meal was going to come from, who's going to put a roof over my head . . . it would have been very difficult to take that leap of faith.

The other most beneficial tool in my life is a deep commitment to truth. Growing up in my home, telling a lie was the absolute worst sin you could commit. You could've done something horrible, but if you admitted it, the punishment would be almost nothing. On the flip side, you could've done almost nothing, but if you lied about it there was hell to pay. I wasn't permitted to lie even about little things. There was no such thing as a white lie in my house. This "truth at all costs" belief was really ingrained in me.

That's the second very powerful tool I have. That is why, when I was given the extraordinary experience of spiritual awakening and oneness on the banks of the Ganga, when I knew that this was where I was meant to be, there was no way I could *not* live it. I *knew* it was my truth and hence could not turn my back on it. People say to me, "God, it's amazing that you decided to stay, it's amazing that you left that Western world, it's amazing that you came here." But for me, there actually was no other option. I could not deny the truth that I had seen. I could not deny what I had experienced.

The life happiness I found didn't come in the form or manner in which I had anticipated. I was on a path, I was getting a PhD in psychology. I was married. I was going to live a normal life—house, kids, career, vacations at resorts. I was not expecting that the happiness of my life was going to come in renunciation, in celibacy, in spirituality, in service to others, living in an ashram in India. But when it happened, when I had that awareness, when I had that opening, there was no way I could deny it.

Truth was the biggest tool in my toolbox—it stared me in the face every time I opened my toolbox. There was no way I could deny that I had had that experience, no way I could turn my back on it and say, "I didn't see that." It is that commitment to truth that made me stay here.

How do we deal with people who have grudges and anger and are reacting with a tool that is not helpful for the situation?

The first aspect is to really recognize this and to realize that person is not deliberately trying to hurt us. Our pain stems not so much from what people do, but from the fact that we feel like a victim of it. We ask ourselves all the time, "Why me?" When we understand it's not about us, but it's about their insufficiently stocked toolbox, it takes that sting out of whatever they've done or said.

In Buddhism they speak about the *second arrow*. The first arrow is the one that actually pierces your skin, and it hurts! It may even draw blood. That pain is physical and neurological. It's automatic and nearly inescapable. But the lingering suffering is caused not by the first arrow but by the second arrow—the emotional reaction to the arrow. The mind says, "Why me? It's not fair. I'm always the one these things happen to. The universe hates me." The piercing of the second arrow lasts a lot longer and is a lot more damaging than the first arrow. The good news is that while we can't always avoid the first arrow, we can develop tools to avoid the second one.

Imagine you are walking through a park, and you get bitten by a mad dog. What are you going to do? You're going to go to the doctor, get the wound bandaged, and get a rabies shot. Would you chase the dog down the street to bite it back? Would you require psychological therapy to get over your mental anguish of being bit by a dog? Of course not. You understand that the dog didn't wake up in the morning planning to bite you, or lie there waiting to ambush you. You were just in the wrong place at the wrong time. You intuitively understand that. Even though you have a real wound that causes real pain and needs a real bandage, it doesn't create an emotional problem that breaks your heart.

The way we understand the dog is the same way we need to understand people in the world. The dog bites because it is sick.

That's why we say *mad dog*. Mad means not that the dog is angry but actually that the dog has rabies. It is sick with an illness that makes it crazy. That's why it bites. We can understand that the dog is sick, and though our leg may hurt for a few days, we do not suffer the mental trauma of being attacked because we understand that the attack was not about us. The same is true with most people who hurt us. They're not doing it *to* us, they're not plotting and scheming about how to make us miserable. They are sick, just like the dog is sick. They may not have an illness that's diagnosable with a blood test or curable with an injection or a pill, but they are living in a state of *dis-ease;* they are not in ease, not in joy, not in peace. They're upset. They're resentful. They're jealous. They're angry at the world. Their toolbox doesn't have love, patience, courage, or compassion at that moment. So in that state of dis-ease, lack of ease, what they've got in their toolbox is anger, grudges, violence, and meanness, and that's how they respond to the world.

When we truly and deeply understand that, their words or actions don't harm us psychologically any more.

This doesn't mean, of course, that we keep walking on the same path through the park, knowing that there is a mad dog sitting there. It doesn't mean that we allow ourselves to become victims. Spirituality does not make us doormats on which people can stomp their boots. Spirituality does not mean that we let ourselves be attacked, literally or metaphorically, over and over. We most certainly do whatever we can to avoid the mad dog or people who act like that! But spirituality enables us to not react when someone hurts us because we realize they are in a state of dis-ease. With clarity and compassion, we're able to respond effectively.

What is an effective response? Does yelling back at them work? Never. Does criticizing them work? Of course not. So when we know what doesn't work, we have to start looking at what might work.

If someone is mean to us, we have to understand that they are miserable. People who are happy spread happiness. This is why we like to be around happy people. People who are in love, even if they are not in love with you, are still really nice to be around. When a friend of yours falls in love, you can feel it, even though you are not the one they are in love with. The love seems to overflow. People in peace exude it. Pujya Swamiji always says, "When you are in peace, you exude peace, you spread peace, you manifest peace. When you are in pieces, that's what you spread—you spread pieces, you share pieces."

If somebody flings hurt and pain at us, it means that's what they have inside. Air conditioners give cold air because that's what they have. Heaters blow hot air because that's what they have. Whether it's helpful in that moment or not, that's all they have and so that's all they can give us.

If what someone has is pain and anger, that's what they're going to give you. You could scream all day at an air conditioner, "Hey! I'm getting pneumonia!" But it won't matter. You can start coughing and sneezing, you could get a fever, you could drop dead in front of it and it's going to keep blowing cold air, because that's all it has. The minute we recognize this, difficult people may not get easier to handle, but our understanding prevents us from reacting to the person and losing our own peace.

Imagine that someone in your office or school is really sick, coughing and sneezing constantly. You know that if you stand near them you'll catch whatever they've got. We all learned the importance of social distancing during Covid. We learned to keep a physical distance from people who seem sick, lest we also catch it.

But with that sick person who is coughing and sneezing, you know that they are not doing it purposely *to* you. They didn't manufacture a virus to come in and give it to you. It's festering inside them. If you get too close, you're going to get coughed on and you might even get sick. But it's not about you. It was never about you. This is true for dis-eases of pain, anger, grudges, and ignorance just as much as diseases caused by a virus or bacteria. We need to maintain an energetic distance so they don't metaphorically cough all over us, but we also need to realize that their dis-ease is not about us.

Sometimes it seems that someone is deliberately trying to harm us. However, even if someone is plotting and planning against you, it is still not about you. Imagine what must be going on in that person's heart for them to waste their time and energy planning to harm another. Imagine what their own heart and mind must feel like if they keep producing hatred. Whatever is produced inside of us affects us first. So if someone is producing anger, hatred, and revenge, that's what's flowing through them, long before it comes out in the form of words or actions directed at you. Although it may not be random, this sort of situation is also a sign that the person is suffering from dis-ease, from lack of ease and peace, from lack of wellness, and we must respond accordingly.

The first step is to understand that they are dis-eased so we can properly protect ourselves—physically, energetically, and emotionally. The second step is to share as much compassion, love, and peace as we possibly can, and to never give up. If we give up, then we let go of our own dharma, which is to share love and peace. That's who we are. If we recognize that we are one with the Divine, that we are soul, spirit, consciousness, love, and truth, then exuding that *is* our dharma.

There's a story I love about a sadhu who is bathing in a river, where there's a scorpion flopping around, drowning in the river. The sadhu goes to pick it up to save it, and tries to put it on the shore. When he does that, the scorpion stings him. The sadhu instinctively flails his hand in pain, dropping the scorpion back into the water. Then the sadhu goes to pick it up again, and the scorpion stings him once more before he can get it to the shore. Again he flails his hand, and again the scorpion falls in the water. This happens several times.

Finally, a man sitting on the edge of the river cries out, "*Baba, chodo usko!* Let it go! It's a scorpion. He's going to keep stinging you! Forget it! Let it drown."

The sadhu replies, "It is his dharma to sting, but it is my dharma to save, so if he's not leaving his dharma, why should I leave mine?"

So don't give up exuding love and peace, because that is our dharma. Love is the very core nature of who we are. Don't react. Don't justify your own bad behavior by saying, "He started it." But also don't keep sticking your leg into the bush where you know the mad dog is. The key is to figure out ways to protect ourselves, not by reacting, not by biting back, but simply by effectively taking care of ourselves, whether it's creating physical or emotional distance. Don't do it out of anger. Don't lose your dharma, but recognize that you must protect your own physical and psychological space.

Breaking Out of Negative Patterns

Why do I think so negatively? How can I break out of negative patterns?

Negative thinking is a tragic pattern that afflicts many of us. We do it because we've been programmed to.

One part of this conditioning stems from our system of education and discipline, based on punishments rather than rewards. Children who do well and behave well are frequently ignored, and kids who cause problems are the ones who get all the attention. In schools, in homes, and out in the world, we constantly hear, "You're stupid, you're bad, you're lazy, you're irresponsible, you're ugly," and we internalize it.

The other part of the conditioning comes from our popular culture—media, marketing, advertising, and politics—that is predicated upon convincing us that we are lacking something vital in our lives that they, or their product, are going to fulfill. This is called marketing. If you already have everything, how can anyone sell you something? If you're already satisfied, you're not a very good customer. Marketers need you to feel that there is something missing in you or your life, which their product is going to solve. Either you are too dark or too fair, your hair is too straight or too curly, you're too fat or too thin, you're wearing last year's model of jeans. This is how advertising works.

Here is my favorite example: What does soap do? It cleans us. We all need it; it's a great product. An honest advertisement would say things such as, "This brand of soap cleans so many parts per million of bacteria more than that brand," or, "Lathering up with this brand of soap for five seconds is the equivalent of lathering up with that brand of soap for thirty seconds." Instead, what do soap commercials look like? There are beautiful people singing in the shower as they lather up in the morning, the bathroom is all cozy and steamy, and their spouse is also in the bathroom singing. They go out together and their child has miraculously got himself up and had his breakfast and done his homework. Then the family walks out the door hand in hand and all you see is just a little logo bearing the soap brand name. Nobody said anything about cleanliness or bacteria. They're not selling cleanliness. They're selling happiness.

Another great example is car commercials. They're selling freedom, driving off into the horizon. How many among us feel stuck in our jobs or our marriages or our responsibilities? We see the commercial and we say to ourselves, "God, freedom looks so good. If I just had that car, I too could drive off into the sunset. Leave everything behind." They're not selling airbags, brakes, and seat comfort; they're selling freedom, romance. Want to sell a sports car? The guy with the car has the right lady. You want to sell an SUV? Kids in the back seat are singing together. When your kids try to strangle each other in the back seat, the subliminal message is that you have the wrong model of car. If you just buy this SUV, your kids too will sing in the back seat.

Wherever we look, we are being told in every magazine, TV show, movie, commercial, and advertisement on websites that we need something to be right, to be full, to be happy. And even worse, they are selling us a scarcity mindset. "Twenty-four hours left of this sale," "Only two left at this price," "Get them now or they'll be gone tomorrow!" "You're growing old, better get the right car, have the right family, take the right vacation, drive your car off into the sunset while you still can." It's all about scarcity. We are indoctrinated and brainwashed to believe that: 1) we're not enough, and there's something wrong with us; 2) these people have it and want to give it to us; and 3) we're running out of time or the supply is very short. Even if we don't internalize the message about the car or the soap, we *do* internalize the message that we are not enough. And we move through our lives with that as our truth.

Additionally, media research has shown over and over again that negativity keeps us glued to the screen for longer. Whether it's TV news or social media, violence, outrage, and fear are the best ways to ensure we keep scrolling and watching. Since the business of media is founded upon advertising income, and the longer we watch the more likely we are to "click here and buy now," negativity is what we get shown over and over until we accept it as the new normal. Tragically, our thoughts are generated by what we intake in our lives. So the more negativity we ingest through our eyes and ears, the more negative our minds become. So when we sit to meditate or pray or be with a loved one, or we lie down to sleep in the night, we find we are assailed by wave after wave of negativity. It's like food poisoning for our minds! If you eat junk all day, you are going to have a hard time meditating or sleeping because of the pain in your stomach as the toxins of junk food wreck havoc upon your digestion. In the same way, the toxins of negativity we ingest all day wreck havoc upon our thoughts and emotions.

If you want to free yourself from negative thoughts, you must stop mindlessly ingesting negativity all day long. It's like saying, "I want the cheeseburger but without the stomachache." Impossible. They are a package deal. Similarly, you cannot aimlessly scroll social media all day or watch "recommended" video after "recommended" video without suffering the ramifications in your mind.

That will help a huge amount. But it won't remove negativity all together, for the very nature of the mind is to be negative, even if we don't have the constant negative input. Another important way to deal with negative thoughts is to make a commitment to compassion and loving-kindness. Then make sure that you are also a recipient of that compassion and loving-kindness. So frequently we forget to include ourselves in our efforts to live more lovingly. Don't make that mistake!

Then, identify the negative voices in your mind. As the negative voice starts to harass you, ask it, "Who are you? Are you a commercial, are you my fifth-grade teacher, are you my mother who always asks, 'Why can't you be like your sister?'"

Most parents mean well; they don't mean to give their children complexes. Look at anyone aged twenty-five or twenty-six. They're kids. That's how old most of our parents were when they gave us these messages that we've been carrying within us for decades. They were doing the best they could, but they were so young. They were trying to do their best, but their best was not always so good for us. They didn't mean their words exactly how they came out, but we internalized the messages as scriptural canon for our lives.

We also internalized the message that our worth is based on what we achieve. People who are successful, rich, and at the top are the ones who society glorifies. The message is that our value and worth are inextricably linked with how much money we make, how high we have climbed on the career ladder; whether we're the president or CEO, or the mail clerk. It's not just our salary that's dependent on our position, but our entire self-worth.

So we internalize that, and even if we don't go down a traditional path, even if we're not climbing a ladder to be a corporate VP or CEO, we still internalize the message that we are only as worthy as what we achieve. Today, sadly, living a regular life is seen as substandard. We are told that our focus must be on doing something that has never been done before, doing something that sets us apart. It's a disease afflicting pretty much everyone between the ages of ten and fifty.

Look at your parents, your grandparents. Did your grandmother do something that nobody had ever done before? Probably not. She wanted to raise a family and cook a great meal that would feed her family, and maybe have a garden. That was enough. Maybe do some charity. Invite the neighbors over for dinner. That was what life was about. She did not worry about her life's purpose. Today, you have to do it *all*: a fantastic, meaningful, lucrative career, a family, perfect health as you squeeze your own organic juice, get to the gym, meditate, do yoga, and stay peaceful and loving and happy while you do it all. And remember to sleep eight hours a night too!

The standards for what counts as a successful and meaningful life have become insane, so it's no wonder we're all telling ourselves over and over again that we're not good enough. We've created standards that none of us can possibly achieve.

But the good news is that when we look at it closely, this indoctrination tends to dissipate. The negative voices in our head get quieter and quieter the more carefully we examine them. We can look at it and say, "Oh my God, I can't believe I got sucked into that model, I can't believe I've been brainwashed." We can just look inside and recognize we are enough. It's not about what you do, it's about *who* you are and *how* you are! Let that be your gauge—not *what* you do, but *who* and *how* you are. Who you are at the very deepest core is divine. So how do you live that? If you live with compassion, love, kindness, and generosity, if you live as an instrument in God's hands, it's a fantastic achievement. Just remember to extend that same compassion, love, and kindness to yourself.

As you move through the world, challenge yourself to see something positive in everyone and every situation. You don't have to be Pollyanna to be able to shift your focus from the negative to the positive.

Are there more ways to break the cycle of negative thinking?

This is where the practice of mindfulness comes in. Mindfulness gives us conscious control over our thoughts, attention, focus, and emotional states. It is not, however, a master-servant type of relationship. Rather, mindfulness enables us to befriend the mind, to see it as a dynamic structure that has been created with our best interest at heart. Unfortunately it doesn't actually know what our highest best interest is! The mind's function is to make sense of things and to protect us. But that leads to patterns of thought that can be actually detrimental to our growth, awakening, and expansion. Fear, contraction, negativity, judgment, suspicion, and pessimism are all quite functional tendencies for survival of the body in a threatening environment. But they absolutely ruin our mental, emotional, and spiritual experiences. Mindfulness enables us to see these patterns, to appreciate the mind for the role it is trying to play, and then to withdraw the conditioned mind's control over what we think, how we think, and when we think. Mindfulness enables us to consciously choose where to put our attention and focus at any moment and to create our own state of mind.

But first one must simply practice being aware. A very simple practice of mindfulness is just being aware as you are doing things. As you are going about your daily activities, say in your mind, "Now I'm doing this, now I'm doing that. Walking. Chewing. Smiling. Washing. Driving. Judging. Expecting. Dreading. Hoping. Sweeping." This brings the awareness back. Then, as a second step, draw the awareness to your breath. Don't try to change it. Just become fully aware of it. You can even begin by saying to yourself, "Here's what I'm noticing now, here's my breath now. Inhaling. Exhaling." Can you follow your breath through the body on each inhalation and exhalation? The breath is probably the easiest and the best way to stay present in the moment. It's nearly impossible to lose yourself in lamenting something that happened twenty or thirty years ago when your awareness is anchored deeply in your breath. Conscious connection to our breath brings us right into the present moment.

Can we permanently change our habits of thought?

Absolutely! The good news is that the brain keeps changing. There's an expression in neurology: "Neurons that fire together, wire together." For example, let's say there was a young girl who shared a room with her brother, and he beat her every time their parents turned off the lights at night. This young girl is going to associate darkness with pain, fear, and terror. Now, thirty years later, she's still afraid of the dark, but doesn't understand why. Her husband or roommates say to her, "Why in the world do you need a nightlight? You are an adult. The nightlight disturbs me. Can't we turn it off?" It creates great conflict. Those neurons in her brain, which fired together so many nights in a row back in her childhood, have wired together *darkness* and *pain*.

The good news is that we can actually rewire our brains. A few decades ago, when I was studying neurology, we were taught that the brain basically stops changing after late adolescence. We now know, however, that our brains keep changing. If you are right-handed, and you strap your right arm to your chest for a week and start doing everything with your left hand, your brain will change. If you are used to wearing shoes all the time and you go barefoot everywhere for a week, your brain will change. If you begin a practice of meditation and practice every day for a few weeks, your brain will change. We can absolutely undo patterns that have plagued us for decades and create new patterns with some tenacity and dedication. If we fill our brains continuously with positive associations, positivity will become the new pattern. Automatically the negative thoughts will dissipate. It's not about fighting our thoughts. We must change the entire landscape of our minds so that there's no place for the negative thoughts to grab hold, as the soil of our minds is no longer fertile for negativity.

In Vedic spirituality and yogic philosophy, we speak a lot about mental impressions, or sanskaras, which are patterns in our mind and consciousness the way that neural networks are patterns of activity in our brain. Our neuronal patterns are functions of chemicals and electricity, which become habituated over time as we start having the same thoughts over and over, or as we react over and over in the same way to the same stimulus (for example, every time you throw a temper tantrum when your kids' room is messy, you become more likely to throw a temper tantrum the next time their room is messy. You are training your brain. Remember, "Neurons that fire together, wire together"). Similarly, when we speak from a spiritual and yogic philosophy level about the mind as the storehouse of our habitual patterns of thinking, reacting, identifying, and feeling, it brings us to the same conclusion. The more you think in a certain way, the more likely you are to think in that way in the future. Whether you look at it on a level of energetic impressions in the mental and intellectual sheaths, the *manomaya kosha* and *vijnanamaya kosha,* or on a purely neurochemical level, the fastest and best way to break a pattern is simply to lay a new pattern. It's never too late to change your brain or to change your mind!

The Mind and Conditioning

How does conditioning take place in the world around us? How do we deal with it?

Conditioning happens in many ways in many places. It begins in our families when we understand and internalize what is important to our parents. If every time she looked in the mirror our mother said, "Oh my God, I can't believe I'm so fat, I'm so ugly," and if we heard her constantly say to our dad, "This makes me look fat," that's conditioning. It becomes a neural pathway and we will likely grow to think that being thin is beautiful, and means we will be loved and loveable.

If every time we drive home from a social event, our father yells at our mother, "I can't believe how you interrupted me in front of the others! Don't you realize that's what makes people not respect me? Why can't you be more like Rajesh's wife?" we will become conditioned to learn that if you're a woman you have to be quiet. If you're a man and are interrupted by a woman, your entire self-worth is in jeopardy. This is conditioning, and it forms the basis of our sanskaras, or patterns in the psyche.

In school, children are told, "Be quiet; speak only when spoken to. Write neatly." What gets valued is how well you conform to rules. In order for society to operate, there have to be some rules. But there are very few places where what's valued is looking within and knowing who you are and having the courage to share that and to be that. So we move through our world judging ourselves based on how well we've adapted to conditioning. Conditioning is different across cultures, families, and jobs, but frequently it is what ends up suffocating us, because there's no room for the true expansive self.

I'll give you a personal example of this. India has a lot of spoken and unspoken cultural rules, particularly regarding women. They're not rules laid down in any law book, but they're cultural standards of how women should be, particularly women in a spiritual world—how you should sit, speak, what you should look like and think about, what your values and priorities should be. For me, coming from the West, particularly progressive California, it was really difficult.

When I had been here only a few months, we went on a trip to Gujarat, including a day in the beautiful and sacred coastal city of Dwarka. It was evening and we had visited many temples in the day. I was so excited to be staying in a town close to the ocean and couldn't wait to be back on a beach. I said to the religious leader I was with, "I'm going to go take a walk on the beach." And he said, "Oh wonderful!" and then instructed two men to go with me.

I said, "Oh no, I don't want people to come with me, I'm going to walk alone on the beach."

And he said, "Yes, they'll come with you."

I repeated that I didn't need them, and he repeated that they'd go with me. I was twenty-five, a backpacker, a trekker. I had spent countless hours walking on trails in the mountains, on the beach, by myself. For me, that's how it was supposed to be done, just me and nature, me and the trees, me and the ocean. But here in India, you don't do that. Here, women should be taken care of and protected.

It's a real dance to figure out which aspects of our conditioning are issues to be addressed and changed and which are merely simple, innocuous socialization. It's important to keep checking and asking ourselves, "Is this really how I feel, or is this how I've been conditioned to believe I should feel?"

The answer to conditioning is not anarchy, it is not being a renegade in every way, because then that becomes my identity and keeps me stuck. It just becomes a different type of conditioning. Under the guise of being free, if I rebel against all conditioning, that rebelliousness becomes my new identity—I'm still just as stuck. All I have is a different label.

In many cases, the highest freedom is to realize that I can still be myself in the situation. I can connect with my soul on the beach even with two guys trailing ten feet behind me. Even though that wasn't my first choice and wasn't how I would've wanted to do it, freedom is not found in saying, "No, for God's sake, don't send them, I need to be free!" Rather, it's about finding my freedom within those roles, because freedom is internal.

Every time you hear yourself saying, "You're so stupid, you're worthless, you're too old, you're not worthy" and other self-deprecating messages, ask yourself, "Where did I learn that?" That is not the voice of the self. It is a conditioned voice. When we're able to step out of our conditioned, automatic beliefs and say, "Yes, I remember, this is the voice of my mother, my teacher, or a commercial," we will see the voice for what it is, not the truth, not our divine voice, but simply an internalized pattern from the way we were conditioned in our youth. We then have the opportunity to say, "No. I don't actually believe that. I know my teacher was going through a rough divorce when she told me I was stupid and worthless. It's not really true." We have the opportunity to say, "I remember my mom was stressed out about having three toddlers and she didn't mean to shout at me. She didn't mean what she said." Then we have found freedom and we can let go of these internalized messages. Our highest freedom is in knowing that who we are is full and complete, and we must refuse any conditioning that encroaches upon that.

Withdrawing the Senses

If God made us perfectly, why do we practice pratyahara, or the withdrawal of the senses? God gave us eyes to see, ears to hear, a nose to smell, hands to touch, a tongue to taste. So why should we withdraw the senses?

Pratyahara is a practice in which we withdraw the senses from objects in the outer world and turn them to the inner world. It's not a dulling or negation of the senses; rather, it is a shifting of the direction of the antennae. Picture an old TV set with the rabbit-ear antennae. If you were born in the 1990s or later, you may have to search on Google to see how TV sets used to work with these big antennae sticking up to properly catch the transmission waves. If the picture got fuzzy, you just adjusted the antennae. Now imagine taking those antennae, which are pointed outward, connecting with the TV waves in the outer world, and turning them to point *inside* the TV to connect only with the internal waves! That is what pratyahara is. It shifts our sensory antennae from the outside to the inside. It is an important limb among the eight limbs of yoga outlined by the sage Patanjali.

Our five senses are a beautiful gift, given to us by the Creator. However, just because God has given us a gift doesn't mean that we were meant to use that gift indiscriminately. Yes, we have tongues that taste, but that doesn't mean we should eat everything, all day long. We have fingers that touch, but it doesn't mean that we should touch everything. Anybody who's ever touched a hot burner, a cactus, or a sharp edge knows clearly that this is not what God intended when we were given the ability to touch.

Just because God has given us something doesn't mean we are supposed to use it with reckless abandon. Everything we've been given is for a purpose, and the sense organs have been given to us so that we can know the outer world, so we can experience the beauty of creation and protect ourselves from injury.

You need the organ of touch so that you can navigate the external world. If you didn't have sensory neurons that worked immediately in your spinal cord, connecting to the motor neurons that pull your hand off the hot stove, you would leave it there. You would burn yourself, and after a few seconds you would give yourself such a burn that it would become infected, it could get septic, and you could die. If you're driving your car and you hear a loud horn, your sense of hearing puts you on alert and helps you notice the car that ran the red light so that you react in time and don't get hit. The sense organs are very important to help us interact safely and effectively with the world around us. They also give us the gift of being able to appreciate and love the beauty of creation—the sunset, the smell of jasmine, the sound of the rain on a lake. Our senses are a gift to experience the outer world.

Yet, as we are reminded over and over again, the real world from a spiritual perspective is the inner world. This is where pratyahara comes in. It is necessary to dive into this inner world if we want to achieve meditation (dhyana), enlightenment (samadhi), divine yogic union, bliss, and ecstasy. But before you can meditate, you have to take this mind that is in a thousand places and put it in one place—focused on a mantra, a candle flame, an image, your breath. And even before you can do that, you have to stop your organs of sensation and perception from being anchored in the outer world. You need them to withdraw inward so you may become aware, attentive, focused internally.

That's why it's very difficult to meditate when you're in the middle of a football game, in a supermarket, or driving your car. You've got to keep your eyes open! Anything you're doing that requires you to be focused outward is a very difficult situation to meditate in because in that moment your perception is rooted in the sense organs that face outward. This is why when we meditate, the first things we do are choose a place to sit that's quiet and close our eyes. Because you have to be able to draw your senses inward to focus them on one thing, whether it's a mantra, a candle flame, an image of the Divine, your breath or the simple question "Who am I?" From that single-pointed focus you will be able to merge into a state of meditation, and from that you will be able to, with grace, experience samadhi. But pratyahara is a crucial first step.

For the outer world, we need our sense organs. We thank God for the fact that we are able to hear, feel, see, taste, and touch. But also, we are grateful for this inner world where we can experience the Divine. We need both.

PART 3

Our Emotions

So much of our lives is hijacked by our emotions. How many times do we hold our head in our hands and moan, "Why? Why did I say that? Why did I do that? How could I be so stupid? I've ruined everything!" We apologize to loved ones for our misdeeds and unskillful words by saying things like, "I didn't mean it. It wasn't me." Of course it was you! Who else could it have been? But it was you under the influence of a mind on emotions. Remember those advertisements to scare us away from drugs? The eggs in a frying pan? *This is your brain on drugs.* The image was awful. I mean, for a nonvegan breakfast dish it looks fine, but for your brain? Who wants fried brains? Still, emotions work the same way. Our emotions are just cascades of chemicals into different neural pathways. Whether it's a "feel good" chemical like oxytocin, or stress-response chemicals like epinephrine and cortisol, everything that we label *happy* or *sad* or *angry* is a chemical and electrical reaction. When we act in ways that we later say are "not us," it means that there has been a pattern, a domino-like cascade of reactions from something we saw or heard into a thought pattern of judgment, resentment, pain, and ultimately anger. The correlating chemicals released into our brain and bloodstream have turned on the sympathetic nervous system designed to either fight or flee, so naturally everyone becomes a threat, and we act the way we would if we were being attacked by a bear.

Many of us take our emotions as ultimate truth. "I am sad." "I am depressed." "I am anxious." We wear our emotions like identities and use them as filters through which we see our self and our entire existence on Earth. In our sadness, depression, anxiety, restlessness, resentment, and negativity, we write entire scripts for our life's drama. Then we complain that we are somehow a victim of circumstance or of other people's wrong actions. Yes, absolutely, there are challenging and disastrous circumstances that befall us. Yes, absolutely, there are plenty of people we meet who are mean, rude, irritating, selfish, and unskilled in so many ways. And yes, in the face of all of this over which we have no control, we *do* have the ability to keep ourselves balanced, calm, peaceful, and anchored—through understanding and working with our emotions, rather than seeing them as captains of our ship charting the course and direction of our lives.

This section focuses on the intersection between psychology, neurology, and spirituality in our understanding of emotions and provides specific tools and techniques to work with yours. See your emotions as a window. They are not to be suppressed or repressed or denied. They offer us a glimpse into the workings of our psyche. They show us where we get triggered, where we forget ourselves, where we lose our anchoring. But as the wise ones have always said, "Don't believe everything you think! Just because you think it, doesn't mean it's true!"

Using Anger as a Positive Tool for Action

How can we experience emotions such as anger and still react reasonably?

We get angry when we're not present, when we're not conscious in this very moment. When we are deeply present, deeply aware, deeply mindful, we don't lose ourselves in fleeting emotions.

Anger nearly always arises out of unconsciousness. You cannot be consciously angry. If I say to you, "On the count of three, you have to become furious. One, two, three, go!" Can you do it? Just try it. Try to become furious. You can't. This is actually really interesting, because how many of us lose our tempers? All of us! It's part of the human condition. How many of us lose our tempers more frequently than we'd like to? And yet, we can't do it on command. This is because our anger comes when we are not conscious in that moment. That's why being present is such a good antidote to it.

This doesn't mean that we approve of everything that's happening in the world. Most of us vehemently, passionately disapprove of the violence and terrorism in the world, of the injustice to our sisters and brothers starving to death or dying of thirst. Injustice, poverty, oppression, environmental destruction, and inequality make most of us quite angry. But that anger is conscious, not unconscious. We don't lose our temper over it. It doesn't cause us to act in ways we later regret or lead to high blood pressure and heart disease. That's not the anger we need to overcome. We rarely regret what we say or do when we are fueled by righteous, conscious anger.

In fact, we *should* be angry at injustice! The anger that ruins our life stems from unconsciousness. It's the anger in which we shout at loved ones or even physically harm them. It's the anger in which we tell off our boss or our subordinate or some random person on the freeway. It's the anger that leads us to say and do things we later regret—including trying to douse the flames of our anger in alcohol or drugs or cheesecake or gambling or pornography. This is why being present and mindful is the greatest solution. If you are truly conscious in each moment, it is very unlikely you will fall victim to the poison of anger that burns you and others and causes you to act in ways you later regret. So consciousness, awareness, presence, and mindfulness become the answer to unconscious anger (and to so much else!).

There's another way to address the problem of anger as well. Typically when we feel anger, it is accompanied by a tape that plays on a loop in our mind, reminding us of the person, situation, acts, and words that made us angry. As we keep thinking about it, we fan the flames of anger, causing it to grow. This harms us in two ways. First, it keeps us out of the present moment, because we are thinking back to ten minutes, an hour, or ten years ago to the moment that made us angry. The past is always a dangerous place to be if you are trying to live a spiritual life. Also, this sort of unconscious rumination turns our brain on autopilot. It is simply a tape repeating the story. For all that plagues us—whether it's anger, depression, addiction, general angst—the bottom line is to let go of our attachment to the record of the betrayal or hurt that plays over and over in our mind, keeping us trapped in anger. Anger, like any other emotion, surfaces, builds, peaks, and dissipates, like a wave in the ocean. The only way it grabs hold of us and doesn't let go is because of our attachment to the story of what or who made us angry. When the wave of the emotion begins we start replaying the narrative. Then the story creates more anger and we never become free. To let go of it, we must stop replaying the story.

Whether we get furious about it or depressed, or become an alcoholic or drug addict, it's all based on our drama, our story.

So, instead, as the wave of anger grows, you need to pull yourself out of the story. When your pulse starts to race, your heart beats fast, your palms get sweaty—the minute your attention focuses on that person or that situation, shift your attention to the actual experience of anger itself. This is a very subtle change but it's very important. Focus your awareness on the emotion itself.

That fully focused attention ironically makes the anger dissipate because being attentive and mindful brings you into the present moment, where there's no story, only the wave of emotion. If you can face that wave, what you'll find is that as you fix your awareness on it, it just starts to fall apart right before your eyes.

Most of these emotions are secondary emotions. If you focus on the anger itself, you will find that beneath the wave, beneath the "how dare you," is fear and pain. So we look at the fear and pain then, and allow them to dissipate too. This practice brings us into pure awareness.

Anyone who has ever gone swimming in the ocean knows that you can't outrun a wave. It's just going to crash on you. With anger, it crashes on those around you as well. The way to deal with a wave in the ocean is to dive into it and then the wave passes over your head quickly and you come up safely and happily on the other side. Similarly with the wave of anger, rather than trying to outrun it or push it away, just watch it like a witness sitting on the beach watching the water, and as the wave comes closer, dive deeply into that awareness of the emotion, without acting on it and without getting caught up in the drama. The wave will peak and then recede, and you will emerge safely on the other side.

The last piece of the puzzle is to connect with your breath. Your breath is your greatest ally in working with anger and so many other emotions that destabilize us and unground us. Your breath brings you into the present moment and immediately pulls you out of whatever emotion has hijacked your mindfulness, presence, and peace. Let the awareness of the breath be low in the abdomen, below the belly button. There is a powerful chakra (energy center) called the *swadisthan* chakra. Swadisthan literally means "the place of the self." It is about two inches below your naval. Allow your awareness of your inhalations and exhalations to be from that energy center. Let it be slow, let it be mindful. The minute you bring I-wareness there, it automatically grounds you. You will notice the impact immediately.

But what if the people around us are doing things that are inconsiderate? For example, I have not been able to sleep because my neighbors create so much noise, and because of other unpleasant circumstances that have been thrust upon me. How do I free myself from my natural negative reaction to that?

First, realize there's a difference between pain and suffering.

Sleep deprivation is a physical state, like wintertime or summertime or rain or sun or heat or cold. There's no subjective value of it as good or bad. It just exists. For example, if it were Maha Shivaratri or some other sacred holiday and you had made the decision to stay up all night chanting mantras, you'd be exuberant at 4 a.m. If you had a 3 a.m. flight to catch to visit a loved one across the world, you'd be filled with joy to see your beloved and more than happy to stay up all night to catch your flight. How many times have you stayed awake all night in the arms of a beloved, or cradling your precious child? It's not the actual state of sleep deprivation that creates anger. Sometimes sleep deprivation coexists with joy. It's the lack of control. It's the voice inside that says, "This is not how I want things to be."

The fastest way out of that is to realize that *nothing* is how we want it to be.

Nothing is as we choose. If what we want happens to coincide with the divine plan or the law of nature, great. But neither nature nor God nor other people are going to change their plans for us. Today we have ATMs, online shopping, immediate delivery of anything we may desire, giving us the illusion that everything is at our fingertips and in our own hands. It is an illusory world where you get exactly what you want—order today, refund tomorrow! We falsely believe that the world functions according to what buttons we push on a keyboard or on a vending machine.

That's not how the world works. We are happy when we are in alignment with what the world has offered, but get angry when what we want is denied. This is a recipe for misery and it's why our sages, rishis, mystics, and prophets of all religions have emphasized letting go of attachments and expectations and surrendering to the divine will.

So, you need to shift your perspective and realize nothing is in your hands. Your neighbors were loud at 4 a.m.; it's not what you wanted. Okay. But your not wanting it does not change the situation. Some people prefer summer to winter, but that doesn't stop winter from coming. Nobody wants to grow old, but that doesn't stop it from happening. The sooner we realize that the very fundamental truth of life is that we have no control over the world around us the sooner we become free from anger.

The only thing in the entire universe you have control over is your response to the universe. The faster you can take a deep breath and realize, "All right, I guess I'm going to be sleep-deprived," and get up to meditate and watch the sun rise with a cup of hot tea, the quicker your suffering will end.

You cannot choose other people's actions. Your only choice is to be miserable or not to be miserable. We must work to align our own will with the will of the universe rather than try to bend the universe to align with our own will. That is merely an exercise in frustration and futility.

In chapter three of the Bhagavad Gita, Bhagawan Shri Krishna says that anger and hatred are the greatest enemies of man. How do we control anger in a situation where there is a question of justice? For example, when Draupadi was humiliated in front of the Pandavas in the Mahabharata, how would we control anger toward the sin and the sinner?

This question demonstrates the other side of the previous question. Even though we don't have control over other people's actions, we must not be complacent or indifferent in the face of injustice and harm. In this example, Draupadi, the wife of the Pandavas, was nearly disrobed in the crowded court due to Duryodhana's anger, rage, and ego. It was an act predicated simply upon malice and therefore we *should* be angry about it. How to deal with anger toward sin and sinner?

First, recognize that anger is not evil or inherently wrong. It can be a powerful catalyst for essential reform. Spirituality does not make us complacent and disconnected. It enables us to act mindfully and purposefully so that we are effective in responding to injustice in the world without losing our inner peace.

Without spirituality, we simply react. Someone says something that makes you angry so you react instinctively. Maybe you slap them or shout at them. Or maybe you punch your hand through a wall, injuring yourself instead of the person you're angry at. Or maybe you go home and beat your kid because you couldn't talk back to your boss when she angered you. This is all mindless reaction and none of it serves any beneficial purpose. Rather it harms us and others. In life we must act, not react.

These days our social media and digital worlds make us more distracted and irritated than ever, and our modus operandi has become to react immediately to everything. From the time we wake up to the time we go to sleep, how many of us make lists of things to do that day? And when the day's over, we realize we've been busy nonstop, but nothing on our list got done. We sit there and scratch our head and think, "But I haven't stopped! I haven't been wasting my time. I haven't been idle, so what's happened? Why did nothing on my list get done!"

The reason is that we have spent all day reacting to emails, phone calls, text messages, the incessant notifications and distractions. We're *reacting* instead of *acting*. That's where we lose our freedom. We become slaves to the beeps, buzzes, and rings.

The key to success in life is to react less and act more. We must act according to our own priorities and values rather than react to whatever comes our way or whatever notifications pop up on our phone or computer.

Anger can either lead us into unconscious reaction or it can be a catalyst for right action. Injustice *should* make you angry. So should violence against those unable to defend themselves. But your anger should not debilitate you so much that you hit your child, or throw your computer out the window after reading the news. Rather, it should be a source of energy to *do something, to serve, to respond to the situation that needs you.*

If your anger at injustice catalyzes right action leading to reform, that's perfect. There is nothing wrong with anger, emotion, passion, or desire, as long as we are able to experience them in freedom rather than being enslaved to them.

When you get lost in the throes of unconscious anger, you become the first victim. Instead of igniting positive action, the fire of anger burns you. Duryodhana did something evil, so now you are going to punish yourself by burning with anger inside. That anger doesn't solve the situation, nor impact Duryodhana, nor protect Draupadi, nor prevent the situation from happening again. All it does is burn you and give you ulcers and high blood pressure. It's worse than useless. Instead, let the anger be a catalyst for mindful, positive action, which can only happen if you don't lose your own mind in the process!

There are a lot of things happening in the world today that we really *should* be angry about. But losing control and burning up inside doesn't serve anyone. It doesn't help our world, it doesn't help us. Instead, we need to acknowledge the anger and realize it's there because something is not in alignment with truth. Then we recognize that we can be a vehicle for change. The energy that wants to set it right is powerful and motivating.

This is what Lord Krishna tells us: "Whenever there is darkness in the world, I incarnate to bring back the light. Whenever there is adharma, I incarnate to bring back the dharma."

Maybe God is trying to incarnate through every single one of us. I believe the situation is so dire today that every one of us is here to be a vehicle, to be the one through whom the light and healing can flow.

If you can acknowledge that experience of anger and not push it away, not eat it or drink it or gamble it or shop it away, not release it through punching the wall or your child, but actually experience it and open yourself to see what it wants you to do, then you can be a vehicle and that energy can use you to be an instrument toward righteousness.

The last aspect to consider here is hatred. Hatred comes when we identify the sin with the sinner, the action with the human. Anger tends to come and go, whereas hatred sizzles and festers.

The antidote to hatred is to understand that just as you are not your fears, your confusion, your upbringing, your desires, or your ego, neither is that person at whom your hatred is directed. Even though this horrible act flowed through them, it's because that's all they've got. Based on their upbringing, experience, and karmic package, what they've got in their karmic toolbox is fear, anger, jealousy, competition. So that's what they give. People don't wake up in the morning deciding that they're going to commit vile sins to cause suffering. Even those we call terrorists have very righteous explanations for what they are doing—to restore justice, to please God. Charles Manson, the serial killer, had a complex rationale for his heinous crimes. People we label as evil, horrible, crazy all think they're doing the right thing. Their karmic toolboxes just don't have compassion or understanding or empathy, or even clarity of thought and mental health.

Additionally, many people who hurt us or commit vile acts against others do it out of a pathological effort of their psyche to work out their own trauma. This is why children who are abused frequently become abusers. It's their psyche's attempt to bring their own trauma to the surface so they can finally work through it. Tragically, however, rather than healing, they tend to cause suffering and trauma for others. It's helpful, though, to realize that nearly everyone who commits violent and horrific acts was a victim of abuse and trauma, and they are incapable of not perpetuating that trauma until and unless they look at their own suffering. This is true not only for physical abuse but also for mental and emotional abuse.

Our understanding of "why" they commit horrific acts doesn't condone the acts, of course. It doesn't mean what they did is okay, but it means that you don't allow hatred to ruin your life or convince yourself that hating is somehow the right thing to do. Because that just kills you; it doesn't change the other person.

How to Deal with Disappointment

How do we deal with being disappointed or let down by someone we loved, trusted, and respected? We must have some expectations from people, otherwise how do we learn and develop ourselves?

We have to have some expectations in order to move through the world. Pujya Swamiji always says, "Expectation is the mother of frustration." But what he also says is, "Acceptance is the mother of peace and joy." The reason it's important to remember both these aphorisms is that the opposite of the frustration we get from expectation is the peace and joy we get from acceptance. The answer is not to never expect; it's to always accept what happens even if it wasn't what you expected.

For example, in order for us to live in this world, we have to expect that our house won't burn down while we're asleep. If you weren't sure that your house would still be standing in the morning, or that your loved ones would still be alive, you wouldn't be able to go to sleep. When we cross the street, we have to expect that a car is not going to run us over, or we'd never be able to cross the street. As we sit in a room, we have to expect that the roof is not going to fall on us, that whoever built the room had knowledge and expertise, otherwise we'd rush out immediately. So in order for us to live, we have to have some expectations.

Similarly, in our relationships, in order for me to give myself fully to you, I have to expect that you're not going to hurt me. If I'm going to give you my heart and love you with all that I am and all that I have, I have to expect that you're not going to take a knife and stab it in my heart, either literally or metaphorically. I have to expect that you're going to take my love as a precious gift and not stomp on it.

Expecting that people are not going to hurt us or that the airplane is not going to fall out of the sky is not the problem. The problem arises when the unexpected happens. You didn't think your new love would hurt you, but he did. You didn't think that a fire would burn down your house, but it did. This is when spiritual practice allows us to find acceptance even in the most difficult circumstances.

Acceptance is simply awareness that we have no control. Anger bubbles up within us when an expectation is not met. For example, I plan a picnic for my birthday with the expectation that it's going to be a sunny day. On my birthday, it rains. Most of us would be slightly disappointed, but we wouldn't lose ourselves in fury. Why? Because we didn't have an assumption of control. We anticipated sunny skies, but we knew that the weather doesn't abide by our wishes. We may be disappointed at the rain, but not furious.

When people disappoint us, though, we are deeply hurt and angry because we assumed that we had control. We assume that being a good person should mean that bad things don't happen. You assume that people you love should treat you well. This is what leads to not only disappointment, but also to fury because we cannot accept the outcome. Very few of us would look up at the clouds and shout, "How dare you?" if it rained during our picnic. We understand that nature has its own patterns. But with people in our lives, we expect they will behave the way we want and the way we deem proper.

We must remember that we have no more control over the people around us than we do over the weather. Everyone is living out their own karmic journey.

Acceptance doesn't mean everything is exactly as you want. It just means that you realize you don't have control over anything except your reaction. Until and unless you can create space in your heart, mind, and life for this fact, you're not going to be able to experience peace or joy.

What are some of the best ways to deal with disappointment and frustration?

Acceptance and gratitude. We love our loved ones, and we expect that they're not going to fall sick or get hit by a car tomorrow, but we don't have control over these things. That doesn't stop us from loving or from living our lives. The awareness of our lack of control can serve as a powerful inoculation against disappointment and frustration. If we're able to hold on to the awareness that every day of health is just grace, that our house is still standing is just a blessing, the more gratitude we will have. Gratitude brings us constantly into the awareness that it is all only God's grace.

If you owed me a hundred rupees and you finally pay me, I'm not going to say to you, "Oh, thank you so much, you're so generous!" You owed me. I was entitled to it. It was my money. Gratitude stems from the awareness that that which I've been given is not something I was entitled to but which I have received due to the generosity of the universe, due to an abundance of grace and blessings. The more we can cultivate gratitude, the fewer expectations we will be burdened by. Inherent in gratitude is the awareness that it's all in God's hands.

By bringing gratitude into our lives, we realize that by the Divine's grace we woke up today. By the Divine's grace what we eat is digested. By the Divine's grace our house has not yet burned down. By the Divine's grace an earthquake has not yet swallowed us up. Then we drop even deeper into awareness and gratitude, and realize that our peace, joy, and fulfillment are not rooted in those things. Our peace is not dependent on whether our house is still standing. Our joy is not dependent on whether it rains or is sunny, whether our picnic will go well or not. Our peace and joy are only dependent on our connection with God, which gratitude strengthens day by day.

The more grateful you are, the less disappointed and frustrated you will be, and the fewer expectations you will have. Going deeper, the more grateful you are, the more you will connect with the Divine, and your happiness and peace will be less dependent on people around you. They will have less power to make you depressed, frustrated, happy, or elated, because you'll be grounded in something much deeper.

Overcoming Fear and Anxiety

How do I overcome fear when it comes to connecting with others and myself? How do I face my past, instead of dwelling on it?

You can't overcome anything until you look at it. You can't overcome your fear until you know what you're afraid of, or why you're afraid.

For most people, the deepest fear is death, extinction. This is pure Darwinism. Our core instinct is to survive. This is true for a mosquito, an earthworm, or a human being. With our fears, let us picture a worst-case scenario, with our fears manifesting in the worst way imaginable. Then ask, "Okay, that happened. My worst fear happened. Then what?" Invariably, our answer will be, "I will die." This conclusion may not happen in only one step. It may take three or four steps of "Okay, that happened. Then what?" to get to the ultimate conclusion of "Then I will die." But it always ends with death. All of our fears fundamentally are rooted in the fear of death or obliteration. Let's take an example of fear of confronting one's boss at work:

I am afraid to confront my boss about unfair working conditions.
Why?
Because then I might get fired.
Okay, you get fired. Then what?
Then I won't have a job or any money.
Okay, you have no job and no money. Then what?
Then I'll be homeless and hungry.
Then what?
Then I will die.

Here's another example in line with your question on connecting with others:

I am afraid to connect deeply with others.
Why?
Because if I really love someone, they might leave me.
Okay, you love someone and they leave you, then what?
Then I'll be all alone.
Okay, you're all alone. Then what?
Then I'll crumble with grief.
Okay, you crumble with grief. Then what?
Then the grief will swallow me, and I will cease to exist.

It all ends with the fear of death. We fear connection because in that connection, we may lose ourselves. Sometimes our fear is slightly different. Watch:

I am afraid to connect deeply with others.
Why?
Because then I may fall deeply in love.
Okay, you fall deeply in love. Then what?
Then I will be so absorbed in the love and the connection that I will lose my own individuality.
Okay, you lose your individuality, then what?
Then I will dissolve into the love entirely and cease to exist.

It may not always be about death or dissolution of the physical body. Sometimes it's ego death that terrifies us the most. Interestingly, the number one fear of people polled from across the world is not sharks or bears or earthquakes or climate change or lack of water or guns. It is public speaking. People are more afraid of public speaking than guns! Imagine. That is because humiliation feels like death. We even say, "I will die of embarrassment!" No one has ever actually died of embarrassment, but somehow everyone thinks they will.

Our identities are so dependent upon other people's assessments of us, that we feel we will truly cease to exist if we fail in their eyes. It begins when we're in our mother's arms—babies look at their mothers, the mothers look back, make eye contact, smile with love, and these babies grow up feeling good and stable about themselves. But when a child looks into the mother's eyes and Mom's upset, stressed, and not making eye contact with love, the child grows up feeling insecure.

On a psychological level, we are constantly judging ourselves based on other people. If I tell a joke and nobody laughs, something inside me plummets. If we run into someone and they greet us with joy, we experience ourselves as worthy and valuable. Alternatively, if we see or speak with someone who turns their head the other way or gives us a weird look, we are crestfallen. We may not even know the person, or understand why they are upset or in a bad mood, but it doesn't matter. We are constantly readjusting our sense of self based on how people respond to us. Think of the last time you went to a party, all dressed up, but no one noticed you or complimented you on your clothes or hairstyle. Did you come back feeling something was wrong? Did you keep looking in the mirror to find out what must have been the problem? There's something deep within us that is constantly getting cues of our identity and worthiness from other people.

It all comes back to the fact that our deepest fear is that we will cease to exist—in body and in ego-self. This leads to a lifetime of fear of failure and hence reluctance to take risks. Let's examine that internal conversation:

I'm afraid of taking this huge risk with a new project, idea, or opportunity. *Why?*
Because I might fail and then people will laugh at me.
Okay, you fail and people laugh at you. Then what?
Then they will know that I am worthless and stupid, and no one will like me anymore.
Okay, they know you are worthless and stupid and no one likes you. Then what?
Then I will just die with humiliation and cease to exist.

On a very deep level we believe that if people don't love us and acknowledge us, we don't exist.

Think about the selfie obsession. Psychologically it is fascinating. We don't just take pictures and keep them. No, we take them to post on social media.

Look at the actual selfies: It's not really a picture of the Grand Canyon or the Eiffel Tower; it's a picture of our face occupying 80–90 percent of the frame and some rocks or steel or a concrete wall behind us.

Once we post it online, we keep checking how many people have liked and commented on it. We think, "Oh my God, nobody commented, nobody liked it. What happened? What's going on?" We post pictures of ourselves in indistinguishable random places and then wait to see what others think and say about it. Our enjoyment of our holidays has become significantly impacted by the responses, or lack thereof, that we get for the selfies we've taken during the trip.

If nobody likes or comments on the picture, we feel that we don't exist. We keep posting to remind people, "Hey, I exist." The more responses I get, the more I exist; the fewer I get, the less I exist.

This is all happening on a subconscious and very deep level, and it's ruining our self-esteem, our confidence, and courage. To overcome fear, we have to first break the myth that making a fool of ourselves will obliterate our existence. Having an auditorium laugh at us will not actually cause us to melt and dissolve.

We will only have the courage to take risks when we realize that our existence is not dependent on people's approval or love. If your well-being is contingent upon others' approval, you're always going to live in fear, playing it safe, saying and doing exactly what you think others want you to. You'll constantly doubt yourself and judge yourself based on others' assessments.

Instead, you must ground your awareness in your own self. You have to know who you are. This is why the core teaching of so many spiritual practices is to simply ask, "Who am I?" and to meditate upon the true nature of the self. Then, regardless of whether others think you're the biggest fool who has ever walked the face of the earth or you're the greatest person they have ever met, it doesn't change how you understand yourself. Being anchored in true understanding of the self is the only way to overcome this fear.

Also, it's important to recognize that life's greatest tragedy is not failing, but rather never stepping up to accept the opportunities in your life. The greatest tragedy is looking back on your life knowing you were paralyzed by fear of failure and humiliation. *That's* the tragedy; *that's* something to be afraid of. We have this incredible gift, this incredible life, all these moments brimming with potential, and it is tragic if we don't use them.

There's a great story about Swami Vivekananda, who was always teaching, "Stand up! Be fearless!" One day, a few of his disciples decided to test him and find out if Swamiji was really so fearless. They dressed up as bandits and stormed the lecture hall, carrying fake guns. Everybody screamed and hid behind the chairs or ran out. Swamiji kept delivering his talk, unfazed as fake bullets whizzed by his head. Finally, humiliated, the fake bandits fell at his feet, took off their masks, apologized, and said, "But Swamiji, how is it possible? Were you not even a little bit afraid? How did you do that?"

He replied, "The bullet that is meant to take my life will take it even if I'm surrounded by a hundred guards. The bullet that is *not* meant to take my life will not kill me even if you fire at point-blank range."

If we can really hold that level of faith in our hearts and move forward with it, it's the best antidote to fear.

I'll leave you with a true story of Pujya Swamiji. He was on an airplane about forty years ago, before I knew him. This story was narrated to me by a professor named Dr. Rao, who was on the airplane with Swamiji. Dr. Rao was the chief editor of our *Encyclopedia of Hinduism*. Having just started the encyclopedia project, Swamiji was flying all over the world, raising awareness about Indian culture and religion, and helping people build temples.

There was a horrible storm during their flight. They were flying over Chicago, known for facing such storms. There was thunder and lightning, and lots of turbulence. The pilot announced for everyone to brace in crash position, warning them that there may be a crash landing. The plane was dropping hundreds of feet at a time. Overhead luggage compartments opened and bags fell out. The plane kept plummeting, and everyone thought it was going to crash. People were screaming, crying, holding on to each other. Swamiji kept writing calmly on a notepad. The plane fell another thousand feet, and everybody was shouting, "We're going to die, we're going to die!"

Finally, Dr. Rao couldn't take it anymore and exclaimed, "Swamiji, what are you writing?"

Swamiji replied calmly, "My speech."

Swamiji never ever prepares a speech in advance, so the idea of writing a speech under any circumstances was unusual. In this moment it seemed preposterous.

Dr. Rao exclaimed, "Swamiji, there will be no speeches. We're all going to die, this plane is crashing."

Swamiji replied, "Well, see, here's the thing. I know I'm not going to die, and since everybody else thinks they are going to die and you're telling me this plane is going to crash, it means I'm going to be the sole survivor of this plane crash. Then naturally they're going to want to take my interview, and since my English isn't so good and you're sitting here next to me, I figured that I would use this opportunity to put some thoughts on paper so that if I need to ask you about some English word, I could ask before the plane crashes."

This is what fearlessness looks like. Most of us may not actually reach this degree of fearlessness. Don't worry. But to be able to move through the world with faith, the kind of faith that a child has in her mother's arms, to deeply know that there's knowledge, wisdom, a Divine Plan, and therefore a Divine Planner who is so much wiser than I am who's taking care of it all—that is living without fear.

There's a beautiful line in the prayers that we chant every morning at Parmarth Niketan that says, "*Tu akele nahin pyare. Ram tere sath mein,*" meaning, "You're not alone, dear one. God is with you." If we can live knowing that we're really in the Mother's arms, that we're being carried by God, that faith will replace fear in our life.

How do we deal with irrational fear?

First of all, you must realize that the fear is irrational. If you really, deeply, in the cells of your being know that something is irrational, you're not going to be afraid of it.

In order for there to be fear, there has to be some part of you that believes in the fear. So when you recognize an irrational fear, first become deeply aware that it's irrational. When the impossibility of your fear actually manifesting is affirmed deep within your being, the fear will dissipate.

Step two is faith. Think of the Swami Vivekananda story. The faith and awareness that you are being taken care of is what will give you strength. It doesn't mean you're going to get every job you wanted, or that you're always going to be healthy, or that people you love aren't going to die or leave you, but it means that at the core foundational level you're being taken care of and there is nothing to fear. Look at children. They may fall, they may be scared, or hurt, or crying, but the minute their mother picks them up and holds them, they may still need a bandage, but the fear is gone.

When we live with the real awareness that we're in the Divine's arms, our fear dissipates. Again, that doesn't mean everything's going to be perfect, but it means that we're being carried by the Divine and so we can exhale deeply and allow ourselves to relax on the deepest, cellular level.

How do we build confidence?

There's no other species that is unsure of its own ability to be what it is. We never see a bird on a branch starting to flap its wings and then backing out in fear of not being able to take flight. When a mother bird kicks her baby bird out of the nest, halfway down as it falls to the ground, the baby realizes it can fly and it soars upward rather than crashing down. After that, there's never a time they don't remember their ability to fly.

Only humans have this lack of confidence, and that is because we are unaware of who we really are. Our stress and despair arise because we're trying to mold ourselves to be something that we are not.

We spend most of our lives trying to be and become who we think society wants us to be, to live in accordance with what others are doing or to follow our favorite influencers on social media. We allow others' projections on us to become our self-identity.

Since we don't fully understand who we are, we don't have confidence in ourselves. Who we truly are at our core is not the role we are currently playing. Our truest self is not a student or an employee, or someone's husband or wife. We are not our bodies or our races or religions, or abilities or talents, or how well we fit society's prescribed standards of beauty. Who we are is consciousness, divinity, one with the supreme reality, one with the Creator and the creation. One with all of existence. *Sat-chit-anand.*

It means ultimate truth or infinite existence, consciousness and bliss. That is our true nature.

Our confidence needs to come from knowing that we've been created *by* the Divine, and *of* the Divine, who is infinite, who doesn't make mistakes. None of us is half-baked or half-done. It's not as if God forgot to put salt or sugar in some of us. Sometimes that's how it feels, but we have to understand that there's a perfection in the universe, and when we realize that we are a perfect, crucial part of that universal perfection, confidence comes automatically not from what we do, nor from how good we are at something, but simply in who we are and from our ability to experience love, share love, and our ability to connect with that one consciousness. That's what we're here for. It's all there and accessible to us; we just have to turn inward to tune in to it.

Self-love and self-confidence are not meant to be based on our physical, temporary existence with our looks, our income, or our areas of expertise. These things are constantly changing. There will always be people who are more beautiful, more successful, more intelligent, more capable than we are. Our self-love, self-confidence, and self-esteem are deep and powerful only when they are anchored in the very perfection of our self as inseparable from all of existence, as *sat-chit-anand.* Yes, of course we should also love and appreciate our physical bodies, our unique skills and abilities, and the experiences we have had in life that give us our unique personality. When we love this individual self, we do so out of faith in the perfection of the divine. We are each exactly as we are meant to be. But the highest level of that confidence and self-love arises when we love not only our individual temporary body-mind-personality complex but also when we love the very divine truth of our being.

I feel anxiety in many situations. Is anxiety a bad thing?

It's important to remember that nothing we experience is bad. The only bad thing is the idea that our feelings are wrong, because then we end up separating ourselves from ourselves. We want to be good, we want to think and act in good ways, so the minute we label something inside of us as bad, we've cut ourselves off from it.

The whole point of a spiritual practice is integration, union, and oneness. Therefore, nothing is bad. Certain thoughts and emotions are conducive to experiencing an elevated and expanded view of ourselves and our place in the world. They help us get in touch with the truth of who we are, the divinity of ourselves and the divinity of the universe. In contrast, some emotions, and thoughts make us contract and feel small and separate.

Those thoughts, feelings, or mental patterns take us out of the expansive spiritual realm and into the flesh, into the narrative drama of our temporal, physical human existence. That's not bad, but it is not the full truth. It is based only on a tunnel-vision view of one's self, one's life, and one's place in the universe. On a spiritual path our practices help us access oneness and union, love and consciousness, rather than a tunnel-vision experience of separation that inevitably includes greed, lust, and anger.

So when we examine anxiety, it is not inherently *bad*. However, it leads to a cascade of physical and emotional experiences that further shut us off from truth. When we feel stressed and anxious, our heart rate increases, our blood pressure skyrockets, all of our energy rushes to the extremities. It's the fight-or-flight sympathetic nervous system response. We are biologically primed and ready in that moment to either fight, flee, or freeze.

That response would be very useful if we were living in a cave and had to protect ourselves from tigers or bears or warring tribes, but it's not helpful in the world we inhabit. We need that rush of adrenaline, that tunnel vision, that heart-pumping anxiety to be able to outrun a bear or to climb a tree or fight off a tiger. But today, the situations in which most of us feel anxiety are everywhere and every day—social engagements, parties, work, family gatherings, looking for a parking spot, trying to grab the last carton of our favorite oat milk before the other shopper takes it. Life has become a series of life-or-death, fight-or-flight situations, and that's harmful on every level. We cannot live in a state of openness and expansion while simultaneously fleeing or fighting. Either the world is something to be afraid of, or the world is something to be one with, but it can't be both.

Every minute that we feel anxiety, our body is telling us that this situation is dangerous. And that's not a healthy way to live. So, how do we stop feeling anxious? The anxiety we feel these days stems from the illusion that we *are* what we look like, we *are* how we perform, we *are* what other people think of us, and we *are* how well and quickly we can get through our day's to-do lists. Therefore, if people don't like you, or you don't get the promotion at work, or someone steals your parking spot, the very nature of your self is threatened. Hence you get anxious. The minute we can go beyond that false identification and truly know that we are divine, we are consciousness, we are infinite, we are existence itself, then whether someone laughs at our jokes or smiles at us, or tells us we're fat or stupid, or asks us out on a second date, it doesn't create anxiety.

Every time you feel anxious, ask yourself, "Is this really a situation where I want to separate myself from the universe?" And if not, then ask yourself how you can expand the way you think of yourself. Ground yourself in your breath. Try to experience a state of oneness with the people around you, rather than a sense of separation, because where there's oneness, there's no fear. Where there's fear, you feel separation. Anxiety takes us away from the truth of who we are. On a spiritual path, we want to be closer to truth.

How do we redirect ourselves in a situation that is causing us anxiety?

There are two possible situations. One, is a situation from which we can literally remove ourselves, and that would be a good thing to do. Let's say you went out with some friends to dinner and it turned into a drinking party, but you're not a drinker. Everyone at the table is drunk, they're starting to get boisterous, and you're feeling very anxious and uncomfortable. You're no longer enjoying yourself in this moment. The best thing you can do in this moment is physically remove yourself from the situation. Just literally get up and leave. And this is true for every situation in which you have the ability to just walk away. If you can walk away, do so. Have compassion for yourself and take care of your anxiety. Just leave.

However, in many cases the situation we're in is one from which we can't remove ourselves so easily. You definitely don't want to become so fragile that there are a very limited number of situations in which you feel comfortable. If you try to create cocoons of peace around yourself, allowing in only that which helps maintain your peace, you are drastically limiting yourself. People will tell me sometimes, "Oh, I can't see that person, I can't do this, I can't go there, I can't listen to that, because it ruins my peace." Our peace should not be so shallow and fragile. We must dive deeper to experience a peace and connection with the Divine that can coexist with a visit to your parents, with getting yelled at by your boss, with getting stuck in traffic. To have a narrow and shallow realm in which we can exist peacefully requires us to micromanage our environment, our relationships, and our experiences. This becomes a huge burden and massive waste of time. The goal is to be able to experience peace in the maximum number of situations. There are some situations, such as the one I described previously with the drunk friends where it's perfectly fine to say, "Okay, everyone, hope you have a wonderful time the rest of the evening. It's time for me to go home," and we excuse ourselves. But mostly, the situations that steal our peace arise in our families and at our workplaces. We don't need to abandon our family or our job and run into hiding in order to find peace.

The answer is to change how you identify yourself. Anxiety is caused because you have internalized someone else's words or actions. Maybe you made a joke, and no one laughed—it means you're stupid. Or maybe you said something that was serious, but everyone laughed—it still means you're stupid. All they've done is laugh or not laugh. You're the one who's made up the whole story of being stupid. You're the one who's internalized the situation and made it all about you.

The way to be in those difficult situations is to just tune back in to your true self. It's important to remember that people who try to make us feel bad are miserable. This is as true in sixth grade as it is in boardrooms, offices, living rooms, kitchens, yoga studios, parties, and gyms across the world.

If you're in a situation where you're feeling anxiety, check in with yourself: "Is this person's truth really *my* truth? Is what I'm feeling in this environment really who I am? Or is it just that these people or this person is using me to feel better about themselves?"

There's a great story of a teacher who draws a line on the chalkboard and asks his students, "Without using an eraser, can anyone make this line on the board shorter?" Of course no one can. It seemed like the only way to make the line smaller on the board was to erase part of it. But then the teacher says, "No, there's another way to make the line appear shorter," and he draws a longer line above it. The lower line hasn't actually changed, but now in comparison to the longer one, it seems shorter. Sadly, this is exactly what happens to us. We are who we are. We are perfect in and of ourselves. Yet we judge ourselves based on those around us.

This is another reason why meditation is so important, because it shows us the truth of who we are. In meditation, as we learn to still the monkey mind, as we learn to simply be aware of the constant vacillations of the waves of thought, we discover that we are not who we think we are!

Without meditation, our identity is based on others' actions, reactions, and projections. Whether you laugh at my jokes, or touch my feet, or give me an A or a gold star. That becomes who I am. So whenever we're in situations that make us feel anxious, we need to reconnect with ourselves. Reconnect with our breath, deep and low in the abdomen, just grounding ourselves back in our truth.

The last but crucial component is to find compassion for that person in front of us and an awareness that the reason they are making us feel bad, the reason they are making us feel low, is because *they* feel low. This is why bullies in school are usually just miserable children.

People who bully others—physically, emotionally, mentally, in any way and at any age—do it because they feel badly in their own lives. So check in with who you are, connect with the Divine in yourself, and then try to feel some compassion for whoever is making you feel bad.

Overcoming Temptations

We live in a world where there are temptations on all sides. How do we strengthen the intellect to control the mind?

There are many temptations in the world, but they all fall into a few categories. They are either things that make us feel better or things that we *think* will make us feel better. There are temptations to eat and drink things we shouldn't eat and drink, to have relations with people we shouldn't have relations with, to do things we shouldn't do. Those form the most superficial layer of temptation. If I eat that, I will feel good. If I drink that, I will feel good. If I smoke that, I will feel good. If I engage in sexual relations with this person, I will feel good. For a lot of people, these temptations are very difficult to resist.

I remember when I was young, my mother was always on a diet. It's what people in Los Angeles do; everybody diets. My mother's always been very thin; nonetheless, she was always on a diet. I remember one time when we went out to eat on holiday. My dad really loves desserts. He's got great discipline and he's a very healthy eater, but we were on vacation, so he ordered a hot fudge sundae for dessert. He and my mother were sitting side-by-side in the booth. I was on the other side.

My dad is very methodical and slow, very peaceful, and he takes his time, while my mother has more frenetic energy. They were sitting next to each other and the hot fudge sundae arrived. As my dad sat surveying it, perhaps taking in how beautiful it looked, my mom had already picked up her spoon and was eating it! Of course, he was very happy to share it—the bowl was huge. By the time my dad finally picked up his spoon and took his first bite, my mom had already eaten three or four spoonfuls. At that point, she decided that she had had enough. She remembered she was on a diet and shouldn't be eating it, so she picked up her glass of water and poured it over the entire hot fudge sundae so she wouldn't be tempted to eat any more! That was, of course, the end of my dad's dessert.

I share this story to show you how strong temptations are. Why didn't she just stop eating it and let him eat? Why did she have to ruin the rest of his sundae? When we're in the grips of temptation, particularly when we are depriving ourselves, disciplining ourselves, or controlling ourselves, temptation takes on a life of its own. My mother is a well-educated, intelligent, wonderful, caring woman. What had the hot fudge sundae done to her? Once she decided she was not going to eat any more, that should have been enough. She could have just put down her spoon and been done with her meal. But temptations take on a power of their own—"I *have* to eat the sundae!" So once she decided she shouldn't be eating it, the only way to overcome her temptation for the sundae was to ruin it completely.

That's our superficial layer of temptations. We are drawn toward things that are going to make us feel physically good for a very short time period.

If we go one step deeper, we face temptation in the form of things we're going to do that may not be physically gratifying or rewarding in the moment, but that are going to make us feel good later on. The temptation to cheat on an exam, for example, we know is wrong, but it can be overpowering. There are temptations to cheat in so many other ways as well—to cheat on our taxes, in our workplace. The world gives us so many opportunities to be dishonest for what seems to be our own best interest.

We tell ourselves that if I get an A on this exam, whether through merit or through cheating, I'll do well in the course. I'll get into the right university, get the right job, and be successful and satisfied. If I cheat on my taxes, I'll have more money and be happier. Every temptation looms over us with this hypnotic call. Even the urge to go shopping. You're walking down the street and see a new coat or a pair of shoes shouting at you, "If you just wear me, you'll feel better about yourself!" You have no intention of going in, but the temptation to feel better becomes overwhelming.

There's a wonderful story shared by meditation teacher, Eknath Easwaran. His friend would go to a pastry shop on his way to work every day. One day the friend decided to stop eating pastries. He would pledge every day to not eat sweets, but even so, he found himself heading back into the pastry shop on his way to work. So he went to Eknath and said, "I don't know what to do! Every day I pledge to not buy pastries, yet every day, without knowing what happened, I find myself with a bag full on the way to the office."

Eknathji told him, "Well, a good solution would be to leave your wallet at home. Then you couldn't buy pastries."

And the guy was stunned. "What?!" he exclaimed. "You want me to steal them?" The idea of *not* giving in to temptation was inconceivable for this man. He thought, "If I have money, I will buy them. If I *don't* have money, I will have to steal them."

The solution is not to control each individual temptation. Then we simply control the pastries, then the cake, then the hot fudge sundaes . . . it is a never-ending cycle. The universe is full of temptations everywhere we look. It would take all our time and energy to control and withstand each individual temptation every time it arises.

The only solution is to understand that, within ourselves, we're already full. The solution is our intellect—not the intellect we gain in university or from books, but the real power of discrimination that makes us understand, "I am *not* my senses. I am not this chemical and electrical pattern of drive for reward in my brain that says eat or drink or smoke." That's what's going on in our brains. It's just a pattern of electrical and chemical firings, a neural circuit within our reward pathways. Every time we give in, we establish that we are merely lightbulbs that can be flicked on and off. The switch goes up and I'm on; the switch goes down and I'm off. No! We are more than that. We are divine. The best way to overcome any temptation is not only to discipline yourself in the moment about the individual temptation, but also to re-recognize who you really are, as a full, complete, whole being who lacks nothing.

This is where spiritual austerity comes in. In the Hindu tradition, there are so many practices of austerity—fasting, staying up all night, meditating as still as a stone, practicing yoga.

When Pujya Swamiji was young and living in the jungle, he spent eleven hours a day standing on one foot. Why? His guru was not in the muscle-building business. It was not as if he were training Swamiji to win some yoga competition or athletic contest. It was a spiritual lesson, not a muscular one. It's the same reason we stay up all night on certain sacred holidays. The body needs sleep; we know that. We know we will sleep again. But on that night we stay awake despite our body's cry for rest. Or we fast. Why do we go without food? Food is not bad. We know we will eat again. So why fast? Swamiji's guru knew that he would not spend his entire life on one foot, so why make him stand in tree pose for most of his waking hours? These disciplines are to give us mastery not over the body but over the mind, mastery over temptation. They teach us that we are not simply a stimulus-response reaction. We are not Pavlov's dogs. There's a purpose to our lives that is not just to eat, drink, and procreate.

We gain that mastery in our spiritual practices. We practice austerity to learn that we are not simply a chemical reaction or an urge or hunger. When we fast, we feel our stomachs growl. Our brains are flooded with chemical signals to eat, but we know we are fasting today. The signals come, and so do the temptations but we do not eat. That practice develops a deep realization within ourselves in which we realize I am the master, not the slave. I watch the urge. I notice it. I do not give in. This deep impression in the psyche of knowing that I don't have to give in to my temptations is one of the most powerful lessons we can give ourselves.

Please remember though, I am not advocating torturing yourself! These austerities are not because we've sinned and need to be punished. People see penance and austerity as a form of self-flagellation. No. It's simply to give ourselves the experience of having all our neurons firing—saying, "Eat, drink, sleep!"—and then not doing any of it. In that experience, we realize, "Wow, my body and mind are screaming at me to give in, and yet I'm still here. I have not disintegrated or imploded or ceased to exist simply because I didn't give in to my temptation. The wave that commands me to eat or sleep washes over me, but I don't react. The wave rises, eventually breaks and recedes, and I'm still here." That teaching is very deep.

We must learn that there is a self that is not merely a response to a stimulus. There is a self that is not just the feeder of my desires. When we connect with that self, it stays with us throughout our lives even though, of course, we go back to sleeping and eating. The awareness and the learning impact us forever.

When I first came to Rishikesh, the prayers held in the Satsang Hall from 5 a.m. to 6 a.m. were compulsory. I was not used to sitting on the floor, and I could sit for barely thirty minutes before my knee or hip would start hurting. But the prayers last an hour, so most of the time I would just switch and re-cross my legs half-way through, or I would change to a different posture altogether. But I developed a meditation technique that I used every once in a while: It was a technique to develop that same awareness of not being my body or my instincts. I told myself, "I will not move, no matter how much it hurts or burns. Whether I itch, whether there is a fly on my nose, I will not budge." It was actually an incredible experience, one I recommend practicing every now and then. Normally in meditation, if you need to uncross and recross your legs, you do it so that you can go back to retaining your awareness on your mantra, or your breath, or the Divine. Usually we don't want our awareness in our meditation to be distracted by our aching knees or hips. But every once in a while it's a very powerful practice to just set an alarm and commit to not moving at all until the alarm goes off. The pain comes, the itch comes, but you just look at it, you don't push it away.

This is really the main point. When temptations come, don't push them away. Don't tell yourself, "I'm not going to think about chocolate," because then what are you invariably doing? Thinking about chocolate. Your consciousness is still filled with chocolate. If I say to you, "Meditate now, but whatever you do, don't think about ice cream," what are you going to think about? Ice cream! So the answer is not to push anything away. It's about recognizing and seeing it, acknowledging it, but not giving in to it, knowing that it's just a temptation to itch or move or eat, to smoke a cigarette or drink alcohol, to cheat on your spouse or cheat on your taxes. Whatever it is you're tempted to do, you don't get anywhere by pretending it's not there.

When we really win is when we can look at the temptation, see it, acknowledge it, and not be overpowered by it. That was the technique I developed in my Satsang Hall meditation during my early days in Rishikesh. Instead of trying to ignore my hip or my knee, I would literally turn that pain into my meditation. In my mind, I would stare at my hip or knee that was hurting and just be fully aware of it. And I discovered that when you actually look at a temptation (in my case the temptation to change the cross of my legs or to move in some other way), you find that the power of the stimulus becomes much less. Temptations act very macho when your back is turned, shouting at you and taunting you from behind, but the minute you turn around and stare them in the face they're nothing but an itch or a pack of cigarettes or a piece of cake or whatever else may be tempting you.

We must recognize that we are divine. This is what all of our mool mantras, the foundational, fundamental mantras teach us—like "*Aham Brahmasmi* (I am the Divine)," or "*tat twam asi* (thou art that)," or "*so hum* (I am that)." We are constantly reminded that we are one with the universe. We are not slaves to chemical and electrical reactions in our brain.

Here's the exciting part: We can change the habits formed in our mind. These habits are what we call in spiritual semantics a sanskara; in scientific semantics, we call it a neuronal network or a neuronal pattern. *We can change them.* If every time you are tempted to eat chocolate you do, you strengthen the pattern that says, "When this network fires, I eat." If every time you feel angry you throw a temper tantrum, you're doing the same thing.

The Western model of psychology says, "Let it out; you need to get it out," but the problem is that you're not actually getting anything out. Your anger doesn't actually go someplace else because you shouted or punched a punching bag. You can't eat to stuff down or vomit out your anger or pain. People try, but they cannot do it. I tried for many years, so I know it doesn't work. All that does is create an even stronger network or pattern that says, "This is how I respond to anger. I eat. Or I shout. Or I bury my feelings in alcohol." Every time you do it, you strengthen that network, you deepen that sanskara.

The way to be free is actually to lay down a different sanskara, a different pattern. Instead of having a temper tantrum every time you get angry, sit down, close your eyes, chant your mantra, take a walk in the park, listen to classical music, have a cup of hot tea or cool water, or light a candle. Whatever it is, set a new pattern that will slowly get ingrained deeper than the previous one.

This is the way to do it. Not by pushing away anger or temptations or controlling them through willpower, because that just causes us to contract. Spirituality is not about contraction. It's not about withdrawal. It's about openness, with the awareness that the path of divinity, spirituality, devotion, and yoga has so much more to offer. The joy I get from a piece of chocolate is nothing compared to the joy I get in my spiritual practice. It's not a path of renouncing joy. It's a path of experiencing greater joy. It's not about pushing things away, but rather embracing something that is much deeper, much fuller, and much more real. Then the temptations just drop off automatically.

Nonjudgment

We are taught to not judge other people, but how can we control this when we see educated, wealthy people harming others?

First understand that judgment is a defense mechanism. I point my negativity outward because there is something I don't want to look at inward. So whenever you find yourself judging others, ask yourself: "What am I avoiding in myself? What darkness within me do I not want to look at?" Judgments are our projections onto others, and frequently the very thing you judge negatively in someone else is that which you judge even more negatively in yourself but you're repressing it from your consciousness.

So judgments are defense mechanisms and ways of deflecting negativity off of ourselves and onto others. Second, judgment is violence. It causes harm. If I sit here and judge someone, whether it's something superficial and silly ("Oh, that person's really ugly"), or on a deeper level ("God, that person is really not very spiritual, they are telling lies"), my judgment harms me first, because it fills my mind and heart with negativity and the illusion of separation.

It also harms others because we're energetic beings, and even if I don't say, "You're ugly," or, "You're telling lies," it will impact you and affect you. Thoughts are things. Thoughts go out into the world as energy, and they impact and hurt people. Also, it doesn't benefit the world in any way. No humans, animals, trees, or water are saved because I judge you. So it causes harm and no benefit.

Third, it is a colossal waste of time. If I sit here judging you, I'm harmed, you're harmed, no one is helped and I've wasted precious minutes I could have spent helping the world and doing something positive. I've thrown them away sitting around judging you instead.

We need to stop judging, for our own sake and for the world's sake. So much mental time and energy is wasted in judging others.

However, just because we don't judge doesn't mean we sit back, complacently and allow violence, destruction, or harm to occur. Whether it's destruction of the environment, racism, prejudice, inequality, injustice, violence against women, or any other type of harm, we must stand up and act. But still we don't judge. We simply need to be aware, as a witness is aware, that what is happening is not right, and then—without judgment, criticism, or negativity polluting our minds—we must intervene in with awareness and clarity in a way that is effective and skillful. Maybe we suggest to someone that they might consider an alternative way of reacting. Maybe we teach, help, and encourage someone to make right choices. In such situations we are not meant to stand by blindly and our ability, our resources, our power and impact, to bring about a change for the better in the world. But if we're judging, then all we do is bring forth negativity without any positive benefit.

Sometimes people think that judgment and criticism are necessary in order to effect change. But actually science has proven it works the other way. We've all been in situations where we've done something wrong and been criticized for it. The criticism hurts us and causes us to shrink up and contract inside. It does not make us want to go out and do the right thing. It does not inspire us or catalyze us. All the criticism does is hurt our hearts. We know this implicitly from being on the receiving end of criticism. It hurts! When we make a mistake and someone says to us, "You're stupid and worthless," we feel horrible. We don't feel empowered to change, nor energized to find a new way, nor inspired to act in a different manner. We feel like crawling into a hole and crying. Thus, when we are on the other side, when we see somebody doing something that we know is not right, we have to remember that ultimately our goal is to improve the situation, not to hurt that person, not simply to vent our outrage. We may be right, but being right does not give us the right to hurt people. Research has also shown that the carrot is a much more effective means to bring about lasting change than the stick. The stick might lead to momentary behavior change, but it doesn't lead to lasting change in thoughts, values or ethics. Therefore, first we must free ourselves from the tunnel vision of judgment, and then will we be able to see the most effective way of communicating so the other person feels empowered and energized to change for the good. That's the best thing we can do—for people, for animals, for the land, for the whole planet.

Compassion

How can we develop true compassion?

The world today faces an epidemic of separation—separation between us and God, between us and the universe, between us and our own selves, between us and those around us. Compassion reconnects us.

Compassion is very different from pity or sympathy, which stems from separation. Pity is when I say, "I feel badly for you. Poor thing." That puts me in the viewer's box watching your life. It may stem from good instincts, but it is rooted in separation.

Sympathy then stems from pity, and is rooted in separation. In sympathy I say, "Oh, I'm so sorry to hear what you're going through. Here, you can cry on my shoulder." Again, it's not a bad emotion; it arises out of kindness and care, so that is beautiful, but it is still rooted in the myth of separation. There's a very safe line between us, a boundary between me and your pain. I can even feel good about myself for being such a sympathetic being. My ego gets inflated, but I'm not of any real use to you, because having someone say, "Oh, you poor thing, I'm so sorry for you," doesn't actually help much.

The only thing that really helps when we are going through a difficult time is to have someone be there *with* us; someone who really feels our pain, someone who travels into the sadness and darkness with us and can hold our hand in the deepest depths of despair because they are not reaching down to us from someplace high above. They are with us, in full oneness and togetherness, as we suffer. Whether they've got words to say or not, whether they take us in their arms and we cry in their lap or they just sit with us and our tears, that connection and comfort of having someone with us, feeling us, in this deep, dark, horrible place is actually the greatest life preserver.

Compassion connects us. It is the bridge we use to walk from *I* to *we*, and therefore from illness (*I*-llness) to wellness (*we*-llness). We all know we should serve and help others, but if we're doing it from a mindset of separation, the benefits are superficial. But if I can actually connect with you and recognize that you and I are one, then I am able to enter the river of compassion. This doesn't mean that I turn your pain into my pain and now it's all about me. Compassion simply means that I'm able to be there with you, fully, and I can respond to your pain as though it were mine.

If you are hungry, compassion teaches me to respond to your hunger in the same way I respond to my own. I will try to feed you. If you're sick, I should serve you as I would serve myself. In true compassion, you and I are connected; I'm not serving you as the giver, with you as the receiver. I am not serving as the great humanitarian to one who is needy. Compassion brings us into the space of oneness. I serve you as self.

It's the same example I gave earlier—that if I fall and hurt my right leg, my left leg will pick up the extra weight. We call that limping. No one has to beg or applaud the left leg for being such a great humanitarian. It picks up the extra weight because it understands that the right leg is self. There's a connection, a oneness. The left leg never says, "Oh my God, me again? I just limped last week! Why is it always me? Why doesn't the right leg ever pick up extra weight? Forget it, I'm not going to do it anymore!" If I injure my right leg every week for the rest of my life, my left leg will limp every week for the rest of my life. That is what real compassion is. Compassion pulls us out of our small, separate ego-self and opens the door for us into the experience of union, oneness, an expanded experience of self.

We serve with compassion when we recognize the other as self, when we realize the universe is not separate from us—none of the humans nor any of the animals or plants. Compassion is not about perceiving oneself as a martyr, a good person, or a selfless person because those definitions again keep us in boxes of labels and separation.

We also have to remember to extend compassion to ourselves as well. In the world we are connected to, the world we serve, the world for which we meditate upon lovingkindness, we exist too. The compassion we develop for others should allow us to feel it for ourselves as well. We must open our compassionate heart to make space for our own shortcomings, our own failings, our own needs, our own humanity. So frequently we work on developing compassion for others but we forget ourselves. Then we berate ourselves when we don't live up to the highest goals of serving others. "You'll never be spiritual! You're a failure at this compassion practice as well! You are worthless!" Can you see the tragic irony? The very practices of compassion can become yet another way for us to denigrate and harm our own selves. As we strive to live and act from a compassionate heart, we must ensure that heart includes ourselves as well.

How can we help others become more present and compassionate?

On a spiritual and emotional level, the only people we can really help are ourselves. Many people come to satsang and ask me, "How can I make my spouse (or children, or in-laws, or boss) more spiritual?" This desire is understandable. When we embark on a spiritual path and begin to experience more peace, more joy, more spaciousness, and calm in our life, we naturally want to share this jewel with our loved ones. We also want to share because it can become a challenge to live with someone who is not spiritual when you've committed to a spiritual path. It's much easier if your loved ones share your values, priorities, and belief systems, so we have a double incentive to try to bring them onto the path.

The difficulty, however, is that this usually cannot be done directly. There are several challenges. First, compassion, presence, a spiritual mindset and viewpoint are virtues that arise from deep within us. We feel oneness with other beings. We feel the presence of spirit, of limitless awareness, of deep connection with the Divine. These are not merely actions or behaviors. They are deep internal experiences and they are also conscious intentions about how we want to think, choose, and live. We cannot change someone else's internal experience or life intentions. There is no way to *make* another person experience compassion or the presence of the Divine.

Second, in our attempt to try to bring them around, we actually create more separation with our loved ones because now we become the teacher. They are the student. That seemingly altruistic and benevolent impulse has pushed you into a place of separation while the intention is to give you an experience of oneness! The only way I can help you experience compassion is through being deeply connected with you and helping you *feel* connected with others.

The third challenge is that frequently our loved ones don't *want* us to teach them or convert them. They may see us as being patronizing or condescending or arrogant. Our very efforts end up backfiring and pushing our loved ones farther away. No one likes to be preached to, especially by a family member or coworker. The more we try, the more they will harden their heart against us in annoyance. Then, even if they are inspired at a later time to start walking a spiritual path, they may dismiss the impulse because it feels to them like giving in to what we have said. This is especially true with family members. The more you push, the farther away they go. So the only way to bring others onto the path is to live our spiritual values so strongly and so authentically that people are automatically drawn to the energy that emanates from us.

You cannot teach or force someone to love. I can only love you and create a space of deep love and invite you into it. To make someone feel compassion, presence, or spirituality, the only way we can even begin is to connect with them deeply from our heart and spirit and be a powerhouse of compassion, love, and spirituality so that the person may feel those things too. When they do, it will awaken something inside them.

If my goal is to help you feel love, then through loving you, I may be able to unthaw the part in you that is blocked from love. But to do this successfully, I have to love you. I cannot help you experience love if I cannot love you. Similarly, the only way to help anyone experience spirituality is to emanate and exude spirituality, so that in our presence others feel that presence of compassion, spirituality, and love. We can create an energy of spirituality around ourselves and gently invite others into that. Our very energetic field can be a magnet that draws people, wordlessly.

There was a beautiful young boy, about eight or nine years old, who came from London to our ashram. He was here for about a week, and when he was leaving, Swamiji asked him how he had enjoyed the visit. He said, "I feel like someone has reached into my heart and turned the switch from off to on!"

That's not something we can teach. We cannot sit a young boy down and say, "Close your eyes and experience love and spirit." We can only invite him to attend the sacred ceremonies and teach him chants, but we have no direct path to his heart and spirit, other than through our own heart and spirit. By being in the presence of such a powerful connection to spirit, to love, to divinity, to compassion, he felt it within himself. That's why, when our goal is to help someone else become spiritual we need to radiate such love, spirit, compassion, connection, and presence that people around us automatically feel it.

When an air conditioner is on, if you stand near it you feel cold, not because you have done something, not because the air conditioner shouted at you from across the room, "Become cold!," but because it emits so much cold air that if you get close enough to it, you walk away feeling cool. In the same way, we have to first experience compassion and love in ourselves before we can offer it to others. Only when we manifest and transmit that love and spirituality and compassion will people around us also feel it naturally. So it's all up to us.

I'm very sensitive and find myself getting hurt a lot. What can I do to manage my emotions?

We are all sensitive to the world around us. We are energetic beings and hence we literally feel the energy of the world around us, whether it's the hot energy of the sun or the forceful energy of the wind or the vibrational field of the person sitting next to us. Some of us are more sensitive than others, so we may experience more suffering when we are hurt by someone or when negative things happen in life. But we can change that hypersensitivity into a quality that can benefit us and the world rather than hurt us. How?

First, recognize that we can only properly respond to other people's actions and words if we are balanced, grounded, anchored, and peaceful.

Imagine this: You're in a room with people you don't know. Maybe someone in that room has had too much to drink, or they've had a bad day, and they call you stupid, or criticize you in some other way. You rightly reason, "I don't know this person. They must've had a bad day, or one drink too many," and it doesn't affect you deeply. Similarly, if you're walking down the street and someone on the corner who is clearly mentally unstable or under the influence of drugs shouts crude remarks at you, you don't take it personally. You may walk faster to get away or cross the street, but you don't get wounded by their words. You understand that person is unstable and what they are saying has nothing to do with you and everything to do with them. However, if it's a loved one who has said or done something hurtful, you take it to heart. Why? When someone else's actions or words have the power to uproot me, to anger me, to make me doubt myself, it means that I have allowed that person and their own experiences of life to define me.

I always emphasize that if somebody hurts us it's because they are in pain. Instead of allowing ourselves to be hurt by their words or behavior, we must try to feel compassion for what they are going through, and understand that if they were in peace they would exude peace. The pain they are exuding is because that is what they are generating inside themselves.

We are not just receivers of energy, but also generators and transmitters. When you say you are sensitive, you're implying a one-way street where your responses are determined by stimuli from the world around you. In a stressful situation, you get stressed. In a peaceful situation, you are peaceful. If somebody's miserable, you are miserable. If they're angry, you are hurt. But you're not a one-way street; you're a two-way street. So a beautiful way to turn your sensitivity into a positive quality is to focus on what you can give out instead of focusing on what's coming in.

When we can be generators of love and compassion, we become the first recipients of it! If I'm generating love, I benefit inside. That love fills me and flows through me before it emanates into the world for others. If I'm generating anger, though, I suffer first. This is why it's said so beautifully that to be angry is like drinking poison but expecting the other guy to die! We have the fullness, goodness, completeness, divinity, and infinite power within us to generate love, peace, and compassion. So why are we generating frustration, hurt, and anxiety?

When you feel yourself being too sensitive, ponder this question: "How did I become a one-way street?" Shift your focus from the incoming energy to the outgoing energy. Shift your focus to the generator of energy within yourself and allow that to heal you, and then to heal others.

What can we do for people who are suffering?

Compassion opens up our hearts so wide that the world comes inside. When you're suffering, you just want someone to be with you, to be really with you in the depths of your despair; you don't need them to fix you. You just need their loving presence.

We don't have to be miserable with the person who is suffering in order to be compassionate. We just have to be fully present. In that full presence, we open up to them and their experience, and their misery doesn't scare us. When, instead, we try to fix people, when we tell them, "Everything will be okay," or, "Don't worry." What that really means on a deep level is: "I'm so uncomfortable with your sadness that I need us to get out of this quickly, so let's start talking solutions." But what people need is for us to be fearlessly present with them in their misery and pain. That's not easy, but it's usually the best thing we can do for people who are suffering.

Our presence, in compassion and connection, actually holds the presence of joy. When someone is in pain, it is very difficult for them to remember the possibility of joy. And it's not something they want to hear us say. If someone is suffering, they don't want you to tell them, "There's light at the end of the tunnel," or, "This too shall pass," or, "You should just think about the happy times." Platitudes do not help in times of grief. But your full, courageous, and compassionate presence that holds the experience of joy allows them to gently remember that there is another possibility.

But I feel guilty when others are in pain and I'm happy. What can I do?

When we see people who are in pain or are suffering, we have to acknowledge them, take them into our prayers and do whatever we can for them. That is the deepest expression of compassion. There is nothing about compassion that dictates you must be equally miserable. You should never feel guilty about being happy, because there's always something to be happy about. Just because a loved one is having a difficult time doesn't mean that you should feel guilty for finding happiness. You can help them, hold their hand, and be present with them through their difficulty, but you do not need to get lost in the darkness of misery yourself. You can hold someone deeply and truthfully while they are in misery without drowning along with them. The fact that you are able to access joy in your life is the gift of remembrance for them, a light pointing toward another truth.

Love

What is the essence of love?

Love is energy. Love is the energy of the universe. It's the power of love between Creator and creation that causes flower petals to open as the sun shines upon them, that causes seeds to sprout into trees, and those trees to grow and give fruit as they are nourished by the soil, the sun, and the rain.

Love is what enables us to grow as well. In fact, there is a medical condition called *failure to thrive* in which children may be given all the proper food, medicine, clothing, and shelter, but their growth lags significantly behind that of other children their age. Through much study spanning many years, researchers discovered that an absence of touch, an absence of the felt experience of love, was one of the significant factors that leads to these children's stunted development. In orphanages, lack of loving touch is the number one cause of this condition. If children are not held and loved enough, there's a chance that they won't grow properly. Love is the energy that helps hold it all together.

When we love we tap into the sacred, divine source of love. It's not only that I'm in love with you, but in loving you, you become the medium through which I tap into the boundless source of love within me.

When someone is showering us with love, appreciation, support, and nurturing, it's very easy to love them. You become like the flower opening its petals, the tree growing in nourishing soil. Yet, if you've ever spent time in the forest, you'll know that even though most trees grow straight upward, if there isn't light right above them, or if there are too many other trees blocking the sun, the trees grow sideways instead. Receiving sunlight is critical for the process of photosynthesis through which trees receive their energy, so they adapt and grow in whichever direction is necessary to access light. There is a wisdom in the universe that shows the tree how to grow sideways instead of straight up in order to access the light it needs.

How can we access that same wisdom? If we aren't showered with the love we need to survive, just as the tree needs the sun, how can we tap into that source? As the tree must find light, we must find love. But that doesn't mean we have to grow sideways. We can find love wherever we go, if we are willing and courageous enough to open ourselves to it. Love does not only mean romantic love or the love of a parent for a child. Love is something we can connect to even in the eyes of a stranger or in hugging a tree.

When you look at someone, try to connect with their content instead of only their form. Instead of seeing only the outward appearance of a woman or man of a certain skin color, age, height, and weight, wearing certain types of clothes, can you see their true content, can you see the Divine in them? Can you see essence, consciousness, soul? Can you see your very self in them? If you can, you will find that, even without knowing them on a personality level, you can immediately love them on a soul level. In that soul connection, you enable yourself to connect to the true source of love within you.

How do we love unconditionally? How can we avoid being hurt?

The only way not to get hurt is to stop living. There is a beautiful saying in Hindi. It works much better in the original language, but I'll give you the translation: "That which bends is that which is alive; that which is rigid is a corpse." When we are alive, we bend. We bend in humility, surrender to the winds and waves of life. This is a hallmark of being alive. The only thing that doesn't bend is a corpse. If you want to stop being hurt, you have to shut yourself off from life. When we love someone and they don't treat us or speak to us or act the way we want them to, we feel hurt. Therefore we decide to stop caring, to stop loving, thinking that will prevent us from getting hurt. But that just hurts us more because it shuts us off from the very flow of life. Instead, we need to accept that getting hurt is just part of the package deal of caring and loving.

There is a way to keep loving without getting hurt, but it requires us to love unconditionally.

We may think we love unconditionally. Ask people to describe how they feel about their children or spouse, and frequently you will hear,

"I love him unconditionally, but oh my God, he is such a slob. If he would only pick up his stuff, then I'd really love him!" That doesn't sound unconditional. In true unconditional love, we are not attached to what the loved one does or says, and therefore we don't get hurt when those actions or words are out of alignment with our wishes. Unconditional love is love for the very essence of who they are, not how they behave or conform to our desires. It is love for the unchanging, eternal spiritual core of their being.

However, unconditional love is certainly not synonymous with apathy. Freedom from attachment is not indifference. You may love someone, but if you need them to behave in a certain way for you to feel happy, that's a recipe for disaster. You're going to get hurt. We don't have control over anybody else's thoughts, words, or actions. We only have control over ourselves. And the only way, ultimately, not to get hurt is to stop having the expectation that others will conform to your wishes or beliefs.

That doesn't mean we stop caring; it doesn't mean we let our hearts turn into stone. Instead, we work within ourselves to allow love to be its own reward.

If we look carefully at what hurts us, it always has to do with an unfulfilled expectation. Sometimes it's a small thing, such as remembering a birthday; sometimes it's a big thing, such as not being betrayed. But for love to be our path to spiritual awakening, we have to recognize that the love we experience is its own reward. Love comes with no guarantees. Just because you love someone, it doesn't guarantee that they will love you back, bring you flowers, or make choices in their life that you want them to make. If the focus of your love is making them dance to your tune, today or tomorrow you're going to get hurt. Or alternatively they'll just become your robot and you'll squeeze the life out of them. Many of us do that unconsciously—we pressure and nag the people around us so relentlessly that they just give up.

If all you want is someone who will do your bidding, there's no point seeking a relationship in the first place. You don't want to live with a disempowered person who has simply adapted their behavior to your demands. That's not how love should be. Love has to be alive. And for love to be alive everyone must have free will. So your focus needs to be on love as its own spiritual reward, and not on how you can manipulate your beloved to do your bidding.

Yes, you will get hurt sometimes, but you must keep going back to love, opening your heart again and again to allow yourself that experience of love.

That's what life is about. Again, I don't mean only romantic love. Love your friends, love the trees, love humanity, love your pets, love God. But we've got to love, and being hurt is part of loving until we can unhook our own heart from other people's actions. That's the real secret to loving and not getting hurt—unhook your own heart from other people's actions and words. The only other option is to turn your heart into a stone, devoid of life, which is no solution at all.

How do we practice giving and receiving unconditional love?

We're taught from early childhood that giving is more important than receiving. But here's what's interesting: This teaching holds true for everything except love. I cannot give love unconditionally until I'm able to experience it in myself. My intention may be very pure, I may want to love you unconditionally, but as long as I'm not able to love myself, I'm not able to fully love you. I may need you or lust for you. I may be attached to you. I may depend on you. But I'm not able to actually deeply love you until and unless I know how to love myself. Love is something where, no matter how selfless or spiritual we want to be, we have to start with ourselves.

When we talk about loving ourselves unconditionally, it's important to recognize that we are loving the capital-S Self. It's the core of who we are. It's our soul, spirit, essence, consciousness, and it *is* love. You don't have to love the fact that you're addicted to smoking or that you beat your children or cheat on your taxes. You shouldn't love any of those things. You should work to change them. The practice of unconditional love holds that all these things you do stem out of your inability to see your true self, to understand yourself or love yourself.

If I don't love myself and feel empty, I may drink alcohol or use drugs or eat an entire chocolate cake in one sitting or max out my credit cards at the store. I'm trying to fill myself, numbing myself, escaping from myself. When I feel empty, I need others to act in a certain way for me to feel okay. When they do, I feel great. When they don't, I'm furious. That, is where my anger comes from.

All of these things do not stem from my being a bad person, but from the fact that I haven't yet seen the truth of my own fullness and divinity. They arise because I'm living behind a veil of illusion.

When I'm really able to see myself, what I see is consciousness, divinity, and love. Yes, this body, this vehicle, has been through a lot. It's faced a lot of challenges, a lot of things have happened to it, which have created patterns of ignorance and illusion in my own mind, patterns that make me feel small and cause me to contract away from the world. When I allow these patterns to run my show, I feel horribly about myself and act in ways I later regret.

When we are young, we establish a set of beliefs in our mind in which we blame ourselves for everything. It's a stage of child development called *magical thinking*, wherein children think they have power over everything. If they cry, their mom picks them up and everything is better. In this phase of magical thinking, we think everything happens because of us, even if it is not something directly related to us. If a sibling or parent passes away, parents get divorced, or the house burns down, in the child's mind, she or he is to blame. Very frequently, although typically unconsciously, we think, "If only I cleaned my room, then Mom would be happy and she wouldn't fight with Dad, so they wouldn't have gotten divorced," or, "If only I hadn't lied about eating the cookies, then God wouldn't be angry and He wouldn't have given my sister cancer and taken her away from us." This type of logic seems illogical to an adult mind, but it is the magical thinking of childhood and it plants its roots very deep in our psyche.

If we don't work through these incorrect beliefs, we carry the patterns into adulthood. We move through this world with patterns that prevent us from loving ourselves, because even though we may have become CEO or founded an NGO that feeds five million people every day, on the inside we still don't feel worthy. These patterns are deep and usually unconscious. They have nothing to do with today's reality, and yet they are the cause of our subconscious thoughts and behavior.

When we speak about receiving love, first we must understand that we are divine and all of the rest of the chatter in our mind is ignorance. It is this ignorance and the ego that says, "I am this body; I am what's happened to it." The ego mind has absorbed all the messages of our culture, the marketing, our parents, everything that's happened to us. The sum total of these messages is that you're not worthy, you're not good enough. "Why can't you be like your brother? Why can't you be like your sister? When I was your age, I . . ." We all have a different way in which such messages got through to us, but the result is the same: We're not good enough and we're not worthy. And that perception is what needs to be corrected first.

When we become able to actually love ourselves, we experience something that we always thought we needed someone else to give us, something we were always looking for outside. What that teaches us directly, instinctively, experientially, and automatically is that we don't need others to behave in a certain way, or speak in a certain way, or do something in a certain way so that we can be okay. Because here we are, experiencing love in our own heart, alone on our own couch, completely independent of anyone else. That awareness that we can tap into the source of love within ourselves shows us that we are not dependent on others' actions or words, so we can let go of the death grip of expectations we hold on the world and our loved ones. The minute we let those expectations go, we are able to love unconditionally.

Imagine you go out to eat with friends. If you're sitting at a table with others, isn't it more fun to also have a bite of this and a bite of that, and to share dishes you think taste really good? But, if someone doesn't want to share their food with you, it's okay because you've got a plate of food in front of you. But if you were starving and your plate was empty and you needed someone's food to live, you wouldn't be able to accept their refusal to share. Your plate has to be full first. Only then is it okay if someone doesn't want to share their food with you. In the same way, your inner plate of love has to be full in order to love someone who refuses to love you, or who may say they love you but doesn't act the way you want. You can only love unconditionally if you are aware of the overflowing cup of abundant love within yourself.

How do we maintain harmony in relationships?

People we have relationships with help us experience the love that already exists within ourselves. Loving someone becomes a catalyst for our own internal love manufacturing plant to be switched on. That person may be the stimulus for us to start intentionally producing love, but the love is being produced within us. It is not dependent upon the other person.

Let me explain this because I know it *seems* like the love we feel is coming from the other person. When your beloved stands up and leaves the room, do you feel any less love? Do you fall out of love every time they go to get a glass of water or when they go to the office or the grocery store?

Of course not. So it's not dependent on them. It's not coming *from* them *to* you. Rather, your feeling of love for them has switched on love within yourself. That state of love is now a place that the two of you cohabit. Your love invites them to also create love within themselves.

You can also think about it logically like this: If you're standing near an air conditioner, you feel cool. But the farther you walk away from the air conditioner, the less cool you feel. The coolness is coming directly from the air conditioner; you are not generating it inside yourself. So you must stand near enough to receive the cool air from the air conditioner. Your coolness is dependent on the air conditioner. The closer you are, the more coolness. The farther away you are, the less coolness. But love doesn't work that way. Love exists actually within you. Through the relationship, the beloved has enabled you to experience the place within yourself that is love. When we talk about a *soulmate*, this is what it means. The soulmate is one in whose presence you are able to experience the truth of your very self, which is love. It doesn't matter if it's a spouse, a friend, a sibling, a parent, a child, a guru, a tree, or a pet.

Unfortunately, we've filled up our relationships with a lot of baggage and a lot of expectations. These pull us from the deep heart into the planning mind. When we move from an experience of love into the everyday logistics of life—who is going to wash the dishes, go grocery shopping, change diapers, scrub the toilet—that is when we lose connection to the love within ourselves and think we are falling out of love with the other person. What is actually happening is that you are no longer able to access that deep place of love within yourself because your thinking mind, busyness, numbness, distractions, and expectations have jammed up your internal love manufacturing plant. Probably the same has happened to your loved one. Rather than realizing that, we blame each other for not giving us the love we think we need. We expect the beloved, then, to act in certain ways to seemingly fill the illusion of a lack of love we are feeling. This is the problem.

No matter how much the beloved may try, if we cannot stay in our loving heart and we get stuck only in the planning and thinking mind, we will never feel that love. They may shower us with love, but if we are not able to access our own love-manufacturing plant inside, we will never feel satisfied. But we will continue to blame the beloved.

The solution is simple. The only way to have harmony in relationships is to stop expecting the other to behave in a certain way, speak in a certain way, and live a certain way in order to fill our holes. We need to become aware that the deep, satisfying love we feel is generated within us. The beloved is an awesome vehicle, the one who has catalyzed it, but it's not their fault if we are no longer able to access the place of love within ourselves. It's within us, which means it's our responsibility to turn inward and find that place within ourselves again. The beloved was just the one who showed it to us.

Harmony in relationships doesn't come from two halves becoming one, or two beings coming together with pegs that fill each other's holes. If I've got a square hole and you've got a square peg, we fit. Yet, over time, because I change, my square hole becomes a triangle. Your square peg, because you change, becomes round. Now you've got a round peg and I've got a triangular hole and the two no longer fit each other. This is when we start to fight and fall out of love. But we have to recognize that we are not those holes; we are not even full of holes. We are whole; what feel like holes are just impressions upon our psyche that can heal and transform. When we enter relationships as a full, whole being, then it doesn't matter what form our beloved is. We don't need them to fill us.

My dad is a successful divorce attorney. He has spent more than fifty years working with couples who are getting divorced. He has also spent more than four decades married to my mother, a wonderful woman but not an easy woman. Despite being married to a vibrant and amazing but difficult woman, he lives in a place of deep peace, which has been such a guiding force and pillar of support in my life.

His teaching is simple: You can either be right or you can be married. You cannot be both. You must choose if it's more important to be right or more important to be happily married. It's not just about our marriages, of course. It's about all relationships. It is our attachment to being right that keeps us from being happy. We can be right or we can be peaceful. The choice is ours. We have to make that decision in our relationships. In every situation, when we run into conflict, we really have to ask ourselves: In this moment, is being right more important than being in peace? Am I prepared to relinquish my attachment to proving I'm right in exchange for peace? We have the ability and the freedom to choose peace in each moment, to choose love in each moment. But we have to choose consciously. If we can do that, if we can let the other be right so that we can both be peaceful, what we find is not only are our relationships peaceful, but we're also peaceful inside.

How to Deal with Loss

How do we overcome the fear of loss?

We overcome the fear of loss by recognizing that nothing is ours to begin with. The fear of loss is rooted in the illusion that we actually own something. If I don't own anything, I'm not afraid of losing it. For example, I don't have a fear of losing my diamond earrings. Why? Because I don't have diamond earrings. The fear of losing something is founded upon the idea that we have it. But when we think more deeply, we realize that nothing is ours. Every single thing, every single person, every ability is being lent to us.

Look over the course of your life. You gain so much—you learn how to be a fantastic cricket player, a great doctor, an engineer. But give it a few decades, and as the body and brain start to degenerate, you're no longer a fantastic athlete, your hands shake too much to be able to perform surgery, you no longer remember engineering equations or formulas.

We're so attached to our beauty, our degrees, our titles, our careers, but time inevitably snatches them from our hands. Even if nothing drastic happens and we simply age, we still lose everything. Everyone retires unless they die early before retirement. Everyone's body degenerates. The same is true of our money. We'll eventually lose it, whether now or once we pass away. God may decide to give us a lesson a little bit earlier—the stock market might crash. But that's just to teach us, "You thought it was yours. I needed to remind you it was never yours."

People tend to bemoan their fate and ask, "Why did God take everything from me?" But it was never actually ours; it was lent to us for a while.

The same is true about our relationships. Eventually, whether through breakup, betrayal, divorce, or death, we're going to lose everyone. It's deeply sad, but until and unless we recognize that as an ultimate truth of life, we can't really live because we're grasping at something that is slipping inevitably through our fingers.

Instead, if we are aiming for enlightenment, spiritual awakening, self-realization, or just peace in life, we must ask ourselves, "What is it that I don't lose? What is it that does not degenerate, die, and slip away? If I'm going to lose everything, including my loved ones, then being attached to these things is an exercise in futility and frustration. I am going to lose them regardless of how hard I hold on." So the question becomes, "What should I be attached to? What should I make so dear that I become afraid of losing that? What is it that's not going to dissolve, divorce me, or die?" The answer is our spiritual connection, the presence of the Divine, and the very truth of our selves. And here's what's beautiful: You don't need to be attached to the Divine *instead* of your loved ones. Be attached to the Divine *through* your loved ones, and through everything in the natural world, because everything is pervaded by the Divine.

This does not mean, of course, that we love our loved ones any less or care about them any less. We don't announce, "Okay, honey, I'm not going to love you and be attached to you anymore; I'm going to love God instead." What actually happens is quite beautiful. We realize, "Okay, instead of being desperately attached to that really beautiful, youthful face, the way she looks in those clothes, or the way she dances, I'm going to be attached to her essence, her spirit, her soul, and the presence of the Divine flowing through her." We shift our connection and attachment to essence, to soul, to the Divine in ourselves and in our loved ones, rather than to just their physical form, how much money they make, etc.

This is the only way to overcome that fear of loss. You can cut yourself off from life, deciding that you're not going to care about anything, but all that does is contract your heart. What the heart does is love. You could say the dharma of the heart is to love. If you block it from loving it atrophies. It hardens and shuts down, and that is not the way to live. Instead, love the essence of your loved ones, love their divinity, love the presence of God through them. There is nothing wrong with enjoying their form in this moment, of course. I don't believe God would have created such beauty if we weren't supposed to enjoy it. But don't get attached to that physical form, just as we don't get attached to a sunset because we know we have only about forty-five seconds before it dips below the horizon. We must never fall prey to the illusion that by grasping hard enough we can prevent the sun or the moon from setting. Nor can we prevent the inevitable dissolution and loss of our own bodies, our roles, skills, careers, and relationships. So focus on that which is unchanging, the presence of the Divine.

When we experience hard times and hard things, how can we keep our hearts open?

No spiritual scripture or guru promises that if you follow a spiritual path you will never be hurt, or no one you love will ever leave you, or everything will always go your way. We must open our hearts despite the near surety that we will be hurt, because to live with a closed heart is to die while alive.

There is a story of a man who goes to his guru after his son has died. The man is as miserable as one can imagine. He's furious at God, and cries, "I've been a good, devout person. How can you hurt me in this way?" He goes to his guru and says, "You're my guru. Bring my son back to life! This is unfair, this isn't right, I shouldn't be hurt like this, bring him back to life!"

The guru says, "Okay, you're right. You are a good devotee, you shouldn't be hurt in any way that is more than the way other good people have been hurt. I will bring your son back to life, but I need one thing from you. I need you to bring me one grain of rice from the home of someone who has never lost a loved one. With that grain of rice, I will bring your son back to life." So the man rushes out to find that family. He goes from house to house, village to village, and of course he cannot find any house in which they haven't lost a loved one. Finally, he comes back to his guru, bows at his feet, and admits, "I'm so sorry. Forgive me for demanding that of you. I've spent the last several days immersed in the pain of others who have also lost loved ones, and I realize this is inevitable."

In life, sometimes we lose. We get hurt. It's the nature of the universe, it's the nature of nature. If we love a certain type of tree, we can worship its green leaves as much as we want, but come autumn those leaves will fall to the ground. We may love the snow, but we're going to lose it to spring. We can love our youth, but we're going to lose it to middle age and then old age.

Whatever we love, we lose. It's the nature of life and we have to accept it as it is. An open heart is our opportunity to accept the invitation of the universe to join it in co-creating our life. Closing your heart doesn't change the nature of nature; it simply means that you're in pain every day, rather than just on the days you lose something. Closing your heart means 365 days a year you hurt. Opening your heart means you may hurt sometimes, but certainly not all the time. It is your only opportunity to truly experience love and joy.

We don't experience deep joy from hugging our money, car, or house. Has anyone ever actually embraced their house? Or the fender of their car? Or their wallet?

The things we embrace are people, animals, trees—things that are living. Yes, we will lose them someday. They may also hurt us knowingly or unknowingly, maybe just by dying, maybe while living. Or we're going to hurt them. But our only chance to experience any joy, any meaning in life, is in staying open-hearted. To close our hearts is to say no to life itself, to turn down the invitation of the universe.

It's not always easy; I know that. This is where courage is needed. We usually think of the words *bravery* and *courage* as synonyms, but they're not. Brené Brown explains so beautifully that soldiers are brave because they have steel plates shielding their chest, steel masks over their heads, and long spears in their arms. They are able to approach a warring army with bravery because they are armed and protected.

But the word *courage* comes from the Latin root *cor*, meaning heart. It's the same root of the French word for heart—*coeur*. The root of courage is literally an open heart. So courage becomes our only choice. It's not a matter of "how to"; it's a matter of "I have to."

You should love people, nature, your work, your talents and achievements, but the safest thing you can do if you don't want to be hurt is to love God. God's not going anywhere. God's not going to betray you, tell your secrets, leave you for someone else, or insult you. Saints and sages who lived in caves were blissful. They had no family, no friends, and no social life. You'd think they must have been lonely, especially in those days before smartphones, social media, and messaging apps. But their inner connection was so strong that even living far from other humans, with just the river, the deer and snakes, the sun and moon for company, they were blissful, peaceful, and deeply fulfilled.

This doesn't mean you must go live in a cave, but you should realize that spiritual connection is the only inoculation for the pain of loss, betrayal, and loneliness. It grounds and anchors us, and gives us something deeper than that which we've lost. Remember that beautiful line in the prayers we sing every morning that I told you about? *"Tu akele nahin pyare. Ram tere sath mein,"* meaning, "You're not alone, dear one. God is with you."

There is also a beautiful line that we sing each night in our Ganga aarti on the banks of the Ganga River as we sing and celebrate and pray and meditate. Pujya Swamiji leads the devotional singing and we sing, *"Sabse unchi prem sagai."* It means the highest form of love is love for God. Everybody else may hurt you, everybody else may betray you, but that spiritual connection carries you throughout your life. It gives you the courage to keep your heart open. It doesn't matter what name you use for God or how you worship the Divine. When we connect deeply, we become a child in the Mother's arms—absolutely fearless.

How do we deal with death? How do we deal with people around us dying?

Death is one of those things over which we have no control. We actually have very little control over most aspects of life, but this is especially true with death. The only way to deal with it is through acceptance, because there is no alternative. Our lack of acceptance doesn't change it.

Usually we think that if we don't accept something—our child wants to marry someone we don't like, our loved one is having an affair, we get fired from our job—somehow our anger, silence, or pain is going to change it. So we live mostly in this illusion of our control.

The truth is we have almost no control over anything in life, other than our own actions and reactions. But death is the area that hurts the most. We can't convince anyone not to die, nor bribe them, nor try to rationalize with them, nor beg them. There's nothing we can do to prevent death when its time has come.

Losing a loved one is always painful. But, we also suffer the loss of the illusion of control. If a loved one passes away at ninety-five or a hundred peacefully in her sleep, we'll be sad but we'll understand that her body just stopped functioning. However, when it's someone who has not reached such an age, or if they suffer tremendously, we feel cheated by the universe. "This isn't fair!" we cry out to God.

Whether we accept it or not, deal with it well or not, there is nothing we can do. When we drop into full awareness of our helplessness in the face of death, we realize it's true not only about others, but also about ourselves. One day we, too, will die.

The cremation ground for Rishikesh is across the River Ganga from Parmarth Niketan and slightly downriver. During our evening sacred Ganga Arti ceremony, sometimes, if you look downriver, you can see a cremation fire burning. Whenever I see a cremation taking place, I always keep my eyes open, focused and meditating on that fire.

The easiest thing is to ignore it. We're over here celebrating; death is safely on the other side of the river. That is ignorantly cutting ourselves off, though, from the fullness and truth of existence. Yes, today we're celebrating and someone else is mourning, someone else is burning, but tomorrow or the next day or a few years from now it's going to be us standing over a burning pyre, mourning a loved one, and then tomorrow or the day after, or a few years or a few decades from now, it's going to be our body burning in the pyre. To hold awareness of all three—the joy, the despair, and the dissolution—at the same time is an incredible, deep meditation.

Our consciousness expands so fully in that practice. We realize, "Wow, this is all part of the package of life. The joy, the celebration, the mourning, the burning. They are inextricably linked, threads woven together in the tapestry of creation."

From an unwise perspective, the river appears to be a safe barrier between celebration and the despair of death, but just a few feet above the water, flames of the cremation mingle with the flames of aarti and one can no longer tease apart which was a flame of death and which a flame of life. Dropping deeply into that awareness is the only way to deal with the fear of death.

It's also, according to saints and sages, the best way to successfully live life. In the Katha Upanishad, young Nachiketa is instructed by Yama Raja (the lord of death) on the true nature of life, death, and the universe. Yama Raja explains that there are two ways to live: the path of shreya or the path of preya. The path of preya is the path of one for whom the physical life is the only life. It is life lived by the motto of "eat, drink, and be merry." I have seen bumper stickers pronouncing that "The one who dies with the most toys wins." That is the path of preya. It leads to a life of constant ups and downs, fear, confusion, attachment, and despair. And it ensures that we will keep having to come back on earth in birth after birth, form after form, until we learn the true meaning of our incarnation. The path of shreya, on the other hand, is a path of truth. Walking the path of shreya does not deny or ignore the body, but it focuses us on that which is eternal and unchanging—soul, consciousness, truth. On this path, we live surrendered to the Divine and aim to be clear instruments in God's hands. This is the path that leads to moksha, or liberation from the cycle of birth and death, ultimate Heaven.

We cannot deal with death until we deal with life. If we don't understand life, we will never be able to deal with death. So let your fear of death and despair around death be a catalyst to propel you into a study of life! Whenever a loved one passes on, recognize that ultimately it was his essence you loved. You did not love only his body. His body changed so many times during the years you knew and loved him. But your love did not waver as his body aged and changed. If your loved one got plastic surgery and looked different, you'd still love her. If she had an arm amputated, you wouldn't love her any less. What you love is the essence and spirit, and that remains, even after death.

Just as our loved ones' bodies change so many times during their lives but we continue to love them as they go from being young to middle-aged to old, or from thin to fat, or fat to thin, in the same way in death the body again changes form. It is the most drastic change, of course, but that's what it is—a change of form. The body goes back to the earth, back to the elements, but the soul hasn't gone anywhere. The soul was never born, the soul doesn't die. That which you deeply loved is still here. Also, the love you felt for them is still here, because it's in *you*. Allow yourself to feel that.

Sadly, our culture encourages wallowing in the despair that your loved ones are gone. If you say, "Oh, I can still hear them; I can still feel them," people will tell you, "Get over it." But the truth is, you still *can* hear them. Not with these physical ears, of course. What you are hearing is not vibrating sounds in your tympanic membrane, but their very presence resonating within you.

Our culture is so focused on the body that people will tell you that you need therapy if you say you can still hear departed loved ones or feel them with you. People will say that you need help letting go. But, what is there to let go of? Their soul that is one with your soul? The love that is still in you, why would you want to let go of that? There's actually nothing to let go of other than attachment to their physical form and the myth that your loved one existed only in that physical form. That myth is all we need to banish. Of course, keep loving them. Love the memory of their body, but love the presence of their soul.

Why do we feel depressed when we lose someone or something important to us? How can we deal with that depression?

There is an important distinction between sadness and depression. Many times in life, sad things happen. Maybe a loved one dies, or you get divorced, or you lose your job, or something else happens due to which, naturally, we feel sad. Society has now become habituated to seeing sadness as an illness. I know countless people who have been prescribed antidepressants in response to tragic life circumstances, the most natural response to which is grief.

The response to a sad occurrence is to be sad. It is not natural to feel bouncy, ecstatic, or joyous in the midst of death, loss, and tragedy.

We need to give ourselves time and space to mourn and be sad. Mourning is necessary not only when someone dies. We mourn loss of opportunity, loss of relationships, loss of youth. There's so much in our lives that we lose that can lead to natural sadness.

It's important not to dump every moment, week, or month of sadness into the box of clinical depression. We must first ask ourselves: "What have I experienced? What's going on? What have I lost?" That loss could just be the loss of an idea. We had an idea of what our life was going to be like, or what an evening or a weekend would be like. When that doesn't happen, there's a moment of mourning, a natural sadness. We obviously don't want to get stuck in that sadness but before we can healthfully let it go we need to simply observe it and acknowledge it.

However, when nothing adverse has happened yet one is feeling depressed for an extended period of time, there are different ways to understand and address it. The first has to do with the brain. There are certain chemical imbalances and fluctuations that we associate with depression. But there is a difference between being *associated with* and being a *cause of* something.

We know that depression is *associated with* (not necessarily *caused by*) imbalances in the level of certain chemicals in the brain. We know that when we give people medicine that changes certain chemistry in the brain, depression often lifts.

We also know that people who have experienced trauma in their childhood tend to have similar imbalances of chemicals in their brains. This leads us to acknowledge that trauma in childhood can be confidently linked to the chemical-imbalance type of depression. For this reason, I do not advise people to categorically refuse antidepressant medication. If you have diabetes and imbalances in your pancreas's ability to produce insulin, you would likely take medicine to balance your insulin. In the same way, sometimes medicines are needed for challenges in the chemistry of our brain and can be quite helpful in bringing stability to our emotional state. Sometimes medication is exactly the life raft someone needs to not drown in the ocean of depression.

A common and important side effect though of many antidepressant medicines is that they limit the range of your emotions. If one side of the emotional spectrum is great joy and on the other side is great despair, antidepressants can chop off both ends of the spectrum, leaving you somewhere in the middle, feeling numb.

Thus in situations where you would otherwise feel joy, you may feel nothing.

However, there are certain situations, for certain people, for whom antidepressants can be temporary lifesavers. You should never feel weak, wrong, or damaged because you need a bit of chemical assistance to balance your internal chemicals, whether it's your brain or your pancreas.

It's also critically important if you are suffering from depression to reach out for help from a priest, a pastor, a rabbi, a guru, a mentor, or a mental health professional. Do not feel weak for needing help. In the same way that going to a doctor for our eyes, teeth, ears, or internal organs is not a cause of shame, you should never feel ashamed for seeking help. In fact, to reach out for help takes great strength and courage. Be proud of yourself for being so courageous.

The other way of understanding and addressing depression, if it is not severe enough to warrant medication or professional assistance, is to find ways to experience joy again. One of the most powerful antidotes to depression is service.

Serving others is a fantastic way to realize how blessed we are, how much we have to offer and to get ourselves out of the agony of our own thoughts.

It works best when the service is interactive. It can be with children, animals, old people, or trees, but you should try to serve a living being—a plant, an animal, or a person with whom you can connect and whose life is improved because of you.

When you hug a child who is deprived of his parents' love, when you spend time with an elderly person whom nobody has visited in six months, when you plant a tree or flowers or vegetables and watch it grow, when you serve food to the hungry—these moments of service are powerful medicine. If you string enough of them together, they can rekindle your connection to humanity and to the source of joy within yourself. Lying in bed at night, you'll be able to say, "It was a good day."

How do we get over the pain of being left by someone we trusted and depended on?

Pain of loss of love doesn't actually go away. But several things happen through which we heal.

First, our sense of self expands enough to include the painful experience. It stops being a hole within us, and just becomes one of the threads that makes up the tapestry of our life. It still exists but it no longer prevents us from living a joyful, peaceful life.

The sting of the pain you feel when someone leaves goes away like the sting of a jellyfish or a scorpion eventually stops hurting. But the love you felt, and still feel, doesn't go away, and there's no reason for it to.

Whether someone left you through breakup or divorce or they left you through dying, your love didn't depart with them. Take a moment and allow your heart to feel it. It's still there. You were habituated to experiencing that love in the presence of a specific person, catalyzed by that specific person. Now that person has left you. But the love is still there because the love always existed in *you*, even if was the other person who catalyzed your experience of love.

The brain plays all kinds of tricks on us. It will tell you that the love is gone. But it isn't; the love is with you as it's always been. You are simply struggling to locate it. In that person's presence you planted, nourished, and nurtured this seed of love within you that has grown and grown over time. The person may be gone, but the love within you is still there.

Sit quietly with your hands on your heart, feeling the presence of the love, but allow your mind to become quiet. Resist the temptation to get swept away in the drama of commentary in the mind ("He left you." "She left you." "You're all alone."), and just become aware of the love.

Also realize that it is not your fault. There's nothing you could have or should have done differently. That person's karmic package was such that they were blessed with your presence for a certain period of time. Sadly, we don't have control over other people's karmic packages. Making our loved ones do what we want isn't a power that we have been given.

So, instead realize that the love is still with you, and allow yourself to continue to feel the presence of love. Your identification with the source of this love needs to change, though. *You* are the source of this love, not someone else.

Desires and Attachment to the Fruit of Our Actions

We are told not to feed our desires, so what do we do?

Desires are not the problem; desires are simply an energy that propels action. The desire to experience deeper spirituality is what draws people to Ganga aarti and satsang each evening at Parmarth Niketan instead of spending the evening at a bar or pizzeria. Desires are what propel us out of bed every morning!

Most people get up every day because of a desire to keep their jobs, or to keep their house clean, or to make sure their children get to school. Or even simply to go to the bathroom and have a shower or a cup of coffee! Those on the spiritual path get up to meditate or do yoga, to ground themselves in spiritual connection before starting the day. We get out of bed for many reasons, but they are all desires. If we desired absolutely nothing, we might never get up.

So it isn't the desires that are the problem. The problem is the *expectation* that we will get what we desire and the nearly inevitable suffering when we don't. The wanting isn't the problem. But when we don't get what we want, when we want it, we become angry and frustrated. For example, if we want a new pair of pants for our birthday, that is not a problem. But if we don't get them, we complain to our loved ones, "But I told you I wanted a new pair of pants!"

When desires don't get fulfilled, we lose our connection to joy and peace and the truth of our own being. That's a recipe for disaster. In order to live in a state of true joy, the source of that joy must be within us. If we depend on anything outside for our internal state of being, we set ourselves up for misery. Outer conditions keep fluctuating. It's warm one day, cold the next. The stock market is up one day, down the next. People are nice to us one day, mean to us the next. We like the way we look in the mirror one day, not the next day.

Our attachment to the fulfillment of our desires is what leads to our emotional and spiritual downfall and that is why we are constantly exhorted to let go of desires. But it's just the attachment and expectation of the fulfillment of those desires that's the problem, and it's a problem because we have no control over it. The fulfillment of our desires is in others' hands or the hands of Mother Nature or the hands of God or our own karmic package.

This is why Lord Krishna is so emphatic in the Bhagavad Gita about the importance of relinquishing attachment to the fruits of our actions. Imagine that you want to become the CEO of a company and you wake up early every day, go to the office, and work hard, honestly, and sincerely, but you never get the promotions you need so you feel dejected, angry, and bitter. The desire to become CEO is in your mind, but the fulfillment of it is in the hands of your bosses. When they don't do what you want, you suffer. It is to free us from suffering that we are exhorted to let go of attachment to the fruits of our actions, to become desireless, to have equanimity in all situations.

Equanimity doesn't mean you lose energy for life and become dull and listless. You do not have to renounce creativity, initiative, or compassion. It means simply that you are able to maintain an internal balance, internal connection to joy and peace regardless of the constantly changing situations around you. It means that your inner emotional state is not hooked into someone else's actions. That hook is what we must relinquish. Have desires, no problem. But when they are not fulfilled, are you still able to access joy and peace within yourself? That is the key.

Where do desires come from?

Desires stem from the idea that we are lacking in some way. A desire for food may indicate a physical lack of nourishment. A desire for spiritual growth may indicate an awareness of the lack of wisdom and realization in our mind. These are both desires that are very worthy of aiming to fulfill.

But many of our desires are rooted in ignorance. The desire to be more beautiful, more popular, more successful—these stem from an illusory belief that somehow exactly as you are in the moment is less than perfect. The truth of our essence, our real self, is whole, complete, and perfect. Pujya Swamiji always laughs at the advertisements for self-development programs; these advertisements insinuate that God somehow left us half-baked and we need to finish up His work. We are here as perfect creations of a perfect Creator. There is nothing we lack, and desires, therefore, to be more and have more are rooted in ignorance and lead to suffering.

You would never look at a rose and say, "This is not a full rose. It needs further development." Maybe it hasn't fully blossomed yet; the petals might still be closed, but the moment the sun shines upon it and its season arrives, the bud will open fully. It doesn't need a course or certificate or degree to become a full rose. And the rose never desires to be a jasmine. Nothing in nature desires to be different that it is, as there is an inherent wisdom through which everything just plays its perfect role perfectly.

Our problem, and the cause of our insatiable desires, is our identification with our physical body, which is finite, and transitory, rather than identifying as the perfect, infinite, eternal consciousness, which is who we really are.

Such identification leads us to always crave more, regardless of how much we have.

This yearning stems from ignorance of the full, true self. Our essence, our spirit, our consciousness, our soul is complete and perfect, because we are created not just *by* the Divine, but *of* the Divine. All of God's perfection, completeness, and wholeness is manifest in all aspects of the Divine. There is nothing lacking in us.

In mathematics, we learn that infinity divided by any number is still infinity. Infinity divided by ten billion is still infinity. So if we have been created out of the infinite, we are infinite. This is what the famous mantra in the Upanishads teaches us:

ॐ पूरणमदः पूरणमदिम् पूरणात् पूरणमुदच्यते
पूरणस्य पूरणमादाय पूरणमेवावशष्यिते
ॐ शान्तिः शान्तिः शान्तिः

oṃ pūrṇam adaḥ pūrṇam idam pūrṇāt pūrṇam udacyate
pūrṇasya pūrṇam ādāya pūrṇam evāvaśiṣyate
oṃ śāntiḥ śāntiḥ śāntiḥ

This is complete and whole. That is complete and whole.
Everything is complete and whole.
When wholeness is removed from wholeness, wholeness
   remains.
When wholeness is added to wholeness, wholeness remains.
Wholeness is, in fact, all there is.
I am complete. I am whole. I am perfect.
I was always complete.

In our role in the divine drama, we have been given a body. The soul incarnates on earth in a body, with a karmic package and set of karmic circumstances. The body experiences cold, heat, hunger, fatigue, sexual desire, and so much more. We also have a brain that in conjunction with the body's signals and experiences creates cravings and neuroses.

For example, maybe the body sends a signal to the brain saying, "I am hungry." This is a very simple need. Maybe our blood sugar is dropping or maybe the stomach is literally empty and growling and sends a signal to the brain: Feed me! As this signal percolates through the pathways in our brain, the emotional mind kicks in with its commentary: "You're already overweight. You've got to fit into that dress tomorrow. You ate too much for lunch and don't deserve to eat now. Starve yourself!" Or perhaps we begin dreaming of high-carbohydrate, high-fat foods: "I'll have chocolate cake for dessert." We get lost in a food fantasy. One simple physical reaction—the stomach sending a signal to the brain, letting it know that it's empty or that the bloodstream needs glucose—has completely turned us into neurotic, fantasizing, way-out-of-the-present-moment beings. That's what our mind does.

Or imagine you're meditating and suddenly the smell of coffee wafts through the window from the coffee shop below your apartment. Instead of simply noticing it and drawing your awareness back to the breath or your mantra, you get caught in a romantic reverie about the time you enjoyed coffee in Paris in a small café on the banks of the Seine with a superbly handsome new love. One simple olfactory stimulus and the mind takes off across the world without a passport or visa! Now you're yearing for that lost love rather than watching your breath!

Our society also gives the mind a lot of fuel for distraction: "You need to look like this, you need to own that, you need to wear this." If you want to be as satisfied as the people in *that* commercial, you'd better have your dinner *here* tonight. Even if you feel satisfied with life, all you need to do is open up a magazine or turn on the TV or scroll social media to suddenly have doubts and complexes about your appearance, your possessions, your entire life, and even about your very self.

All these things are fodder for mind games. Out of these games stems desire, and that is what can lead to misery. For example, perhaps you are in an airplane reading a magazine in which you see an advertisement of a beautiful woman walking her child to school in their bucolic suburb full of tree-lined streets. Her handsome husband is standing on the porch of the house, waving to them with a briefcase in his hand, as though he's on his way to work. If you are single and wishing to get married, or if you are married and wishing you could have children, or if you are married with children but wish your life were happier, when you see this advertisement it triggers a feeling of yearning for that perfect moment the model seems to have found. If the advertisement is for the shoes the woman is wearing, you suddenly want to buy those shoes. If it's an advertisement for the handbag on her shoulder, suddenly you want that handbag. You may not consciously realize the link between your own dissatisfaction and this ad, but suddenly you are filled with desire for new shoes or a new purse.

Then the drama unfolds in your mind. The desire for new shoes is not satisfied with the shoes once you buy them, because the true desire was never actually about the shoes. It was about happiness. What feeds and fuels the desire is our belief that tells us we are not enough, what we have is not enough, what we look like is not good enough, our lives are not enough. So these desires are rarely about the object of desire per se and more of a way to finally feel complete.

We live in a constant state of yearning. Something is constantly fueling our desires. Yet, the real desire—the desire behind these desires—is simple: to feel whole and complete, to feel we are enough, to experience the expansiveness and fullness of the true self.

This is how ignorance fuels desire: ignorance that we are this body and mind, ignorance that we are *anything* other than whole, complete, and perfect.

When we fulfill our desires, whether it's a chocolate ice cream cone, a new job, a pay raise, or a new mobile phone, we might temporarily feel better. Ignorantly, we then associate feeling better with what we've just achieved—ice cream, a new phone, or more money.

However, this is a very subtle but critical mistake. Obtaining the object of our desire is *not* what makes us feel good. What makes us feel so good when we get what we want is the fact that, temporarily, we are no longer desiring it. It is the temporary absence of desire that makes us feel great, not the actual *object* of desire we've attained. It is the *absence* of a desire that makes us feel better, not the *object* of that desire. But we conclude incorrectly, "Well, that made me feel so good last time, I should do it again," and this leads us to repeat the cycle over and over again.

How do we avoid being controlled by our desires?

Through spiritual practices such as meditation, prayer, and selfless service you can purify your mind, thoughts, and intellect and connect with the fullness and the wholeness of your true divine being. When you are already full, you will be free from chasing desires and can realize the beautiful state of desirelessness.

Imagine that you are at someone's house and you are very hungry. The host passes around a platter of fresh ladoos (a wonderful Indian sweet). Your mouth waters. You will eat ladoo after ladoo until your stomach is full and sick! However, now imagine the same situation with one difference: You are not actually hungry because you've just come from having a deeply satisfying meal. You are absolutely, happily full. Now when the plate of ladoos gets passed around, you are not even tempted because you're already full.

We become a slave to our desires when we feel something lacking in ourselves. We try to fill that emptiness just as we fill our empty stomach, so we are tempted by ladoos. But when we live in an experience of the fullness of the self, we are no more tempted by material objects or pleasures than we're be tempted by a ladoo when we're completely satiated.

Ultimately, our core purpose is to realize the truth of the self, which is boundless, perfect, complete, and whole. We fill ourselves and our lives with material possessions, pleasures, even titles and achievements, in a misguided attempt to experience fullness and wholeness, which is actually the nature of our own being. When we experience that fullness genuinely, deeply within ourselves rather than through external objects or achievements, the sense of fulfillment stays with us because it comes from within.

What about our desires for sex, alcohol, drugs, and other coping mechanisms?

We're not born with a desire for drugs and alcohol. We're born with a desire for joy, peace, and deep connection in our life, and when we don't have these, that's when we turn to alcohol, drugs, compulsive shopping, overeating, indiscriminate sex, or other coping mechanisms. There's no innate desire for any of these substances or experiences. They're simply an urge to numb our awareness of the present moment. We turn to drugs and alcohol to push away our experience of the present moment, to push away what we're feeling or going through.

Addiction is actually a spiritual quest gone awry. The instinct that says, "How I am feeling right now is *not* my highest possibility," is actually true. The instinct that propels us to change the suffering we are experiencing is a healthy, spiritual instinct. The problem arises only with the means we use to change our experience. Drugs and alcohol certainly alter our perception, our thoughts and feelings. But first of all, it's only temporary. You get high and then you come down. Second, the drugs and alcohol have not actually helped you work with the suffering or the thoughts and actions that lead to your suffering. So when you come down you're just going to be in exactly the same place you were before, but now you also have a hangover!

So if you have a burning desire for drugs, alcohol, umpteen chocolate cakes, or to shop till you drop, don't ignore those desires. They are giving you an important message. Ask yourself what it is you're looking to numb, what sorrow you are looking to drown, what emptiness you are trying to fill. Urges for drugs, alcohol, gambling, overeating, pornography, mindless shopping are all wonderful indicators that there is something you need to look at and actually change in your life. If you can change an external situation that is causing you to suffer, wonderful. If not, work to change how you think about that situation, how you interact with that situation.

Otherwise you spend your whole life just drinking, smoking, eating, or shopping your way out of moments. And that's not what you were put here on earth for.

Why do we have regrets?

We have regrets because we are never satisfied. We don't regret choices that worked out well for us. We only regret the ones that didn't. For example, we regret that we didn't work hard on a project, and therefore didn't get the promotion. We regret that we didn't put in extra time or energy on a plan or idea that could have become successful. We regret that we didn't spend time with our loved ones, only after they move away or die.

We don't regret choices that led to success, even if perhaps our actions were not full of integrity. For example, if we didn't put in time on a project but our colleague did, and we claimed her work as our own and subsequently got a promotion, we won't regret that unless our conscience catches up with us or the boss finds out.

Regret comes because we think, retrospectively, that different decisions would have brought us greater happiness. Regret is to blame our present dissatisfaction on our past action. However, the kind of regret that would serve us very well doesn't seem to impact us at all. Very few stop to wonder, "At whose cost have I become so successful? Who have I pushed out of the way to get ahead? Who have I hurt?"

We tend to justify those decisions that benefited us and regret those that didn't. What we should really regret is, "Oh God, I haven't been able to culti-vate as much compassion as I would have liked. I haven't been able to culti-vate enough spirituality. I haven't served as enough of a tool in God's hands. I haven't loved enough, served enough, given enough, meditated enough." Those are the regrets we should have. The more satisfied we can be with what we have materially and dissatisfied with our cultivation of compassion, selflessness, generosity, love, and patience, the better off we'll be, as that regret will prompt us to open our hearts and expand our consciousness.

How can we remember in our day-to-day life not to get attached to the fruit of our actions?

In the Bhagavad Gita, Lord Krishna tells us that we must do our duty, sincerely, fully, to the very best of our ability, but we must not be attached to the fruits of our actions. This is a deep and difficult spiritual injunction. In my life, it's been a constant lesson to be able to remember this at all times. It's not easy at all, but simply the intention to remember it, the intention to serve for the sake of service and dharma rather than for the outcome, is a fantastic spiritual practice. Even before we master it, we benefit greatly, as the mere intention leads to much deeper satisfaction in every aspect of life. No longer are we dependent upon an outcome, but rather on our own sincerity in performing the task, and fortunately our own sincerity is in our hands while the outcome is not.

I'll tell you a personal story from the time I was still in the United States. When I lived in Palo Alto, we had a backyard where I grew a few potted herbs—basil, mint, and a few others. When we moved to San Francisco, we had a windowsill garden instead. There were holes outside the kitchen window where pots could be placed and one could grow flowers or, as I did, cooking herbs. I planted seeds for basil, mint, and other herbs, but they wouldn't grow. I kept getting new and better seeds and replanting them, but nothing would grow. I started to feel really badly about myself. I started thinking, what kind of a useless person am I? I can't even grow basil. I'm hopeless!

One day I came home early from my PhD classes, looked out of the kitchen window, and saw that the cat we had adopted was playing in the pots, tossing the dirt and the seeds all over the place. No wonder nothing would grow! The cat had tossed the seeds on the pavement below. I did everything I could—got the best organic seeds, planted them at the right temperature, made sure the plants got the right amount of sun and shade, watered them properly, but I could not control our cat from jumping into the pots while I was away at school.

It's not easy to detach from those expectations. When you put time, energy and effort into something, it's very difficult not to be attached to the outcome. But the practice of nonattachment is very much like meditation. It is a practice! In meditation, when the mind starts to wander, you bring it back, it wanders again, and you bring it back again. Similarly with attachment. Whenever we get distracted into attachment, we remember and re-anchor in that over which we have control: our own actions, our own responses, our own intentions. Then we get distracted again. And then we re-remember again. It is a process and a practice.

When our minds are focused on the results of our actions rather than on the action itself, we get disconnected from the flow of the universe. We lose the opportunity to hear our inner voice, to receive signals telling us how to perform the action in better alignment. The universe could be shouting: "No, do it this way, not that way," but if our attention is stuck on the results, we won't hear that voice. When we're attached to the outcome, we lose the spiritual benefit of being present, mindful, and aware in the moment, and we also miss the very practical benefit of being in tune with the wisdom of the universe that guides us in our actions. There is an intelligence in the universe, but we have to be open to hear it.

Being fully mindful, conscious, and present while engaged in any action without latching onto the future result is a constant practice, but it transforms our life. Every moment becomes meditation, because as soon as we find that our mind has drifted elsewhere, we simply bring it back.

PART 4

Spiritual Practices

So, what to do, then? How to actually attain these states of understanding, wisdom, grounding, connection, and expansion? Just as reading a menu doesn't fill your belly, and hearing someone talk about water doesn't quench your thirst, reading about truth doesn't give you the experience of that truth. It has to become you. It has to be an internal experience. That's the difference between spiritual teachings and academic teachings. It's the difference between a great teacher and a spiritual guru.

A great teacher can teach you all about a certain subject, and in most cases that is enough. An oceanography teacher, for example, can teach you all about life under the sea—what lives there, what the activity is, how deep the ocean is, how wide it is, how many dead zones we have due to microplastics in the oceans, and so forth. And that's great. It's all you need. You don't actually have to become wet to understand. But spiritual wisdom must be actually experienced in order to benefit us. We can say "Aham Brahmasmi" all day long, but if we don't have a lived experience of truly being one with the supreme reality, that intellectual recitation is going to be of limited benefit. We must actually have the experience to have the true knowledge. In Hindi, the word is *anubhava*, which means *direct perception*, the knowledge one gains from experience. That is what we're looking for.

For that, you must practice. This section is dedicated to that. We talk about meditation and renunciation. Is it necessary? What do we really renounce when we take vows of renunciation? I hope through this section you will be inspired and guided to take direct action on your spiritual path.

Meditation

What is the true self, and how do we realize it in our lives?

The sages and rishis have said that their descriptions go around the truth; what they offer are words that give us an idea, an aspect, a reflection. They offer the metaphoric finger pointing to the moon—but you have to see the moon yourself. The scriptures emphasize that to really know the self, you have to look within and meditate. The rishis and sages can only give us practices to have the experience of our self. They cannot give us the experience. This is why the scriptures, sages, and saints have always pointed us inward. If you want to learn math or science or history, experts can teach you. But you cannot obtain knowledge of the self through someone else's words any more than reading a menu can satiate your appetite or someone's description of water can quench your thirst.

So we are given descriptions around the true self. For example, in the Bhagavad Gita, Krishna explains that it cannot be cut by knives, nor dried by the wind; it cannot be burned by fire, nor wet by water. It is eternal. It was never born and it never dies. It is infinite, complete, and perfect. It is inseparable from the supreme reality. These are certain attributes of it, but none of them is a precise definition that enables us to truly experience the self. For that, we need to go within and actually discover it.

One of the ways to know who we really are is by realizing what we are not. The meditation practice called *neti, neti,* which means, "not this, not this," helps us achieve this. As we remove layers of identification—"I'm not the clothes on my body, I'm not my skin, I'm not my blood, I'm not my muscles or organs"—slowly we reach a place, a state, where there is nothing left about which to say "I am not." And in that spaciousness, which the Hindus refer to as everythingness, or *purnyata,* and the Buddhists refer to as nothingness, or *shunyata,* the experience of the self emerges.

We can realize the self more easily through realizing what the self *is not.* For example, if you ask me, "What does a naked body look like?" I could use words to describe it to you. I could talk about a tone of flesh, hair, orifices, but all of that is talking around it and I'm not going to be able to give you a clear idea of what nakedness really is. The best answer I could give you is to tell you to take off your clothes, layer by layer, and look in a mirror. This is what the practice of meditation does. It helps us identify and remove that which is not self, layer by layer, until we can see the true self. It is the experience through which we can actually know the true self ourselves, and not merely conclude based on what we hear someone else say about it.

What is meditation?

Meditation is a practice to know who we are. It becomes a way of life not merely what we do seated on a cushion for a few minutes or hours each day. Meditation is experiencing, knowing, and living as our true self. It is not a complex, esoteric skill that only experts can perform, such as feats of gymnastics. Meditation is what gets us back in touch with who we really are, without judgment or analysis or drama. Meditation creates stillness and expansive spaciousness in the mind so that we're able to genuinely live and experience the spaciousness and expansiveness of our own being.

Our suffering is not due to the world outside, it's due to the world inside our minds. Our thoughts run rampant and repeat stories about who we are and our place in the universe. Stories that we're too much of this, not enough of that, we should be like this and not like that. Stories about what's happened to us and what it means about who we are. These stories form the foundation of our false self, our ego, which judges and comments all day long. The voice may have come from outside, from something someone else said or did, but we internalize it and then hear it all day long on constant repeat mode.

If you consider yourself intelligent and thoughtful, there's nothing quite as humbling as listening to your thoughts. If you've never done that, you might assume that you think very deeply and are very contemplative and rational. But most of us really aren't most of the time. The mind simply does its thing, running on indiscriminate autopilot most of the time. When we start to listen to our thoughts, we notice that the vast majority of them are utterly useless and make little sense. And they certainly are not helpful.

In the midst of the random cacaphony, there's the internal judge who bellows loudly about what is wrong with us and how we should be.

Then there are thoughts about others, how they should be, what they're doing wrong, All this judgment, yearning, longing, wishing, and aversion clogs our minds. It's not *who* we are; it's just what our thinking mind *does* habitually.

Meditation gives us the experience of what it could be like if this weren't going on all the time. It's not a very complex skill, but the lack of complexity doesn't mean it's easy. Simple, yes. But easy, no. This is because of the games the mind plays. The moment we start meditating and try to quiet the mind, mental patterns and habits rebel and suddenly we are convinced we left the coffeepot on and we must jump up to turn it off. Or we panic about an email we haven't responded to and we jump up to quickly reply. Or the mind convinces us that we are not pure enough, spiritual enough, worthy enough for deep meditative experiences and that this whole thing is a waste of time and energy. Or we use the quiet moments to make shopping lists in our head, or lists of our grudges and how we've been wronged by the world. The moment you sit to meditate you will see a hundred seemingly urgent thoughts cascade through your mind. Do not listen to them. Recognize them as the nature of the mind and simply bring the awareness back to your true self.

A deeply powerful way to re-center ourselves, even in the midst of our daily busy lives, is to bring the breath and awareness to the area right below the navel, about two inches below the belly button. It's a very special energy center, a chakra. It's considered by many to be the core, the source of the self, and the place from which many saints and sages (even from different religious traditions) meditate. The energy center is called the swadisthan chakra. *Swa* means self and *sthan* means place, so it is quite literally the place of the self.

Resting there, connecting in this energy center, grounds us energetically in who we are. It is the place upon which we should anchor our breath and awareness in meditation, but also it's the place we can return to, over and over throughout the day, as we find ourselves getting ungrounded or unanchored.

Meditation invites us into a place of pure awareness—awareness without judgment or analysis, simple witnessing of what is there when we remove the non-self. Through meditation we are able to peel back layer after layer of not self.

Just train your awareness on your breath, and keep bringing your awareness back when it wanders. You can add a simple mantra if you find that your mind wanders too much. There is a beautiful mantra, "*so hum*," which means "I am that." I am one with all. I am inseparable from the supreme reality. There is no place I end and the universe begins. I *am* it all. You can chant "*so*" quietly to yourself on your inhalation and "*hum*" silently to yourself on the exhalation.

You can even add open-eyed meditation if you find that closing your eyes causes the mind to wander too much. Watch a candle flame, gaze upon an image of the Divine that evokes feelings of divinity in you. While you do that, just keep bringing your awareness back to the breath in the body and especially to the breath in the swadisthan chakra. As you breathe, you'll notice there are places that are tighter and places that are freer. Don't analyze. Don't start telling stories of how your body became tight or injured. Meditation is not psychotherapy. You're simply noticing. If something arises in your awareness, just bring it back to the breath.

The breath grounds us in the body, and connects us to a divine consciousness that's both outside of us and inside of us—that entire spirit or soul or divine universe. When we breathe, we are taking in not only oxygen but we are also taking in prana, or the sacred life force. It is the deep, energetic vitality of our physical being, and it also is that which connects us with all of creation.

Why must the mind be controlled?

If the mind is not controlled, life cannot successfully be co-created. Our destiny is the product of our actions, our karma. But what determines our actions? Our thoughts. Our reactions to the world around us. If our mind is jumping all over the place like the metaphoric monkey and is in a constant state of reactivity, we will likely act in anger, lust, hurt, greed, attachment, desire, aversion, fear, and in all the patterns of our subconscious. Those actions determine the quality of our life in each moment—are we calm, peaceful, loving, anchored, grounded, and compassionate?—and they determine our destiny. All outcomes begin with one thought. If we have no way to control our thoughts how can we possibly participate in creating our outcomes? We cannot. This is why learning to control the mind is so important if you want to consciously, deliberately, intentionally craft the quality of your life.

However, realize that the goal is not to control or subdue the mind with a whip. The mind simply needs to be trained to work *for* us rather than against us. The mind is a beautiful tool, organ, and muscle. It simply needs to be understood and exercised. Try to avoid thinking about annihilating or conquering the mind, because that creates an inevitable struggle. It's all happening within yourself, and you don't want one part of yourself trying to suppress or annihilate another part. All parts need the same thing: compassion and love.

The goal is to train the mind to be a tool in our hands rather than master of the show. For example, we may say that we don't want our mind to be impacted by the outside world. Yet, taking cues from the world around us is what helps keep us alive. Imagine that you step off the sidewalk to cross the street when suddenly a car speeds by. If you've quieted your mind so completely that it's not impacted by any external stimuli, you'll just walk right into the path of the speeding car. This is not desireable!

What we're looking to do is train rather than subdue. Let the mind pick up cues from the external world, whether through smell, sight, sound, touch, or taste. The world has glorious experiences to offer us—the fragrance of flowers, the sound of music, the exquisite glory of a sunrise or a star-filled night sky, a newborn baby's face, the taste of cool water on a hot day, or hot tea on a cold day. Our senses are what enable us to interact with and experience the beauty of creation. The challenge is to stay anchored as the one who is aware rather than becoming a slave to those stimuli.

Normally we simply react to stimuli. Our lives become a series of stimuli and responses, akin to Pavlov's dogs. But that is not the highest calling of our lives or the highest use of our minds. That's why the mind must be trained. Imagine that you're walking down a street. You'll see restaurants, cafes, other people, an ATM machine, maybe a music store. The streets are filled with a barrage of visual and auditory stimuli. No one can actually absorb all of it. We're seeing the world through a filter of our personal mind and attention. Imagine you're walking down that street starving.

You've just gotten off work, haven't had anything to eat since breakfast, and it's seven o'clock in the evening. What are you going to notice? The music store? No, of course not. You're going to notice the restaurants. Pizza, or Chinese food, or maybe a sandwich vendor. If you aren't hungry, but are driven by sensual desires, you'll notice attractive people on the street or even a sexy mannequin in a store window.

What we see is actually determined by the mind, not by the eyes or by our environment. If a hundred people walk down the same street, they will experience it in a hundred different ways. It's not that they invent their experiences. They are all equally justified in their perceptions. One person will notice the pizza place, another who may have just gotten a cast off her broken leg will keep her eyes on the ground to make sure she doesn't fall.

Training the mind is about developing control over what gets absorbed. That's what meditation does. It is a practice, a tool, to help us master the mind. When we focus on the breath, what does that do? It takes our awareness from a thousand places and brings it to one. Before we get to meditation, we have to establish ourselves in concentration, full focus upon one object. It doesn't have to be the breath. It could be a mantra. It could be a candle flame. It could be spacious awareness. There are entire schools of meditation based purely on the practice of awareness. We teach that if you sense an itch, bring the mind back to the breath. But there are schools of meditation that say if you itch, allow the awareness to be with the itch and name the sensation itching, itching, itching. They're all just different ways, different mechanisms, to take the mind from jumping aimlessly between a thousand places and make it sit in one place. The various techniques help us get a little bit more familiar with the mind, befriend it, and train it. "Ah, you were in a thousand places, now you're in one." Whether it's your breath, whether it's your mantra, whether it's your itching foot, you're in one place now.

From that one place we're able to take our awareness deeper and eventually come to an experience that who we are isn't the mind. We begin to identify with the one who is aware rather than with the object of awareness. So instead of thinking "I am angry," we realize "Ah, patterns of electrical and chemical behavior seem to be happening in the brain that look like anger." We are simply noticing. We are not the anger. We are the awareness of anger. Similarly, when the anger dissipates and we come back to a place of loving-kindness, compassion, understanding, we realize it is not that "I am now joyful" but simply that "Ah, that pattern has ceased and new patterns of chemical and electrical behavior have started, which look like joy, peace, and compassion." Still, *I* am not the joy. I am the awareness.

In the spaciousness created by removing identification with that which is not-self, the experience of self emerges.

Ultimately, meditation brings us into that experience of pure consciousness. But first, we have to bring the mind to one place. It's hard for everybody in the beginning. Do not worry. The very nature of the mind is to jump all over the place. Consciously draw your awareness and attention to it, guide it to the magnet of your breath, away from the constantly changing thought patterns in the brain, and slowly the space between those thoughts grows. Then when you move through the world, and things happen around you, you no longer automatically react, because you've cultivated a habit of nonjudging, nonanalyzing, nonreacting awareness.

In meditation, we learn to witness without reacting. Maybe my ankle itches. I am aware of it but I do not scratch. I cultivate the ability and habit to simply be, without reacting. My mind may be aware of the itching foot, but meditation helps cultivate an entirely new habit that stays with us, not just in meditation but also in the world. The person in front of me can, metaphorically, become my itching foot. She may be doing something that's provoking or angering me, making me itch to slap her with my words or my hand. But I know I have a choice, because I've cultivated the habit of stillness in meditation. It will take a little time, though, just like learning any new skill.

How does meditation connect us with God?

Another aspect of meditation is that as your mind becomes still, as it withdraws from the habit of reaction into the infinite nature of self and connection with the universe, you become aware of the divinity of others as well as in yourself. If there is not enough humility, surrender, and sincere practice, people may have an experience of divine connection but not gain the full meaning. That experience then further separates them from others. For example, sometimes you hear people say, "I'm living in God consciousness, therefore you should do the household chores and take care of the children, because otherwise it would disrupt my God consciousness."

Or, "I'm living in God consciousness, so you should touch my feet, take care of me, and do the cleaning up every day." That is absurdity. If you really are living in God consciousness, you will realize that everyone and everything is God. That consciousness has to begin with the self, of course, because only then can we recognize it in others.

Sadly, the human mind and ego are so subtly manipulative that if we give them an open field on which to play, that's exactly what they'll do. They'll take a spiritual experience and run with it, but instead of running into surrender, truth, and expansion, they'll run straight into arrogance, ignorance, and separation. This is why we have meditation and other techniques of sadhana or spiritual practice. This is why we go to satsang, pray, sit at the feet of the gurus, do seva (selfless service), and engage in other spiritual practice. These practices help us stay grounded in truth, so that our mind doesn't become an open field for the play of ego, mind, illusion, and ignorance.

Why do people experience the soul differently in meditation?

Meditation connects us with our true self, with soul, or *atma*. The soul is one with all; there aren't actually plural souls, but rather one soul, of which we are all varying manifestations, like different waves in one infinite ocean. However, despite the oneness of the self, the way in which we each experience that self is different. Because we're in different bodies, with different histories, sanskaras, or patterns, and with different functional patterns in our brains, we're going to experience that self differently. Certain meditation techniques will work for me; different ones will work for you.

What runs a microphone? Electricity. What runs a lamp? Electricity. What runs a fan? Electricity. The same thing is running them all. The electricity flowing into the microphone is the same as the electricity powering the light or the fan. However, because the vehicles are different, the manifestation of that electricity is going to be different. Fans give air, lamps give light, microphones give sound. Similarly, when we meditate we're meditating on the self, the soul, but I'm going into it with my specific, personal medium of consciousness, which is my brain, and you're going into it through your medium of consciousness, your brain.

Ironically, that brain, or mind, which can be the greatest obstacle to experience our true self, is the very brain or mind that is *needed* in meditation to experience that truth. The answer to knowledge of the self is not to get rid of the brain or mind, although they certainly can be obstacles to our deepest spiritual experiences. We need the brain. The physical brain is the medium through which we experience consciousness. It is *not* our consciousness, but it is the *way* we experience consciousness, just as our eyes are not sight but they are the medium through which we experience sight. If you didn't have eyes, the world would still have sights to see, but you would not be able to experience them. Similarly, if you had brain damage and no brain activity at all, the self or soul would still exist, but your ability to consciously experience it would diminish.

How can we analyze our thoughts and emotions, and at the same time be in the present moment? I find myself sometimes observing my thoughts, words, and instincts, which leads me to understand myself better, but it removes me from just *being* in the present.

We balance this by doing both at different times. For example, when you take a shower, it wakes you up entirely. How can you stay asleep and bathe at the same time? You can't. It's very important to sleep, and it's also very important to bathe, but you can't do them at the same time. In the same way, both understanding and witnessing are very important aspects to our spiritual practice, but most often they don't happen together.

One aspect is the nonjudgmental, nonanalytical, noncontemplative, nonintrospective act of simple witnessing. Just be present in the moment without judgment. Meditate and watch your breath, and when thoughts arise in your mind, don't allow your awareness to latch on to them. Don't analyze them or judge them. A physical sensation, such as your stomach growling, may temporarily distract you, but the witnessing mind simply notices and brings the awareness back to the breath. The thinking mind, in contrast to pure awareness, would get hooked into the sensation, leading to thoughts such as, "I'm so hungry, I haven't eaten since last night. I wonder what's for breakfast . . ." The analytical mind would come in and say, "I read this article that says it's not good for the adrenal glands to go hungry for so long, so maybe I should change my meditation time . . ." Or the even deeper analytical mind says, "Why am I thinking about food?"

Each of those is a very valid issue to ponder. We have a body, and if something in our schedule is not working in concert with our physical health and stability, that's an important point to address. But not during meditation. It's also important, if the same thoughts keep coming back into our meditation, to investigate why that is happening. Why are certain thoughts or certain types of thoughts besieging me? That's important to analyze and contemplate upon. But not while we're meditating. In meditation we simply witness.

Human beings are the only species that has the ability to be aware of their own consciousness. We're the only beings that actually have the ability to watch ourselves consciously. If I start to get angry, but my meditation practice is strong, then I can witness the anger approach. I see it but it doesn't drown me, because I am rooted in pure consciousness, watching the wave of anger draw closer and closer but not actually getting pummeled or drowned by it. If, on the other hand, I haven't cultivated the ability to witness, then as soon as anger hits, I find myself screaming, shouting, hitting, throwing things, drinking, using drugs, stuffing myself with chocolate cake, bottling up the emotion, or developing ulcers. I *become* the anger. This is why we say, "I am angry." We identify so completely with the anger that we feel we have become anger . The witness enables us to simply see it, recognize it, but not identify with it, and therefore not drown in it. It is much like a wave crashing on the beach down below while we sit on a cliff high above the waters. We are aware, but we are still dry and calm while the waves are turbulent.

The act of witnessing gives us, first in our meditation and then in our life, a different place to sit. Most of us sit right in the center of the drama of our lives: "I'm happy, I'm sad, I'm hungry, I'm sleepy, I'm excited, I'm nervous." If I ask you, "How are you right now?" most of you will say something like, "I'm excited about the party," or, "I'm nervous about my exam tomorrow." Whatever the answer may be, it's going to come right from the place of drama. It will be an answer given by the role you play in the cosmic drama or *lila*. Witnessing teaches us to sit in the consciousness of the one who only witnesses instead of smack in the middle of the drama.

Any analytic activity of the thinking mind takes us out of spacious awareness. In spacious awareness, we are *just there*. We're not judging, analyzing, or following our thoughts. We're just aware of them, in the way we watch the waves go up and down at the seashore. There is neither anger nor sadness nor anxiety nor yesterday or tomorrow. There is simply is-ness. Existence.

However, analysis and understanding are also very important; they give us insight into our psyches, patterns, and neuroses. They help us see and work through all the places we are stuck—the negative and dysfunctional patterns of our lives. They require a different time and place, though. If you notice that the same thoughts keep arising all the time during meditation, such as thoughts of food, it is helpful to analyze that. There are two possible reasons for this experience. One, of course, is that you have gone too long without food and your stomach is growling. However, if you find yourself always hungry in meditation, even when you've recently eaten, then that is something worth thinking about. What's the inner emptiness? What are you hungry for? What are you longing for? Why are you wanting to run into the next meal instead of sitting in meditation? What is coming up for you in meditation that you would like to numb with food?

If certain thoughts, fears, desires, or experiences keep coming up in our meditation, they are worth examining because that's the stuff that's preventing us from fully connecting with the Divine within ourselves. So make sure to create time for contemplation, analysis, and insight, but that time should be different from your meditation time.

Lastly, recognize that analysis and understanding take place in the thinking mind, and being present takes place in the intuitive heart, in consciousness itself. The thinking, intellectual mind separates; it thinks *about* things. In meditation, the ultimate goal is union with the Divine, the universe, the Creator, and creation, so if you relegate your meditation to your thinking mind, you lose the opportunity to connect with your heart, to sit in conscious awareness, and to dissolve the boundary between individual self and divine self. We must devote exclusive time for both.

Renunciation

Why did you renounce worldly life?

This question arises frequently and tends to be rooted in the idea that the material world has so much to offer that people cannot understand how I have forsaken it, renounced it, and sacrificed all the good things in life. How could I do such a thing, and why? That tends to be the underlying foundation of these questions.

For me, renunciation was not a decision of my analytical mind. I didn't wake up one day and say, "I know what I'm going to do today! I'm going to renounce all these things and people in my life and go on a spiritual quest." I didn't make a list of pros and cons and weigh the benefits of renunciation. For me, it just happened. I had come to India on what I thought was a short vacation adventure while pursuing my PhD. I had no intention of staying. I wasn't consciously looking for a guru; I wasn't even consciously on a spiritual path. But standing on the banks of the Ganga, something so deep and powerful happened to me on every level of my existence and awareness that I knew I was supposed to stay.

Here's an analogy I use to describe it. Imagine that your feet are a size eight, but you've spent your whole life wearing size six shoes. Everybody gives you size six shoes. In the beginning you say, "But my feet hurt!" and they say, "Yes, yes, don't worry, that's just what shoes feel like." Slowly you get used to it. You are not living in pain; you believe that this is what shoes feel like and you do your best to adjust and get used to it. Then one day someone slips your foot into a size eight shoe and you realize with great joy, "Ah, this is what shoes should feel like!" Then, ironically, people ask you, "Don't you ever want to go back? Don't you miss wearing size six shoes? Are you sure that you always want to wear size eight shoes?"

And you just think, "Really? Why in the world would I go back to something that didn't fit?"

It's not a perfect analogy, because my life was actually good in America. It wasn't like a painful pair of shoes, but it just wasn't the deepest, highest, fullest expression of who I am. So while my life there was rich and fulfilling in many ways, when I came to Rishikesh and had the experience of oneness with the Divine on the banks of Mother Ganga, I received something extraordinary. The experience has been one of receiving not renouncing. The questions people ask about my life almost always hint at sacrifice, at what I've given up to be here. But that has not been my experience at all. For me, it has been an experience of *gaining*, rather than an experience of *sacrifice*.

Every time you order food at a restaurant, you have to make a choice—this dish or that one; you can't have both. When you're getting dressed every day, you can't wear two pairs of pants—you pick one. Everything is a package deal. The worldly life is one option, and the life of a monastic renunciant is a different one. Neither is all good or all bad; neither is all luxury or all hardship, neither is right or wrong, better or worse. They are just different packages.

We only have twenty-four hours in a day, regardless of which package we choose. We only have a certain amount of energy. We have to eat, sleep, and bathe. So we're left with only a certain number of hours in the day that are really in our hands, and the question is, "What way of spending those hours is most in harmony with what's most important to me?" For me, the choice to be in a place that enables me to dedicate myself to spirituality was worth letting go of all the soy lattes, cars, comfortable beds, and cozy relationships that I had been accustomed to. You can have the most comfortable bed in the world, but if you need to take a pill to sleep at night because of your anxiety or depression, the quality of the bed doesn't really benefit you much.

What I have found in Rishikesh, in the life of renunciation as a sanyasi, is not perfect, but on the whole it's much more fulfilling and meaningful to me than the package deal of the life I had before, the life I would have if I went back, or any package deal I could envision.

One of the tragedies of New Age spiritual teachings is this mythical concept that life is a buffet, and that you get to pick and choose whatever you want. Life is not like that. You can't simultaneously live in Paris and in Los Angeles. You can't simultaneously shoulder the responsibility of raising children and have the freedom of not having children. You have to make choices. Each of the options can lead to great fulfillment and has its own challenges. The goal is not to make life a buffet. You can't. The goal is to choose which package deal has the greatest potential to bring you the greatest possibility to unfold, blossom, grow, expand, and share your gifts with the world.

Pujya Swamiji and I were in Switzerland a few years ago, running a spiritual retreat in the Alps. From the Zurich Airport, we drove straight to the retreat center. Along the way, we stopped at a wonderful fresh marketplace, which had a coffee bar. I enjoy coffee, but not instant coffee. When I'm in a place where I can have nice filtered coffee, I love it, particularly after an overnight flight. So I followed the Swiss woman, who was organizing the retreat and had picked us up at the airport, to the coffee bar and said to her, "Please order me a caffe latte, but with soy milk instead of regular milk."

She smiled and replied, "Please tell them yourself."

This woman is a devotee, an incredibly generous, dedicated, selfless woman, and I could see on the counter that they had a carton of soy milk, so her refusal to order my soy latte was confusing to me. I asked her, "What do you mean? I don't speak German."

She said, "That's okay, they speak enough English. Please tell them."

So I ordered my own caffe latte with soy milk, and they gave me a funny look at the counter but made the coffee for me. When we returned to the car, I asked her why she needed me to order my coffee when she was ordering everything else. She explained that in Switzerland you must take things exactly how they are and not ask for any changes.

She went on to explain that a month earlier she had had a group of friends visiting from California. She took them to a restaurant, and they all did what people from California are used to doing, which is to order like this: "Well, I'd like this sandwich, but instead of that bread, can you put it on this bread; instead of that spread, can you use this spread; and instead of this side dish, can you give me that side dish?"

The waiter replied sardonically, "I have a wonderful idea. Why don't you go home and cook your dinner exactly how you'd like to eat it?"

In California, you go to a restaurant and the waiters can handle that kind of order without even noting it down. They're used to it. But in California, we've been spoiled because the world isn't like that. We've really been spoiled to think we can walk into any restaurant and ask for everything to be cooked the way we like to eat it. Life isn't like that. Life resembles dining in Switzerland much more than it resembles dining in California. Life offers us opportunities and options and packages, but it's not a buffet.

When I chose the life of renunciation, I was aware of that. I don't think marriage and children are bad, and I certainly didn't think that saffron was the most flattering color for me. Giving up marriage and children, wearing saffron, these are the pieces that came with the package of life I wanted to live, the life I knew I was meant to live. The full package being offered to me was so much richer and fuller than the life I had previously been living.

It's not perfect, but none of the package options is perfect. The only thing that makes life perfect—whether we choose worldly life or the life of a renunciant—is how we deal with it. That's what's in our hands, and that's what brings peace and joy. There are a lot of people I know who are married with children, and are miserable, and a lot of renunciants who are miserable too. And of course there are many happy married people with children as well as many happy monks and nuns. You cannot decide which way is right by comparing with others.

I discovered that this path was much simpler in the ability it offered me to live the truth I had experienced and the truth I wanted to live, without having so many encumbrances. It's not that you can't live a spiritual life without being a renunciant. Of course you can. The scriptures are full of stories of enlightened rishis and sages who are married and living with families. But for me, life in Rishikesh was so much more beautiful and fulfilling than anything I had known before. So it was not a matter of renouncing, it was not a matter of pushing *that* life away. It was a matter of opening myself more and more to *this* life.

Everything on the menu at a great restaurant may look scrumptious while you're still hungry. But once you're full, it doesn't matter how good something looks, because you're no longer hungry. You don't long for that dish you didn't order. What I have found in a spiritual life is so filling that there is no hunger or thirst or yearning for anything else.

PART 5

Our World

What does spirituality mean beyond our meditation cushions, sacred sites, places of worship, chanting, and prayers? Regardless of our religion or spiritual path, what are we called upon to do if we identify as "spiritual"? Different lineages and paths worship in different ways, pray in different languages, and have different views and visions of the way the Divine manifests—or doesn't manifest—here on earth. But where do they overlap and agree regarding our off-the-mat, off-the-cushion, day-to-day lives? As it turns out, there is quite an overlap! Differences abound regarding the way to worship, but as far as the ethics, values, morals, and priorities of our lives, the tenets are quite similar: be compassionate, be generous, be honest, be loyal.

If you look at the ten commandments of the Judeo-Christian tradition and compare them to the foundation of yogic philosophy, the yamas and niyamas, you will find lots of commonality. Truth, compassion, nonviolence, integrity, and selflessness are core tenets of all religions and spiritual paths. Whether we worship Krishna or Christ or Allah or Adonai or the tree in our backyard or our ancestors or the sound of Om or all of the above, our sacred texts and teachings exhort us to live in harmony, in peace, in love with each other and the planet.

What does this mean today? Today our world teeters on the brink of environmental collapse. We have made great strides in uplifting the human condition. Rates of hunger, poverty, illiteracy, and infant mortality have decreased significantly over the past several decades. More people have access to education, health care, employment, and human rights than ever before in history. However, at the same time, our air, water, and soil are getting more and more polluted and toxic each day. Approximately 7 million people die every year due to air pollution, and 3.5 million die each year due to lack of clean water, sanitation, and hygiene! Our forests are being decimated at the rate of about ten million hectares (approximately twenty-five million acres) a year! Dead zones (oxygen-deprived water) in our oceans have quadrupled in size, growing by more than 1.7 million square miles since 1950, and extinction rates are soaring. So, we have a lot of work to do!

As I mentioned at the very beginning of this book, spirituality does not take us away from the world, rather it brings us closer. It connects us, deeply and inextricably, to every living thing on the planet.

When we pray *oṃ sarve bhavantu sukhinaḥ / sarve santu nirāmayāḥ / sarve bhadrāṇi paśyantu / mā kaścidduḥ khabhāgbhaveta*, it means may all beings be happy / may all beings be healthy / may all beings attain their highest potential / may no being suffer. This is not only human beings. It is all beings.

Spirituality is not about living in mansions while others sleep in the cold. It is not about eating caviar while others starve. It is about recognizing how our karmic threads interweave with those of every other being on the planet into the exquisite tapestry of life.

It sounds like a lot of hard work. But spirituality also reminds us, over and over again, that we are not the doer. We are neither the one who has nor the one who lacks. We are not the ones who have to figure it all out or make it all happen. We are simply instruments in the hands of the Divine, showing up fully every moment—in awareness, in love, in attention and intention to fulfill our unique role here on earth. As St. Francis of Assisi said so beautifully: "Oh Lord, make me an instrument of your peace. Where there is hatred, let me sow love. Where there is injury, pardon. Where there is doubt, faith. Where there is despair, hope. Where there is darkness, light. Where there is sadness, joy." So, we stand up, show up, and do our best while simultaneously remembering that we are merely playing a role in this particular scene of the cosmic divine drama, or *leela*, and that, ultimately, there is nothing but Divine Perfection.

This next section speaks to how to live in the seeming paradox of Divine Perfection and human duty.

Living Human Values in Our Daily Lives

How can each of us live with good human values like honesty, patience, forgiveness, and compassion in our lives, even in the most difficult circumstances? And why should we even try?

Every culture has a set of human values. In Indian culture we call them sanskaras, which means impressions upon our psyche—the values, ethics, priorities, and ways of thinking and live that form most of our subconscious processes. We need these values, and to aspire to live according to them, even if our highest goal isn't enlightenment or moksha but only to create a society of honesty, equality, cooperation, and compassion rather than corruption, lies, deceit, stealing, discrimination, and competition. These values are building blocks of life.

The system of yoga developed by the sage Patanjali, seen by many as the father of yoga, includes eight limbs. It is called Ashtanga Yoga, literally the eight limbs of yoga. In this system, the physical exercises, or asanas, are limb number three. Breathing exercises, or pranayama, are limb number four. The highest limb is samadhi, or the ultimate blissful state of merging into oneness with the Divine. Long before we get into a practice of using our body or our breath, long before we move into withdrawal of our senses, concentration, and meditation, we have limbs number one and two, the very foundation of yoga. These limbs are the *yamas* and the *niyamas,* which are the dos and don'ts of how to live.

The five yamas, the most fundamental root of yoga, limb number one, are nonviolence, truthfulness, nonstealing, nonhoarding, and integrity in our relationships. These are all virtues and values of daily life whether we ever step on a yoga mat or not. These values permeate every aspect of our life. Nonstealing does not just mean that I don't grab someone's shirt off his back. Nonstealing means how I live every day—what I eat, what I buy, what I wear. We clamor for more, more, more and cheaper, cheaper, cheaper when we shop without realizing that this supports a system of production rooted in stealing—stealing land, resources, water, and the health and lives of women and children working in sweatshops to satisfy our insatiable desire for more. When we choose to eat meat rather than a plant-based diet, we make choices that directly cause suffering not only to animals but also to our human sisters and brothers who are dying of starvation or lack of water. The meat industry is a significant contributor to climate change and a huge contributor to world hunger and depletion of our water resources. So these virtues and values become avenues for us to live yoga throughout the day. If we want to live a life that is righteous or yogic, we must strive to bring these values into every aspect of our lives.

So every meal, every shopping trip, every moment gives us an opportunity. How do you speak to the clerk who checks you out at the grocery store? How do you respond to the bank teller who is a bit slow, or to the airline desk agent who is flustered and can't find your reservation? Every moment is an opportunity to get closer to the truth of who we are, and by striving to inculcate these virtues into our lives we get closer to that goal of self-realization or God-realization. It is *not* simple behavior modification. It's not simply putting up a Post-it note that says, "Do random acts of kindness." This shift happens only by bringing spiritual truths into our daily life. Many of us have experiences of oneness and divine connection while on a meditation cushion or on a yoga mat. Striving to live according to our virtues enables us to bring that interconnectedness into every moment of our lives.

All of these virtues—compassion, patience, generosity—are virtues arising from our inherent connection to each other, to Mother Earth, to the presence of the Divine in all. But we must also remember that *we,* the individual human karmic package that we associate as *me,* is not separate from all of creation for which I am aiming to have love and compassion. Whether it's patience or generosity or compassion—remember to extend it to yourself as well!

If your car breaks down on the side of the road, you don't beat it. You know it's not the car's fault. It didn't wake up in the morning and plan to break down; it just happens sometimes. This also happens to us. We make mistakes, we forget things, we lose our anchoring, and act in unskillful ways we later regret. These virtues of love, compassion, patience, caring, generosity are not just for others in the world; they're for ourselves, from ourselves to ourselves.

If your heart is blocked, contracted, and afraid, you cannot connect deeply with another being; you cannot have real compassion for another being, real love, real generosity of heart and spirit.

What does "selfless service" or seva even mean?

Seva is a spiritual practice that purifies our mind and thoughts through service. Typically whatever we do, we do for ourselves. We may give to another, but we do it to feel better about ourselves. Assuaging our own lack of self-worth is not the highest goal of giving and serving. Seva takes us higher. It takes us into the highest goal of realization that you and I are one; that in serving you I am serving my true self that exists also in you and as you.

In order to reach that stage, though, we need to first be able to see the human of me with love and compassion so my heart can open freely. Only then can we drop deeper into our own spiritual experience and into our connection with others.

Often when we are working to stop criticizing or judging ourselves we swing in the opposite direction. In the name of compassion, we simply let ourselves off the hook and condone our own spiritual laziness. To deprive ourselves of our own highest experience is not compassionate.

You can say, "Oh well, you've had a troubled life, you've been abused, you've been abandoned, you've been betrayed"—or whatever your story is—"therefore don't worry. Just sit on the couch and eat potato chips forever. That's okay. Don't worry. Sure, be angry. Hit people. No problem. You've had it tough. Sure, become an alcoholic, become a drug addict. It's okay. You've got a good story to explain it. It's not your fault." That may sound compassionate to an untrained ear, but actually it's the opposite of compassion. It is belittling your own capacity to experience the very truth of your own existence. It is saying no to the sacred invitation each of us has been given by the Divine to wake up to the truth of the perfection of our own selves. That pseudocompassion is telling yourself that you don't have the capacity to connect to the Divine, to your own true self.

Your whole identity, your story, your karmic drama . . . that's not the true self. That's just where your body has been. It's what happened to your body. Not the soul. Not the true self. The true self has never been abused or abandoned or cheated or lied to or forgotten about. The true self doesn't have complexes or depression or anxiety or fears. That's all the stuff of this body and mind. So to allow ourselves to spend our entire lives in the jail of this body and mind is not very compassionate. It's not holding us up to the possibility of who we actually are. The highest level of compassion says, "Get off the couch, let go of the bottle, let go of the cigarette, stop hitting people, this isn't who you are. Wake up! Yes, that stuff happened, but that was act one of your life. The curtain has dropped, the intermission has passed, the curtain has now risen on act two of your life. It's a brand new day, brand new scene, brand new stage, brand new place, but you need to show up. You're the only one that is missing from this act two of your life. And anyway, at the fundamental level you are the actor, not the role. You're not even the one to whom this stuff happened. Stop thinking you're the role and realize you're the actor." That's the highest level of compassion.

Don't berate yourself when you slip into moments of unconsciousness, mindlessness—we all slip. Don't berate yourself for again having fears, judgments, impatience, or pain, but also don't allow yourself to keep slipping into it. Keep holding yourself up to the highest truth of who you are. That's the deepest compassion, the deepest generosity. That's what patience is for. It's not, "Let me be patient while I waste breath after breath, minute after minute of my life." It's, "Let me have patience while I climb these steps. Let me have patience while I open these curtains to let the sun in. Let me have patience while I peel my layers back one by one." That's the stuff we need patience for. And when we learn to have it for ourselves, then we can have it for others.

Appreciating Human Diversity

What do unity and diversity mean, and how do they coexist?

Unity and diversity are like the waves of the ocean. If you took a photograph of the ocean with a wide-angle lens you'd get a picture of many different waves—tall, short, wide, narrow, some that seem to go on forever, some that crashed immediately, some that were blue, some that were half white as they crashed into the shore. That's the external, temporary diversity. But ultimately, fundamentally, all waves are ocean.

It's the same truth with us. The diversity amongst us exists in our different colors, shapes, languages, races, religions, sexual orientations. Imagine that every one of the more than eight billion people on the planet has a different fingerprint. No two faces are the same, no two eyes are the same. There is such reliable diversity in the eyes that they are now used for identification! Imagine! More than eight billion people alive today and no two eyes or fingers are the same!

No two are the same, and yet we're all simply different waves of the same ocean.

Fundamentally, at the core, we are soul. And fundamentally there are not many souls—there is one soul. One unmanifest, infinite supreme reality, what we call Brahman in Sanskrit, but you can also think of it as an infinite ocean. So when we look at the waves, we see and appreciate diversity. In this intersection of time and space, your form has black skin, or white skin, or brown skin. Your particular form belongs to the Hindu religious tradition, or the Christian tradition, or the Jewish one, or the Muslim one, or the Buddhist one. Your particular waveform has a great abundance of water in it. It's a big wave! We call that rich. Someone else's waveform has less water; it's a smaller wave. We call that poor. We can focus on the form of the wave that exists for a split second on the timeless ocean, or we can focus on the ocean itself.

Diversity depends on which aspect of existence we are focused on. If we focus on the outer level, the level of fleeting waves coming into existence, growing, crashing, and retreating, then there is a lot of diversity. There's nothing wrong with that. In fact it's beautiful. The beauty of a garden is dependent upon the variety of flowers. More flowers, more beauty. A safari is interesting because one can see many different types of animals. Humanity is so exquisite because there are so many different types. We celebrate, honor, and appreciate the diversity, but we must also remain aware of the inherent, underlying unity and not get lost in the different wave forms.

Living as Mindfully and Harmlessly as Possible

What can we do about climate change?

There's a beautiful story of three men stranded on a boat in the middle of the ocean. They start to fight, so in order to keep some peace, they draw invisible lines down the boat, dividing the space up so that each of the men has his own one-third of the boat, much like young children do in their bedrooms. Although the lines are just imaginary, each of the men stays in his third of the boat. One day, two of the men look over and they notice that a leak has sprung in the third part of the boat, and that water is now flooding in. They panic and shout at the third man, "Stop up the leak! The boat's going to sink and we're all going to drown!" But the third man turns to them and says calmly, "Oh, don't worry, it's only leaking in my part of the boat."

We all understand that, invisible lines or no invisible lines, a leak in any part of the boat will cause the whole thing to sink. I love that story because that's the situation we are in on planet earth today. Our collective boat of our healthy, sustainable, physical presence on Mother Earth is sinking. It is up to us to plug that leak.

When we talk about climate change, so many of us relegate it to the responsibility, fault, and duty of our governments, of multinational companies, and of the massive transportation industry. We sign online petitions, we march, we picket, we post on social media. It's wonderful to show solidarity, and we must, but there's also a lot more that we can do, and there's a lot more that we *need* to do. The Amazon rainforest, earth's largest carbon bank, stores about 20 percent of the carbon captured by plants across the planet and acts as a major defense against climate change. But, the Amazon is being clear-cut at the rate of a football field every twenty seconds. Not only are we losing a major source of oxygen on earth, we're also in danger of heating the planet by several degrees as this carbon is released.

Take a minute and just breathe. Inhale for ten seconds, let it out for ten seconds. Repeat for one minute. In that minute that you just breathed, three football fields of Amazon rainforest have been deforested. For what? Primarily for the livestock industry, so that those who have the luxury to choose can choose to eat hamburgers and steak, to have teak and mahogany tables and doors.

Humanity does not exist in a vacuum. We are interconnected and interdependent.

Climate change is taking place due to the overproduction of several greenhouse gases but particularly due to carbon and methane. The livestock industry is responsible for more carbon dioxide in the atmosphere than the transportation industry. The United Nations released a report in 2006 called *Livestock's Long Shadow* emphasizing the detrimental impact of animal agriculture on our climate and the huge role (even larger than the transportation industry) played by the meat industry in greenhouse gases and climate change.

How many of us feel a pinch of guilt for the airplane or car travel we do? Perhaps we make a donation to offset our carbon footprint, and yet the impact of our air travel is negligible compared to what we're eating. The production of every single hamburger creates 3 kilograms of carbon dioxide released into the atmosphere. The livestock industry is responsible for more than 30 percent of the methane in our atmosphere, due mainly to cattle. When you include the clear-cutting of the forests to graze the future hamburgers and the burning of their waste, *more than 100 million tons of methane per year* goes into the atmosphere.

It's also critical to look at our planetary water crisis. Water is an inextricable part of our lives and of the climate change we are facing. The less water there is, the hotter our ground is. The hotter our ground is, the hotter our air is. The hotter our air is, the more water is pulled out of the earth.

The United Nations estimates that by 2040 the world will need 50 percent more drinking water than we use now. Where will it come from? Fresh water is being lost every day. The UN also estimates that by 2040 that we could have up to hundreds of millions of water refugees, people forced to leave their homes due to lack of water (or due to rising sea levels). Already today more people suffer and die each year due to lack of clean water than due to all forms of violence combined. We work for peace. We pray for peace. We protest for peace. But today our definition of peace needs to expand to ensuring that our sisters and brothers have access to water.

In India, farmers are dying by suicide due to desiccated fields, and their inability to provide for their families. Yet the amount of water that we are utilizing simply to eat hamburgers, hot dogs, and chicken would irrigate not only the fields in India but the fields throughout the world. Commercial agriculture uses 70 percent of the fresh water on this planet, including a significant portion for livestock. Livestock agriculture accounts for 20–30 percent of the world's freshwater consumption.

Approximately 2,500 gallons (about 10,000 liters) of water goes into the production of that one pound of beef—one meal of hamburgers for a small family or a few friends. If you shower every day for approximately eight minutes, in six months you will use approximately 2,500 gallons of water in bathing—the same amount used in that one meal of hamburgers! That means that every time we eat beef, we have to ask ourselves, "Am I prepared to go without bathing for six months to offset the water that has gone into this meal?" Chicken uses about one-third of that water, so for chicken we'd have to go about two months without bathing to offset the water usage

We have learned to turn off the tap while we brush our teeth, we put low-flush devices in our toilets, we donate to environmental organizations, sign online petitions to stop fossil fuels, but then we go out to a steak house. I share this with you not to make you feel guilty, but simply so that every one of us understands the great power we have. Even if we don't go fully vegetarian, every single time that we choose a vegetarian option over meat, we are freeing up crucial water resources for the planet, we are putting water in parched throats, we are irrigating desiccated fields, we are helping our brothers and sisters survive.

It's important to look not only at what we eat, but also what we buy and what we wear because almost everything we use is produced in a factory, and most factories spew noxious gases into the air, chemical waste into our soil, polluting our groundwater, flowing into our rivers, turning what should be drinkable fresh water into poison that is killing our brothers and sisters across the world. The solution is not, of course, to abstain entirely from shopping, but we must reclaim our power and autonomy to withstand marketing techniques telling us to "shop until you drop" or sending us out for "shopping therapy" every time we're bored, frustrated, or sad. It is entirely a question of consciousness. As we work in our meditation, prayers, and yoga to expand and deepen our consciousness, that expanded awareness must also permeate our actions when we are off the mat and off the cushion. Our conscious, loving choices have the power to mitigate suffering and to protect and preserve our planet.

Lastly, the meat industry is not only killing our planet, it is also killing our hungry sisters and brothers. We produce enough grain to feed more people than even exist! The reason our sisters and brothers are starving is because the grain we grow is not being used to make rice, pasta, and bread to feed people. It's being fed to the cows, pigs, and chickens who later become hamburgers, hot dogs, and chicken nuggets.

It takes sixteen pounds of grain to produce one pound of beef. Sixteen pounds of rice, wheat, soy, or corn are fed to the cow. The cow eats throughout its life, and most of its food is digested or defecated. Only a very small amount of what the cow eats turns into meat. That is why so much grain goes into the production of such a small amount of meat. But to make rice, bread, or pasta, one pound of grain makes one pound of food. So every single time we choose to eat meat, we are saying we deserve to eat for fifteen other people. We deserve their food so we can enjoy hamburgers.

Isn't eating plants also violent? They have emotions too. So then what can we eat?

It would be nice if we could live on air. It would be nice if we could tread through life without ever causing pain or suffering, let alone death, to another being. Unfortunately we can't live on air. Every day we are killing billions and maybe even trillions of bacteria every time we wash our hands, bathe, and clean our homes. Anytime you take an antibiotic, you are killing millions and millions of little living bacteria within yourself. Every time we walk on the grass, we kill tiny insects. In order to stay alive, there is an impact upon other life-forms.

Plants *do* have feelings! Science has shown that plants respond to different tones of voice. There have been studies showing the growth rates of plants that are sung to or spoken lovingly to compared to plants that are yelled at or threatened. The ones spoken lovingly to seem to grow faster and better! We also know that when plants get "stressed" they emit certain unique sounds (beyond the perceptive ability of the human ear). However, that response is significantly less than the response of an animal's nervous system. Without any pain receptors, nerves, or a brain, scientists agree that plants cannot actually experience pain. The more complex a creature's nervous system, the more its ability to experience pain. Humans are highest on the ladder. Our intricate brains, spinal cords, and complexity of nerves gives us a vast spectrum of reactions and responses to the environment. As you move lower on the ladder of complexity, the nervous system becomes simpler and simpler. For example, we know that an earthworm has a less complex system of nerve fibers than a chimpanzee. This is why biology classes in many schools teach dissection on earthworms, but it would be unconscionable to kill a chimp to dissect. The more complex the nerve fibers, the more intricately woven the neurons, the more of an experience of pain and suffering the creature will have. Fruit, vegetables, and grains fall at the very bottom of the list of items that we can actually eat and digest.

Additionally, there is another important aspect: Eating the cucumber is only violent to the cucumber. Eating the cow is violent, not only to the cow, but also to our human brothers and sisters with whom we share this planet. Eating the cow is violent to every farmer whose field is desiccated and is living with thoughts of suicide because he has no harvest and cannot feed his family. Eating the cow is violent to our water supply, our air supply, to every person on earth who lives on the edge of a water body that is rising with climate change. Eating meat is violent to the tens of thousands of people who perish from starvation every day and the nearly one billion people who sleep hungry each night.

Remember that everything is interconnected, and because there's consciousness in everything—even if it's minimal—we must take only what we need. As Mahatma Gandhiji said so beautifully, "There is more than enough for everyone's need and never enough for even one man's greed." We must feed our need, not our greed. Just because a cucumber is lower on the scale of consciousness than our starving brothers and sisters, doesn't mean we should eat more than we need. Wherever on that chain of consciousness we're eating, shopping, dressing, and utilizing, we need to ensure it is as nonviolent as possible. Ahimsa, the first tenet of yoga, the core foundation of yoga, means nonviolence.

When you go camping in America in the national parks, you'll see signs that say, "Take only memories, leave only footprints." Let us think about our life on earth like that. We'd like, of course, to leave more of a positive impact, more of a positive legacy on earth than merely footprints, but what we take from the earth should be as close to just memories as possible.

What can we do to promote vegetarianism?

The truth is a magnet. The most important thing we can do is live it! Live as vegetarians (vegans if possible) and invite others into your compassionate way of eating and living. When I was a teenager my friends called me a "vegeterrorist" because I was so vehement about promoting vegetarianism. It's cute in retrospect and no one ever forgot that I was an ardent vegan, but my vehemence didn't convince even one person. People don't change because other people berate them or criticize them. They change when they are given agency, autonomy, and inspiration to change of their own accord. So be a vegetarian. Be a vocal vegetarian. Share the reasons behind your choices with others, but do so in a way that simply invites them into a space of conscious living rather than demeaning their current choices.

Each of us has a voice. How we use it is up to us. Many of us bemoan what social media has done to our lives, our families, and our communities. There are many downsides to social media, especially around its ability to distract us so powerfully that it can steal our whole day, and its algorithms make us more and more polarized and outraged rather than more and more open and tolerant. However, it's not all bad. Social media is probably the most powerful free tool that the general public has ever had in its hands. There has never been an ability to share and spread so much information so quickly to such a vast number of people for little to no cost. If we can use social media as a powerful awareness-raising tool of inspiration and motivation, rather than as a way to zone out or check out what others are doing, we'll realize we have an incredibly powerful way to effect change.

The challenge with spreading vegetarianism is that most people don't like to talk about what they eat. Everyone wants to be a good person, to be a spiritual person, to do the right thing, but mostly we want to be able to do it in fifteen minutes a day without changing our lifestyles. I can't tell you how many people have asked a question in satsang that sounds like: "In order to be spiritual, what's the bare minimum I have to do every day?" Sadly that is what so many people are looking for. What's the bare minimum? How many breathing exercises, yoga postures, rounds of chanting my mantra do I have to do to earn a spiritual stamp of approval?

This is sadly what spirituality has become for so many people. A simple stamp of approval based on a set of exercises with our breath or body or a certain amount of time spent meditating. Spirituality is actually that which is meant to permeate our entire lives.

But we don't want to change our lifestyles. We want to keep shopping till we drop. We want leather car seats, leather bags and shoes. We want to eat whatever tastes good, buy whatever we fancy. We don't want our taxes raised. We want to keep up every habit, hold on to every cent, and feel good about ourselves at the same time. Unfortunately, if you're deeply honest and introspective it's very difficult to feel good about that type of lifestyle, since so much is *not* in alignment with our spiritual values. A little bit of inner uncomfortableness about what we just ate or bought actually catalyzes necessary shifts in our behavior. And that's what's important.

So this is why spreading vegetarianism is so hard. Most people don't want to hear about what they need to change about their lifestyles. But you must keep sharing the truth. What they *do* with the truth is *their* karma. *Your* dharma is to share it! Not everybody is going to change, but even if people continue to eat meat 90 percent of the time and substitute plant-based foods 10 percent of the time, the sheer impact on the planet would be phenomenal. As Mahatma Gandhi said so beautifully, "Be the change that you wish to see in the world." The solution is not to shove our truth down other people's throats. The best we can do is become the change, to live, embody, exude, and manifest spiritual values and mindful living in our own lives. When we do that, it creates a beautiful invitation for others to also live like that.

There's a lot of crazy human behavior occurring right now all over the world with violence and war. What are some of the best ways to stay grounded in our heart space, and to know the best time to take action?

Our hearts do not prevent our heads from working. Staying grounded in our hearts does not disconnect us from common sense, initiative, creativity, and effectiveness. We anchor in our hearts to connect with the presence of the Divine within ourselves and in others, to remember our oneness and interdependency with all of creation, and to remember that no matter what is happening in the world around us, it is not happening to the very truth of who we are. When we say "Aham Brahmasmi" or "Tat tvam asi"—I am one with the Divine, thou art that—these are teachings not about our physical bodies and karmic packages in this lifetime but about the very core of our self. Whether we say soul, spirit, consciousness, or divinity—that fundamental most-true aspect of self is eternal and unchanging. It is all pervasive and perfect. It is sat-chit-anand, truth, consciousness, and bliss. Anchoring into our deepest heart space reconnects us to that truth in which we can re-ground ourselves and come back into alignment with right action.

A lot of us lose ourselves in stressful situations because we get triggered into fight-or-flight sympathetic nervous system responses that are fantastic for short-term life-threatening situations but are severely detrimental in the long term. Our practices of meditation, especially loving-kindness meditations, prayers, and japa (chanting), reconnect us to our hearts and to our truth. Practices of yoga asanas, nature walks, hikes, and swimming in fresh rivers or lakes or the ocean can all be deeply healing and helpful in reminding us of our sacred place in these physical bodies, on planet earth.

These practices restore us to a place of inner perfection in which we know that we are whole. We are complete. We are loved.

However, we must also remember that this inner, peaceful, expansive heart space is not for hiding from the world. It is the place from which our engaged action should flow. Think of your inner heart as both the very truth of yourself and also the fertile, rich, healthy soil in which right action, karma yoga, can grow.

People frequently ask me, "You're a spiritual person. You believe in God and have faith in God, so why do you work so hard?" We work not because we don't believe in a perfect creation by a perfect, infinite, supreme Creator, but because we realize that we—in this human body, with this human brain, with its ability to initiate, to innovate, to have creativity and compassion—are a perfect part of the perfect creation. It's not that the universe is perfect minus us. It's that *we,* with our eyes that cry when we see starving children, with our hearts that break when we read stories of war, violence, hunger, and human rights abuses, with our yearning to *do* something . . . are all a perfect part of the perfect creation by the perfect Creator. For us not to feel sadness, grief, and anger about the situation in the world is most definitely *not* perfect. However, in order to be truly effective vehicles of change, truly powerful instruments of peace, we must first be able to anchor in our loving heart, in our calm and spacious mind, in our soul, spirit, consciousness. From that place of anchoring and grounding, our right actions spring like sprouts from a fertile field.

When things are happening in our world as they are, we need to be there in both heart and mind. It's not enough to just meditate on it and cry, feeling that our heart is open. It's not enough to post it on Facebook because we are so upset. It's not enough to just sign petitions. It's not even enough to just send a check to an organization that's doing peace work. All of these things are important, but every one of us needs to be a part, in heart and in action—*mindful* action—of co-creating a more peaceful, loving world.

I have a friend who is a renowned author and scientist in London named Lynne McTaggart. She's worked at Princeton, and at other top universities. She has spent the last few decades of her life doing research on the power of thought and intention to actually effect change in the world. Her research has shown that our thoughts are things. This is really important, and it's the opposite of what most of us are taught. It is exactly in alignment, however, with spiritual teachings. *Our thoughts are things.* They do not exist only between our ears; they are not just the mindless patterns of chemical and electrical behavior. They actually have a life that moves beyond our brain into the world and changes matter in the world.

When things are wrong in our world, whether it's war or terrorism, whether it's white supremacists, whether it's people shooting up schools, whether it's climate change, whatever the problem is, we actually have many options of action, and an open heart is a crucial beginning. It's not that *any* thought impacts things. According to Lynne's research, thoughts have to be rooted in an open heart, with a deep connection, and with great intention. What that means is that when our hearts are open and we're able to connect with the world, when we are able to focus our thoughts and intentions, even if we did nothing else, we can effect change in the world.

But the great news is we don't have to stop there. The great news is that in addition to our thoughts, in addition to our open heart, in addition to our intentions, we've got hands, we've got mouths, we've got legs, we've got creativity, we've got initiative, we've got skills, we've got intelligence, we've got technology and talents to put to use. Spirituality doesn't ask, "How can I be in peace while everybody is dying around me?" or "How can I stay blissful while the world is suffering and collapsing?" Spirituality asks, "How can I stay peaceful and grounded so that my heart, mind, thoughts, and actions are in alignment with what needs to be done?" If I'm not able to stay peaceful and grounded, I'm not going to be an effective agent of change, I'm not going to be an effective vessel of God's will and divine flow. So I work to keep my heart open and to stay grounded in love, peace, and truth, because only then can I keep my ego in check. Only in peace does my fear not prevent me from fulfilling my purpose. Only in peace does my desire not push me into unskillful action.

We stay grounded in peace and anchored in our open hearts because in that connection we know what's needed and how to serve. When a baby says, "La la la," the mother will say, "Oh, she's hungry." Then the baby says, "La la la," and the mother says, "Oh, she needs go to the bathroom." Later, the baby says, "La la la," and the mother says, "Oh, she needs a nap." To anybody else, the "La la la" sounds exactly the same each time. The baby's gurgles seem like random gurgles. But to the mother, it is language and she understands perfectly. How does one decipher tears of hunger, from tears of "I have to go to the bathroom," from tears of needing a nap? The mother is so connected to her baby that she knows intuitively and instinctively what's needed.

Our world requires that of us. Billions of dollars have been spent by think tanks, NGOs, charities, and other organizations for decades trying to end the same problems that we're still faced with today, and we haven't gotten any closer. There's no correlation between the billions of dollars that have been spent and world peace or equality or justice or sustainability. What's needed is for each of us to be connected to the world in such a way that we actually know what's needed and are able to take those steps. You don't have to become the head of a country or the head of NATO or the Secretary-General of the United Nations in order to effect change. Each of us is a part of that change every day, in exactly the roles we play. But we have to have our heart open, and we have to stay connected so that we know how to move and what to do. And then we act from love, so that divine will can flow and so we can be effective.

You can think about the best path being one of four Cs: connection, courage, creativity, and compassion. First we stay connected to the presence of the Divine, to truth, to love, to our hearts. From that connection we develop courage to take bold steps and risks without fearing failure or embarrassment. Courage gives rise to creativity, which is critical today. Creativity is not only for works of art. It's not relegated only to paintings or music or poetry or literature. The problems our world faces today are brand new. We cannot use the same solutions from the past. It is, in fact, the decisions we made in the past that have brought us to the problems we face today. So we need new solutions, new creative solutions. True creativity arises only when there is courage in the heart. Lastly is compassion. As our connection, courage, and creativity blossom, we find that we are acting more and more from a place of compassion for all beings. This leads us to action that is both spiritually "right action" and effective and powerful at bringing about the changes needed in the world.

Why is environmental protection important and what can we do about the destruction and deforestation?

Let's look first just at our trees and forests, as the term "environment" encompasses also the water, air, and soil. Forests are the givers of life. Trees provide oxygen, absorb carbon dioxide, provide the shade that cools the planet, transpire large volumes of water back into the atmosphere, and are a necessity for mountain streams that feed many rivers. There is a tragically funny saying that says, "It's too bad the trees don't give off Wi-Fi, because if they did we would plant them everywhere. Unfortunately, trees only give oxygen, which we need to live!"

My time spent in forests has included some of the most precious moments of my life. Being in the soil amidst trees heals us spiritually, emotionally, psychologically, and mentally. Beneath gently swaying branches we find inspiration. We are uplifted. Hug a tree and feel how deeply we are all connected. How deeply we are all one.

Trees teach us that we are interdependent. We know trees give us shade and cool the planet. They give us fruit to eat. Their amazing leaves absorb our carbon dioxide, and in exchange they give us oxygen, which we need to breathe.

Here in the Himalayas, Mother Ganga flows from the Gaumukh Glacier. But along the way, this narrow stream from Gaumukh is met by innumerable tributaries pouring forth from the mountains, becoming the wide, deep, rushing Ganga River. These are fed by trees.

Trees also store water in their roots, which then becomes moisture in our atmosphere and eventually rainfall.

There are two very simple ways to take care of our forest: 1) Plant trees; 2) Protect the trees that are already planted. It's the simplest and the most obvious way. Each evening in our sacred prayer ceremony, the Ganga arti, on the banks of the Ganga River, we all pledge together—the hundreds or thousands who are present raising their hands—that on all special occasions, on all birthdays, anniversaries, and other celebrations, we will plant trees. Instead of giving each other random gifts that go into storerooms and closets, or sit in boxes on our shelves, we pledge to give gifts of life. Try it. For birthdays, Christmas, Hanukkah, Diwali, anniversaries, graduations— whatever holiday you're celebrating—give the gift of a tree. It's the gift that keeps giving. The gift of real life, of sacred and healthy life.

We also need to protect the trees that we already have. For most of us, protecting trees sounds simple. We think, well, I don't cut down trees; I don't have an axe. I don't go into the jungles and chop them down or burn them as firewood. Yet there are so many ways in our lives that our choices, decisions, and lifestyles lead to rampant and tragic deforestation. For example, if you eat meat, your meals are cutting down the forest.

Each year, about twenty-five million acres of forest are cut down. For what? Sadly, one of the main reasons is to feed our lust for meat. We cut trees to graze the cows and other livestock who become food. As I mentioned earlier, the meat industry is the single greatest contributor to deforestation of the Amazon. And across the world, animal agriculture is a major—in many cases, the *most* major—component of climate change.

This is all happening in the name of development. Whether we're building condos or freeways, shopping centers or factories, these precious forests are seen as expendable. We call them natural resources. Our forests are not resources to be used. They are our very lifeline. Would you refer to your lungs as a resource, or your heart as a resource, or your bloodstream as a resource? Of course not. We understand these are critical parts of our very existence. So are trees.

Our current economic vision indoctrinates us into believing that in order to develop our cities and nations economically, technologically, and commercially, we should view nature as a resource, something to be used and discarded. But in the name of economic development we are actually using and losing that which we need to live: oxygen, water, a habitable planet.

Deforestation is also a humanitarian crisis. About 1.6 billion people actually depend on forests for food, for fuel, for timber to build their shelters, for their livelihoods. Deforestation is a massive ecological crisis for our animal family and our plant family in addition to our human family. About 80 percent of the terrestrial biodiversity on planet earth is held in our forests. If our forests disappear, we lose 80 percent of land-based species on earth.

So in whatever way we can, we must pledge to protect and preserve the forests of this world. How? Don't cut down trees and don't buy products made from trees that have been cut down. There are alternatives to wood for everything. We must stop seeing Mother Earth as a commodity.

Trees give us life. We all know this; we all learned it in basic biology. We inhale oxygen; we exhale carbon dioxide. That which we give is exactly what trees need to survive. That which they give is what we need to survive. There is a divine symbiosis.

Our oceans, plants, algae, and other natural photosynthesizers are the only producers of oxygen on earth. We have factories for clothes, electronics, cars, motorcycles, tires, perfume, but we have no factories for oxygen.

With regard to protection of our air, water, and soil, there is so much we can do to curtail the destruction. Nearly every decision we make has an impact upon the planet. For example, what type of car do you drive? Do you carpool, bike, walk, use public transport, or do you drive alone every day? Do you recycle? Does your home make use of alternative energy sources such as solar? When you shop for new clothes do you look mostly only at the price tag and what styles you've seen in advertisements or do you look also at the impact of this particular brand upon the earth? After the meat industry, the fashion industry is one of the greatest contributors to waste and water pollution. We have choices. There are so many new, eco-friendly, sustainable brands of fashion these days. Do you look deliberately and intentionally for earth-friendly options or do you shop on autopilot, driven only by habit and the advertisements you see? The cost of any item is not only the number on the price tag. It is also the cost to our air, water, soil, and forests. Our mindfulness practice and loving-kindness practice is actually the greatest way to help protect and preserve our environment if we can bring it off of our meditation cushion. We learn to walk mindfully and chew mindfully but can we also shop mindfully? Can we dress mindfully?

We speak so frequently about saving the earth. The truth is, though, the earth is going to be fine. The earth existed for billions of years before humans. The earth has existed through ice ages and through five great extinctions. Mother Earth does not require a specific temperature to survive. She does not require a specific ratio of oxygen to carbon to nitrogen to hydrogen. We are the ones who require this very, very special, unique concentration and combination of oxygen in the atmosphere. So it's actually ourselves we are saving; it's humanity we're saving; it's so many other exquisite species with whom we share this planet who are dependent upon that oxygen that we are saving.

Privilege and Responsibility

How do we uphold both our privilege and our responsibilities with balance and commitment?

When we think about privileges on a spiritual level, being alive is a privilege. All that we've been given is a privilege. Some of us have been given additional privileges around wealth, opportunity, education, freedom. This is where gratitude is so important on a spiritual path. If I think I'm entitled to something, I don't see it as a privilege. I see it as my right. The minute I start to feel entitled is the minute I lose gratitude. The minute I lose gratitude is the minute I lose my connection to God and to joy. So many spiritual teachings, teachers, and lineages emphasize the practice of gratitude

Also, we look at privilege as part of our karmic package. Remember, each of us has been given that particular situation that is a) a result of our past actions and b) most conducive for us to walk our next steps closer to God-realization or self-realization. This does not mean that to be born a certain color, race, religion, ethnicity, or socio-economic status is a reward or a punishment. It is simply a result of past actions and it is the environment in which the unique lessons *you* need for *your* karmic journey will manifest. Frequently we have been given privilege in order to utilize that privilege as a catalyst for fulfilling our dharma. Privilege is not ours to just have and sit back comfortably. Whatever we've been given has been given as a tool in our own karmic journey and our own awakening.

Too many of us lose this opportunity, though, and regardless of how much we've been given, we focus on what's wrong. Perhaps we are facing a difficult situation at work, or a pain in our body, or an annoying family member. If we can shift our intention from grumbling to gratitude, we can shift our lives from illusory drama to truth.

Many of us think that the key to happiness is to get what we want. We believe that when our desires are fulfilled we will be happy, and when we are happy we will be grateful. But this is absolutely backward and upside down. Happiness does not come from fulfillment of our desires and fulfillment of our desires does not always lead to gratitude. Gratitude leads to happiness! Psychological research tells us the same thing that spiritual teachers have said for thousands of years. Give thanks. Be grateful. Recognize that your cup runneth over. It is the very mindset of gratitude that leads to happiness. Not the other way around.

Recognizing that our very life is a privilege is the beginning of our gratitude. Everything is a privilege. Has any of us worked for our breath? Have we worked for the water we drink, for the privilege of simply turning a tap and having clean, drinkable water pour out? Have we done something so remarkable that the universe knew it couldn't live without us and reached into our state of deep sleep or faraway dream world and pulled our awareness back into our bodies? No, of course not. Another day with breath in our body, with eyes, ears, and limbs that work, with food to eat, clean water to drink, freedom to love and worship whomever and however we choose— these are enormous privileges we've been given.

From privilege should arise gratitude. From gratitude arises happiness. From gratitude should also arise service and generosity. When we recognize how much our cups runneth over, the most natural instinct should be to serve others, to give, to use our privilege as the springboard from which our right action flows.

When we start to realize that every breath is a privilege, it affects us in two ways. First, it leads to gratitude. Think about the Covid pandemic. When people were in the hospital on ventilators, struggling to breathe, they would have paid anything for one healthy breath. But how frequently do we acknowledge the gift of our breath? The moment we realize, "God, I haven't done anything, I'm just here. There's nothing I've done to truly earn my breath, to truly earn my days and nights, to earn my wakefulness each morning. It is all a gift," this awareness of our privilege gives birth to deep gratitude in us.

Second, we realize what a great responsibility we have. When we realize how much we've been given without having earned it, it catalyzes a sense of responsibility. I frequently marvel at the generosity of the universe: "Wow, all this! For doing *nothing*! All this for just being here. Even with my ego, with my selfish desires, with my negativity, with all the minutes I waste. Wow!" The Divine never says to us, "Well, you wasted your last breath, so I'm not going to give you another one. Look at you in the bar, look at you in the club, look at you gossiping, look at you stealing, look at you lying, look at you cheating on your spouse. Forget it. I'm not going to give you another breath. You clearly don't see the value of it; you clearly don't deserve it. Forget it." The Divine just keeps giving us breath after breath, waking us up day after day. And when we really recognize that on a deep level, it inspires responsibility. We stop taking things for granted. Rather than wasting the breaths, wasting the days, we honor them, we love them. We want to utilize them the best that we can, and we want to share. We automatically fulfill the responsibility of sharing, not because we've put Post-it notes on our fridge that say, "Do random acts of kindness," but because we live with the awareness that we are blessed, and giving becomes our most natural state.

There's a beautiful poem by Kahlil Gibran called "On Giving." In the poem, one of my favorite stanzas is:

> *You often say, "I would give, but only to the deserving."*
>
> *The trees in your orchard say not so, nor the flocks in your pasture.*
>
> *They give that they may live, for to withhold is to perish.*
>
> *Surely he who is worthy to receive his days and his nights, is worthy of all else from you.*
>
> *And he who has deserved to drink from the ocean of life deserves to fill his cup from your little stream.*

What do we have to offer someone? A few dollars, a hand across the street, a hot meal, a bit of help, a bit of advice, a hug? What do we have to offer that's on par with their days and nights that the universe has already offered them? We allow ourselves to simply be instruments in the hands of the Divine to provide them whatever else they may need.

How do you overcome guilt that has arisen from privilege?

Whenever we see the news, whenever we watch TV or go online, we see tragedies and destruction happening in the world. Children are suffering and dying of hunger, of lack of clean water. Women are dying in childbirth. Millions of people are living in refugee camps due to oppressive regimes or famine or drought or climate change. Poverty, oppression, and suffering are so rampant that those of us who are this privileged are naturally going to experience some guilt. We ask, "Why me?" When we're honest with ourselves, we know we're not any more entitled to the good life than anyone else; we see all the ways that we are dishonest, negative, or lazy. When we look at how blessed we've been, it's natural to feel undeserving and therefore guilty. Why do we have such a good life, when so many others are suffering?

This guilt is actually good. It means that we are honest, that we see ourselves clearly, that we are not living in an illusion of superiority. This guilt can catalyze inner clarity and help us bring change to our world. There are two ways to work with guilt—an inner way and an outer way—and both are important.

The inner way is to know that no matter how flawed I am—and we're all flawed—the flaws come only from my ignorance. At the core of who I am, I am pure and perfect and divine, because God—by any name or form or path, however you connect to the divine Creator—is perfect and divine. In the Vedic tradition we believe that God is not just an artist making human beings, animals, and mountains at His workstation. We believe that we've been created not only *by* the Creator but also *of* the Creator. So the qualities of the Creator are the qualities that are in the creation, and that's the core of who each of us is. All of the negative qualities we see in our ego-self—the anger, fear, desires, aversion, negativity—are all due to our ignorance. It is due to our false identification with the physical body, history, and story. When we stop identifying as the body, as the drama of this particular karmic incarnation, then we remember that who we are at the core is divine.

What that means is that you are no less deserving of the bounties of this universe than anyone else. As a manifestation of the Divine, you are entitled to the bounty of the universe; it is your birthright. God is not like a teacher we have to please in order to get an A+ or a cookie. We are children of the Divine, inseparable from the Divine. That's the inner work to realize the full, whole, complete, divine nature of our selves. That work dissolves the guilt we feel in our separate narrative of this ego-self.

The outer work, then, is "Yes, *and* . . ." Yes, I am fully deserving of the bounty of the universe because I am child of God, because I am one with God, *and* so is everyone else. In fact, just as I am inseparable from God the Creator, so I am inseparable from the creation. So if someone else has not received their full bounty from the Universe due to the play of karma, it is my duty, my dharma, to do whatever I can, in whatever capacity I have, to help them get it. Just as I am no less deserving, so are they no less deserving. As we, the human species, have lived mostly in a state of forgetting our true nature and oneness, we have created societies built upon inequality, oppression, and suppression. Our societies are products of this forgetting, of our illusion of separation. If someone else has ended up on the "have-not" end of our societal structure, then an inherent part of my spiritual expression will be to help them have whatever they have not.

But isn't it all due to karma?

Sometimes people say, "Well, isn't it their karma to be poor?" or, "It must be my good karma to be rich or privileged." Karma is not a system of rewards and punishments. Karma is the action that leads to a result that will bear fruit either immediately, later in this life, or in a future life. But there is nothing in the law of karma that speaks about worthiness or deservingness or anyone being less or more entitled. The law of karma ensures that we each receive the very situation that is both the result of our past actions and the most conducive situation for us to take our next step closer to the Divine in our karmic journey. However, it is not frozen in stone. It may be someone's karmic fruit to be poor today. It may be your karmic fruit to be rich today. But that entire karmic scenario may exist so that when you see the poor person, compassion is stirred and awakened in you and you change your way of thinking and living in order to care for others. Karma is not a justification for human rights abuses, poverty, or hunger. If you have been blessed with plenty, it's because that is the most conducive circumstance for you to take your next step closer to the Divine. Very likely that next step may be to realize your oneness with those who don't have, to see your very self in them, and to care for them as you care for yourself.

How do you maintain your energy to continue giving and giving for so long?

The beautiful thing about giving, when you give of yourself, when you give love, is it actually replenishes you. If I have a glass of water of which I've already drunk most, there's only a little bit of water left. If I had to give some of this to a large group of people, it would run out very quickly, or I would only be able to give a tiny bit to everyone because there's a finite amount. But when you give of yourself, when you give of your love, it's infinite. It's not about having to replenish yourself. The giving actually replenishes you.

That which really gives us the energy and enthusiasm to live is deep connection. This is what helps new mothers survive on an hour or two of sleep for years and sacrifice so much of themselves. That sacred connection. The connection to the Divine, directly in our spiritual practice, or through another being or through many beings, keeps us going.

If I withdraw all of my energy, I'm going to need to replenish myself. But from where am I going to replenish? With what am I going to replenish? With my glass of water, in the earlier example, I could go to a tap and refill the water glass. But with my life force, how am I going to replenish that? The only thing that replenishes it is life itself, a life of connection. We need not only food, water, oxygen, and sleep; we need spiritual connection. Food, water, oxygen, and sleep keep the body alive. But what about our life force, our prana (life-force) our *ojas* (vitality)? That's not just from oxygen. That is from a deep infusion of spiritual connection. It is from tapping into the source of life itself.

This is why spiritual practice is such a great antidote to the fatigue afflicting so many. Of course you need a good night's sleep. But large percentages of people, particularly in the West, after long nights of sleep still feel drained, burned out, fried, exasperated, frustrated, enervated, and exhausted. It's not because they're not getting enough sleep, but because what they are doing in their days has cut them off from life. They are suffocating. But it's a spiritual suffocation rather than a physical suffocation. In order to stay energized, we must stay connected to real life, to the

Divine in all forms—whether it's our child, a sunset, a tree, all children in the world, or just every aspect of creation, because it's all the Creator. Whatever we're serving, if we serve as if we're serving the Divine, that connection replenishes us.

How do we take something someone gives us graciously? Do we have to repay them? How do we repay them?

On the highest spiritual level, there actually is no giver and no taker. We fall into this ego-trap both as the "giver" and as the "receiver." This prevents us from giving from the highest place and it binds us into the drama of being a receiver. The goal is to realize that—whether you're playing the role of a giver or the role of a receiver—both are just roles in the cosmic drama. In the Bhagavad Gita, Krishna emphasizes this point to Arjuna and reminds him that whether he kills or gets killed, either way it is only the role, not the true self, that his true self was never born, will never die, and is untouched by the incessant happenings on the stage of the cosmic drama. He encourages Arjuna to simply surrender as an instrument in his hands, in the hands of the Divine. It is similar to the prayer of St. Francis of Assisi that says, "Oh Lord, make me an instrument of your peace." An instrument. Not the doer, not the giver, but just the instrument.

Typically we give to others because we see that we have a lot and they have so little, so we feel guilty or sympathetic and we give. That's the most basic level. It's not bad. It's just the most basic level, the physical, temporal level, the level at which we are separate from others. But even if you are only able to give from this level, don't worry. It is still better to give than not to give.

On the higher level though, we give as instruments in God's hands, as channels through which the Divine flows. So, when something flows through us—whether it's money, medicine, schools, food, or other ways of helping others—we're aware that we are just a channel.

You have to remember this because otherwise the ego starts to create trouble, saying things like, "I'm the one always giving, why don't they hold up their end of the deal?" or, "I'm giving so much more than everybody else; I'm such a good giver." And then you've lost the whole point. We are blessed to be utilized by the universe as a vessel; the universe is blessing us to utilize us in service.

So then, how to receive graciously? With the same awareness that we're not a taker, we're not separate from the giver, we're not less than. Many of us feel ashamed to receive. We say, "Oh, you shouldn't have," and we immediately start thinking, "Now I have to give something back to this person; Oh my God, now the ball's in my court." It's a very stressful situation. Sometimes in addition to the stress of owing something to the giver, many of us feel unworthy of receiving. The act of being given gifts fills us with stress because it belies the way we feel about ourself.

When you've been given something, you've been given a beautiful opportunity to receive, to immerse yourself in the role of receiver.

First, simply receive what is being given. If you start with, "Oh my God, you shouldn't have," you've just separated yourself from the force of giving in the universe. It's not merely that individual person who is giving to you. That person is simply an instrument of the universe. Whether you were hungry and received food, or you were sick and received medicine, or you were down and received a hug. Whatever you received, the opportunity is to allow the universe to flow through you. When you find yourself on the receiving end, don't allow your inner critic to tell you that you are any less worthy or deserving or that now you have to repay them, as that implies you were not worthy to receive. Repay the giver in the highest way by taking the gift in a spirit of the love and gratitude. Instead of thinking about paying it *back*, think about paying it *forward*! Having received this gift, and all the other gifts we receive from the universe, how are you more able to serve others with love? Ask yourself this question and then serve! Whether we're giving or receiving, the lesson is about being connected in love. It's not about the separation between haves and have-nots. It's about each of us playing our part in the cosmic karmic drama and the connection between self and divine that is our entire life's purpose.

The last piece to remember is that giving is the way to be in touch with the truth of who we are, because we are only really able to recognize the divinity that flows through us when we're serving others. Very few of us are able to tap into the divine flow within us on a regular basis, but when we find ourselves blessed to be a vehicle of service, it's a very special experience. It doesn't matter whether you're making sandwiches and feeding them to the poor, whether you're handing out medicine or doing surgeries, or whether you're stuffing envelopes or making phone calls to raise funds for a nonprofit. We're all serving in so many ways, and it's a gift to be used to serve the world.

PART 6

SPIRITUALITY THROUGHOUT OUR LIVES

In the Vedic scriptures, nearly all of the sages, rishis, and yogis were householders. They were married men and women with families. While there is a strong monastic tradition and lineage (called *sanyasa*), it is nowhere written that one must live a monastic life in order to attain God-realization. Even Lord Krishna and Lord Rama—divine manifestations on earth, in human form—had wives and children and lived in the world fulfilling their duties to their family and kingdoms. So why do our relationships seem to pull us down so much? Why is our first instinct to run away from our relationships in order to seek spiritual peace? Relationships are not easy. I always say that relationships are a yoga, a spiritual path, a practice. Standing in shirshasana (headstand) requires not only musculature in the legs, back, arms, and core, but also a delicate and refined sense of balance, an ability to work with the inner subtle muscle groups to make sure you don't lean too much to the left or right, front or back. Similarly, relationships require balance, alignment, presence, and a continual attention to where subtle energies may be shifting one way or another, taking us out of alignment with each other and our higher selves. In his wedding blessings to newlyweds, Pujya Swamiji always says, "May you walk together, hand in hand, closer and closer each day to the final destination of God-realization."

But relationships push our buttons. They trigger us in the worst ways. They provoke us to lose our grounding and anchoring. It can seem impossible to be in a relationship and in spiritual peace at the same time! This does not mean we should abandon the relationship. It means we should *use* the relationship to get free of our triggers, *use* the relationship as the path to freedom from all the places our egos are bound.

But how? This section explores using the yoga of relationship to strengthen not only our human existence but also to help us walk closer and closer to the ultimate goal of realization of the self.

Creating Change

The famous Serenity Prayer says, "God, grant me the serenity to accept the things I cannot change, the courage to change the things I can, and the wisdom to know the difference." So how do we accept the things we cannot change?

There are very few things we can change. We cannot change the fact that it's raining outside. But the rain is not the problem. The rain is just rain. It is my mind that says, "Oh no! Another rainy day!" The problem is our reaction to the rain, and *that* we can change.

In the same way, in our relationships we cannot change another person unless they want to change. But the problem is usually not the other person, but our reaction to them, our attachment to the idea that they should be different. Fortunately we do have control over our reactions. When we change ourselves everything changes.

If you and I grab opposite ends of a rope, and you pull to the left and I pull to the right, there will be a lot of tension in the rope, a literal tug-of-war. If you just let go, even if I am still pulling, all of the tension will disappear. It only requires a person on one side to let go in order for all tension to vanish. This is true with tension in our relationships just as much as it is true with tension in a rope.

In our lives, when there is any problem, it's really important to ask yourself, "Can I change this situation? If I can't change it with my words or actions, can I change it internally? Can I energetically let go of my end of the problem?" Can I stop tugging? I'm not saying you have to love or approve of everything everyone does; but true serenity requires us to realize that the problems we face are due to our own reactions, our own tugging on the rope.

One person could walk into a room full of people and say, "This room is beautiful. The artwork is beautiful. The designing is beautiful. The people are all beautiful." Somebody else could walk into the same room and say, "My God, there's a chip here in the ceiling. Why didn't they paint that? Why hasn't that chip been fixed? Look at these people sitting here laughing with their mouths open! Don't they have any manners?" The issue is not about the room or the people in the room; it's about how you interact with the room.

There are always situations and people around us that could be improved. But you must decide whether you want to look at the world through eyes of negative judgment and disapproval, or look at the world through eyes of acceptance and love, eyes that see what's beautiful. The choice is yours and the choice leads to a life of serenity or stress.

How can I help someone who doesn't want to be helped?

You should not try to change other people, especially people who don't want to change. It is impossible and an exercise in futility and frustration. You can never change anybody. Deep change only occurs when they change themselves. You may be able to influence, touch, or teach them, but change must come from within themselves.

Without a deep internal shift, the most you can get from someone is behavior modification. For example, let's say your son's room is dirty. It drives you crazy, and every time you see his room you yell at him. Eventually your son will learn to pick his clothes up and put his room in order because he doesn't want you to yell at him. He's modified his behavior. However, nothing deep inside him has changed. He has just made a wise decision, consciously or unconsciously, that it's easier to pick up his jacket than to face your wrath. This does not mean, though, that you have turned him into a neat or organized person. It does not mean that his locker at school is neat or that when he goes off to college that his dorm room will be neat. You have not created real change in him, only temporary behavior modification to prevent you from freaking out. In order to create real change, he must actually see *why* keeping a clean room is important, and be motivated to do so other than just to prevent you from yelling.

The flaws in our way of changing others go deeper also. The reason you yell, the reason his clothes on the floor drive you crazy, actually has nothing to do with a sweater or a pair of pants. If you go to a clothing store and see someone's clothes on the dressing room floor, it doesn't upset you. But when you see your son's clothes on the floor, you feel disrespected and ignored. You have bought the clothes with money you've worked hard for, you've put your time, energy, and love into those gifts. When you see them on the floor you think your children don't respect you and you lose your temper.

Unleashing your fury on your children every time their room is messy doesn't make them value you. Has anybody ever respected another person for yelling at them? It's actually the opposite. When people scream at us, we think, "When are they ever going to shut up?" Your children simply conclude that once they pick up their clothes, you will calm down. So you may get a clean room but you still don't get the love and respect you wanted in the first place. Basic behavior modification is not what you are looking for.

Here's another example: If your husband forgets your anniversary every year, and every year you cry and mope, maybe he'll hire a secretary to remind him of your anniversary. So now imagine that he shows up on time, on the right date with chocolates and flowers because his secretary reminded him and she ordered the gifts. All he had to do is bring them home from the office. You know it's all happening only because of his secretary. Are you happy about it? Do the chocolates and flowers make you feel good? No, because your sadness was never about the chocolates and flowers. Your sadness was that you felt ignored. You felt that your husband should remember important dates, love you, think about you, and value you. Forgetting your anniversary means, in your mind, that he doesn't value you. The fact that he now has a secretary who reminds him to take home the flowers she bought doesn't change anything in your heart.

In both examples, you think that what you want is something external—a clean room or flowers on your anniversary—but truthfully you want something deep inside. You want a change, not in how someone acts but in how they feel and think. Unfortunately, however, you can never change that through coercion. By trying to do the impossible, you not only don't succeed in changing others but you also thwart all the great potential in your own lifes, because you succumb to annoyance, irritation, anger, frustration, and judgment. Every time people do that thing that annoys you, you judge, criticize, and get angry. That becomes your nature, which means you're not able to fulfill your own potential because your nature has become warped by this fruitless effort to achieve the impossible.

In most cases it's only our own inner acceptance that can shift a negative situation into a positive one. We cannot force change on someone even if we are sure it's for their benefit. All we get is resentment. Our effort to change them frequently pushes them away and we end up farther from them rather than closer. Instead, we need to look within and ask, "How can I accept this situation?" Acceptance doesn't mean thinking it's great. Acceptance simply means we recognize that we don't have the power to change this situation and our aggression will only make it worse. The goal is acceptance and compassion, both for the person acting in a way we think is wrong and for ourselves.

Acceptance and compassion create space in our relationships, and in that space, people are able to breathe. When they are able to breathe, they often look at themselves and realize they do need help, whether it's for something as detrimental as alcoholism or drug addiction, or something more subtle, such as ego, anger, false identification, jealousy, lifestyle, neglect of their spiritual practice, family, or health. Thus, no matter what seems wrong about how someone else is living, we have to first create the space for them to breathe so they may become aware that they need to change.

Realize that being in love is more important than being right, because being in love is the most right thing you can do. Love has the power to change things. Being right doesn't change anything. Be in love, because when you love, people around you feel love. If you can change yourself, that's great, but if you can't, at least stop trying to change others.

How do we help others who are struggling? I know someone who keeps having challenges, but sometimes it gets really tiring listening to their same old commentary. Help me help them.

Think back to a time when you've shared your problems with someone. What did you want from them? You wanted them to listen, you wanted love and compassion, and you wanted someone to be there with you. Connection is so important, and that's really what we're craving. We rarely go to friends or colleagues or even family members expecting them to solve our problems. If something happened at work and you go home and tell your spouse or your parent about it, you usually don't expect them to solve it. You just want them to listen and understand, to have empathy and compassion for you. Or maybe you want them to sit and have a cup of tea with you or take a walk with you and be together in your frustration or hurt or fury.

I remember when I was young I'd come home from school and tell my parents about things that happened at school that troubled me. My mom would say, "I'll come tomorrow. I'll tell them! I'll fix it." I used to beg her, "No, no! Please don't come to school and fix it!" It was the last thing I wanted. No kid wants their mom to show up at school to fix things. You just want them to listen and understand.

We're not looking for others to solve our problems. If a friend is struggling with their spouse or child, they're not looking to us for the answer. People think about their problems, often all day. They're the ones living and breathing the problem. You can be sure that before they've come to you they've thought about the problem at least a hundred times, and it's unlikely there's going to be something you say that they haven't already said to themselves. What people want is connection and compassion, and to have someone be there with them.

Don't feel as if you have to be a fixer. That's a trap a lot of us fall into. We try to give people advice about what they should do, how they should solve the problem. Usually they don't want to hear it and it just pushes them farther away from us. Whatever may be the outer expression of their struggles, if someone comes to you, realize that they are coming for love and connection. If you can give those, it'll help them, and you will also benefit in the process. Whatever we share with others is being manufactured inside ourselves.

If you become angry with them, you didn't buy the anger off a shelf and swallow it. It's welled up inside you, in your mind and physical body. You're the anger manufacturer, which means that when you get angry at them, even if it is for something that they did, the first recipient of that anger is you. We have to be really careful about what emotions we manufacture. Someone else may have done something hurtful, but that doesn't mean that our anger factory has to go into overdrive poisoning our own selves.

There's a beautiful quotation that says, "Getting angry at someone else is like drinking poison and expecting the other guy to die." On the other hand, if you know that what the other person needs is just love and compassion, you only have to turn on your internal manufacturing plant of love and compassion. You may not have the answer to their health problems because you're not a doctor, and you may not know how to fix their marriage, or what to do with their unruly children. But they came to you, which means what they need from you is not the medical advice they could get from their doctor or even on the internet, but just love and compassion, and that is something you can surely give.

So don't feel frustrated, annoyed, and helpless because someone keeps coming to you with the same problems over and over again. This is just an opportunity for you to cultivate compassion. If it benefits them, fantastic. But the first beneficiary of that compassion and love is you.

I have worked hard to change myself. I've tried to forget the mistakes I made in the past and move forward, but people around me keep reminding me of my earlier mistakes. What should I do?

It's so hard. We try to change, learn, grow, and evolve, but it's so difficult when people around us keep us stuck in old patterns and keep reflecting our "old self" back to us. So what do we do?

Before we can actually change others' perceptions of us, we have to change our own perception. People are only going to accept that we've changed when the change is real. The fact that my mistake was a long time ago does not guarantee I have changed. If I lied a week ago, it doesn't mean I've become honest by today. If I cheated two weeks ago, it doesn't mean I've become loyal by today. It's very difficult to trust, believe, and have faith in people if they have not changed and if they don't take responsibility for their own mistakes.

We have made mistakes in the past. We want to be free of them, but do we want to be free without changing our ways, or do we want to be free because we are a better person now? That's an important distinction, and it's important to the people around us. So if we find that people are not letting us forget the wrong things we have done in the past, or they're not accepting that we've changed, we need to deeply introspect: "Have I really changed? Am I just trying to put the past behind me because it's uncomfortable and I feel guilty, or have I really taken steps to be different?"

If your husband or father or brother has hit you every single day of your life for the past thirty years, you're not going to wake up one morning and believe him when he says he won't hit you anymore. Unless he has really taken steps to introspect, reflect, and understand why he was harming you, and done the deep work to overcome that and change, you're not going to just let it go and forget the last thirty years.

Our ways of interacting with people are habitual. We don't consciously process and plan each word, action, or reaction. Our relationships become a habit. We run much of the time on autopilot in our interactions. If someone changes, you're not going to know they've changed unless that change has been deep, profound, and visible.

So, if people are not letting you forget your mistakes of the past, first check in sincerely with yourself and see if you've done the work to earn their trust. If you are clear that you really *have* changed, that you *have* overcome the habits and tendencies of the past that led you to make those mistakes, here's what you need to do: 1) have patience and faith, both in the other people and in yourself, and 2) know that truth is a magnet. When you live in that truth, people will respond.

Growing up in America, I used to hear people say to their children, "Do as I say, not as I do." For example, the parents may sit around smoking cigarettes and getting drunk, but they tell their children never to touch these things. Or they cheat on their taxes and lie to people, but instruct their children to always be honest and punish the children severely for dishonesty.

"Do as I say, not as I do" is a futile strategy, because children are going to do what you *do*, regardless of what you *say*. This is not only true for children. We all typically respond to what people do more than what they say. Someone may profess love to us, but if they do not act in ways that are loving, the words will ring very hollow.

Therefore, if you're really changing, that change needs to come through in your actions, not just in your words. When the change ripples through your words and your actions, eventually people will see it, will believe in it, and will respond accordingly. Remember, the truth is a magnet. But it takes time.

Dharmic Relationships

How do we have dharmic, spiritual relationships?

We have three types of relationships. The first is with ourselves, and it determines the quality of our relationships with others in the world.

Our relationship with ourselves is the foundation for all other relationships. Even if your goal is a relationship with someone else, until and unless you have a relationship with yourself that is grounded, centered, and full of compassion and understanding, you won't be able to have a fruitful relationship with others.

When we embark on a relationship with ourselves we learn to recognize that we are divine. This is very important, because it's not how most of us think of ourselves. Most of us have been raised in families, educational systems, and societies where we were judged—typically negatively—based on our appearance and how well we performed according to cultural norms. Are we pretty? Handsome? Is our body the right shape? Are we athletic enough, or academic enough? Do we bring home good grades, good report cards, praise from the school or athletic department? From a young age, we have internalized that our value, worth, and identity are rooted in our looks, our actions, and our abilities.

The dissatisfaction most of us feel about some aspect of our body or our abilities is the foundation for our relationship with ourselves. We tell ourselves, "I should be taller, fairer, prettier, more talented." Not only is this a recipe for inner emotional disaster, but it's actually a dishonest, inauthentic, non-dharmic relationship with the self, because it's affirming the false notion that we are the shape of our nose, the color of our skin, the physical dimensions and capabilities of our body.

This is not just painful to us; it's actually dishonest.

Our dharmic relationships in the world must begin with the true awareness of who we are. Every aspect of our physical bodies is constantly changing. And yet, throughout our lives, we refer to ourselves as *I*. At age two, we say, "I, me, my toys." We grow up a little, but still say "I." We grow up a little more and continue to say I." We never say anything but "I," regardless of the changes in our body, our abilities, our roles and relationships in the world. None of the cells that formed our skin, organs, and blood at the time we first learned to say "I" in our early years are still there in our body. Every single cell has regenerated. So who is that I? Where is that I?

The sages, rishis, yogis, and wise masters emphasize that we are not our bodies. Slowly through our spiritual practice—meditation, yoga, selfless service, study of scripture, association with the holy ones—we begin to have an experience of an I that is not bound by the body, an I that is constant even while the body changes. Slowly we begin to realize that this I is expansive, always present, inseparable from consciousness itself. So the foremost aspect of having a dharmic relationship in the world is to have one with yourself— to know honestly who you really are. Who you are is consciousness, soul, divinity, infinity that manifests temporarily through your body but is not bound by the body or defined by the body.

This is the mental shift that I always refer to as the Hollywood-to-Himalayas mindset shift of coming to the truth of our selves. The Hollywood way of thinking, which is how nearly all of us are raised, teaches us we *are* our bodies—the size, shape, color, talents, skills, relationships, roles, popularity, and so on. So we suffer. We suffer from ignorance, which leads to feelings of jealousy, resentment, lack, not-enoughness, competition, and fear. And we bring suffering to others as we see other people as objects to either help us get, have, or be more, or as obstacles on our path to getting, having, or being. The Himalayan way of thinking, which of course does not require you to actually *be* in the Himalayas, teaches us that we *have* a body, but we are *not* the body. We are soul, spirit, consciousness, love, truth. That is the path to ending suffering. It is the path to an authentic, truthful, dharmic relationship with yourself, and therefore the foundation of a dharmic relationship with others.

In our interpersonal relationships, problems arise when we think we need something from the other person. We think we are lacking and carry that mistaken belief into our relationships, which we see as a way to fill the emptiness. For example, if in your childhood your parents or siblings told you that you were stupid and ugly, you might have an inner hole that says, "You are ugly and worthless." Thus the relationship you're going to want is one in which you feel beautiful, brilliant, and important. If you meet someone whose metaphoric peg fits your hole, you'll call it love. It feels so good because you now feel whole; your internal holes have been filled by your beloved's pegs—by their way of speaking to you, treating you. Every time your beloved tells you that you are beautiful and the most important person in the world, you temporarily feel free of the inner holes that have plagued you throughout your life. But this good feeling is very temporary and unreliable. It exists only as long as they keep telling you that you are beautiful and brilliant. This is what we call a honeymoon period.

The problem is that over time your issues begin to take a different form. You grow and change, your way of being in the world changes, what you need changes, your experience of your inner holes changes. And your beloved changes. Suddenly, their way of speaking, acting, and being in the world does not fit or fill the holes you now have. So you think, "I have fallen out of love." But there wasn't really love to begin with.

This is why it's so important to begin with a relationship with ourselves, because only when you know that you are whole and complete will you stop looking for people to fill the emptiness you feel. Only then can you have a dharmic relationship with another person.

Once, a wise man was sitting on a road in the jungle. A traveler passing by said to him, "Baba, that village up ahead—how are the people there?"

The wise man said, "Well, where did you come from?" The traveler answered, "Oh, I came from the village down this way, and the people were horrible! They were evil liars and cheats!"

"I'm so sorry," the wise man replied, "but that's exactly how the people are in the next village up ahead." The traveler was dejected and walked away.

A short while later, another man came by. "Baba, how are the people in the village up ahead?" he asked.

"Well, where did you come from?"

"Oh, I came from the village over there, and the people were beautiful! They were so kind and loving, giving and selfless!"

The old man said, "I have great news! That's exactly how the people are in the village up ahead!"

After the second traveler walked off, a young boy who had been sitting with the old man turned to him and said, "Babaji, there's only one village up ahead. How is it that you told the first man that the people are horrible and evil, and you told the second man that the people are honest, beautiful, and kind?"

The old man explained, "Because that's what they each saw in the last village, which means that's their vision of the world. So that's what they will see in all villages up ahead."

It's not the people or the situations, but our vision that becomes the filter through which we see the world.

In Hindi it is said, "Jaisa drishti, vaisa shrishti," which means, "As is your vision, so is the world." The answer to problems we have with the world is to change our perspective and perception. When we move through the world—whether in a relationship with one person or an organization—and we expect the best, we impact our present reality and our future.

I once saw a sign that said, "Watch your thoughts and you will see the future." This is true. Our thoughts create our future. Hence, as we navigate the world and our relationships with the world, the dharma we bring with us is the power of our own thoughts.

When we speak of dharmic relationships, it is also important to cultivate and sustain an awareness of oneness with all. It's easy to shut ourselves off from the world, particularly from the pain. Yet, that separation, those walls we erect between us and others, are actually the cause of our deepest suffering.

Ironically, we sometimes think that we'll be fine as long as we can create a safe, cozy cocoon and isolate ourselves, away from the world, but paradoxically we just end up suffocating ourselves. Our goal should be to break down those walls and allow ourselves to connect. There is pain in the world, yes, but there's also joy, and opening ourselves up to the pain allows us to be open to the joy as well. For true spiritual connection, we have to let those walls dissolve.

When we look at our bodies, we look very solid and separate from each other, but actually we are connected. Spirituality tells us, "You're not the body; you're spirit, you're soul." Science tells us that we are mostly energy, whirling, twirling energy in constant motion! If we could see our physical bodies on the subatomic level, we wouldn't see borders and boundaries of skin and bones. We'd see whirling electrons spinning in space. There are no borders or boundaries to the atoms that we're made of. We appear solid only because our physical eyes are not sophisticated enough to see on the subatomic level, but even when we can't see it, science tells us it is true. There is no place, scientifically or spiritually, where I end and you begin, where any of us ends and the rest of the world begins. That illusion of separation is what causes our suffering. And by dissolving that illusion we actually alleviate our own suffering and simultaneously the world's suffering. That's the element of dharma in relationships.

Raising Spiritual Children

How do you raise spiritual children? How do I support my spiritual child?

Children, by nature, are spiritual.

Look at what makes them happy. What's their greatest joy? Their own mother's arms, lying on their back and playing with their own toes, having someone stare lovingly into their eyes, connection. When we give them expensive gifts, they are usually more excited about the box or the colorful wrapping paper than the toy that lies inside it. We have to tell them, "No, no, that's not the present! That's just the box! Open it! Open it!" We push the box away and thrust the shiny present into their hands. We teach them to be materialistic. We teach them that their toes are not supposed to be a source of greater joy than the shiny new truck.

So if you're a parent and you have a child who still displays spirituality, fortunately you don't have to do much. Just don't squeeze it out of them. Children come into this world so deeply connected to the universe. No child ever declared, "You're Black, I'm white; you're poor, I'm rich; I won't play with you. You're Christian, I'm Hindu; we can't play together. You're ugly, I'm pretty; you can't use my toys."

We're the ones who tell them, "No, don't play with him. You can't go to her house. They are different from us." We're the ones who squeeze that spirituality out of our children and teach them to objectify themselves and others. So the way to raise spiritual children is to help them stay connected to what they've come into this world with, which is the awareness that we're all one. Let them stay grounded in the love they feel for all those who smile at them; love for nature, love for the ant and the caterpillar.

Several years ago, we had a beautiful launch for our eleven-volume *Encyclopedia of Hinduism* with His Holiness the Dalai Lama. I was sitting just behind him, and I noticed that every few minutes he kept bending down, over and over. I couldn't see why at the time. Later I found out that he had been bending down to pick up little caterpillars, one by one, from the floor of the stage, and hand them to his security guard standing nearby. He was worried that someone would step on them. One of the things that's so beautiful about His Holiness is that childlike connection. Children pick up little insects and save them, and adults tell them, "No, no, put it down. Now go wash your hands."

To raise spiritual children, just help them stay connected with what Pujya Swamiji calls our inner GPS—God's Perfect System. In children, their inner GPS guides them and connects them to the earth and to one another in a much deeper way than the rules of socialization that adults teach them. You'll find that raising spiritual children is actually very easy, unless you have your own conscious or unconscious agenda that they should become materialistic to fit in better with society.

It gets a bit harder as they grow and spend more time with friends and are exposed to more of the culture, media, and social media. You need to re-anchor them at home. Our home is our first school; it is where the foundation for our life is laid. As children grow, as they get more influenced by society, friends, TV commercials, and influencers on social media, we have to re-center them.

What anchors them is our behavior and the example we set. We cannot raise spiritual children if we are materialistic. We cannot complain that our children are not spiritual when we exclaim, "Oh my God, did you see what she was wearing?" or, "My God, he's become so fat!" or, "What is she thinking with that awful haircut?" or, "She wore that same sari last week, doesn't she have any other clothes?" We have these types of conversations at home, in the car, in front of our children. We engage in superficial gossip, and then we wonder what's wrong with our children. To raise spiritual children, we have to raise our spiritual selves first.

I have a friend who's deeply spiritual and is a very committed yogi and meditator. One day, when her daughter was about five or six, my friend saw her sitting in the temple space at home. She said something to her daughter, and the little girl turned around and said, "Shhh, Mom! Can't you see I'm meditating?" She only knew to say that because she had seen her own mother meditating.

Children pick up quickly what we do, so the best way to raise a child to be spiritual is to be spiritual ourselves, just the same way that the best way to teach a child to be honest and have integrity is by being honest and having integrity ourselves. To raise them, we must raise ourselves.

How do you show the young the way to spirituality, especially if they don't seem inclined?

When I was in school in Los Angeles, simply giving the right answer on an exam or in class wasn't enough. The teacher would persist, "And why do you say so? How do you know? What is your reasoning" We not only had to give the right answer; we also had to defend our entire thought process.

That form of education, a more Western model of education, is now more and more common around the world. Good education is less about simply memorizing facts and figures and more about learning to think creatively and courageously. And this is a good development! We want to raise conscious, connected, creative, and courageous thinkers, not robots. Artificial intelligence and technology can give us the facts and figures. We don't need our children to become poor versions of robots. We need them to become the best, most alive, most creative versions of themselves.

The challenge for traditional parents is that children bring these habits home. If we tell them to do something, for example to say their prayers or perform a religious ritual or to be a vegetarian, they will likely ask, "Why?" Most parents today didn't ask their own parents why, so sometimes they don't have the answers. Or the answers they give aren't acceptable to this generation. "Because I said so." "Because it's the right thing to do." These are no longer answers that will satisfy children even if they are the answers your parents gave you. The culture has shifted. The educational system has shifted. But the truth has not shifted. These things are still very true and important, but you have to give better reasons today.

Answers to these questions do exist and they are persuasive. There are specific, clear reasons behind most rites, rituals, and tenets. The tragedy is that because you, as a parent, may never have asked *your* parents about it, because that wasn't the culture a generation or two ago, you may not know the actual reasons underlying the ancient practices.

This is one of the main reasons that Pujya Swamiji originally conceived bringing out the *Encyclopedia of Hinduism*—to put all the answers for Hindu parents in one place, so that when their children ask a question, instead of giving them an explanation that isn't satisfying to them, parents can turn to the *Encyclopedia*.

Frequently children will make excuses and say they don't have time to pray or meditate or read spiritual texts. It's the same excuse adults use. There's plenty of time to be on Instagram or TikTok or WhatsApp, to watch videos, to post selfies, so it's not a matter of time; it's a matter of choices.

When I'm back visiting in the United States, if my friend says, "Let's go to the movies," I'm likely going to say, "I don't have time." It's true. In my mind, I don't have three hours to go catch a movie. But if I say to her, "Come, let's sit, let's meditate, let's have satsang, let's sing *kirtan*, let's work out a proposal for a project for how we can clean the banks of the Ganga," she'll say, "Oh, I'd love to, but I don't have time." She's got three hours to go to the movies, I've got three hours to do satsang or kirtan or social work. So it's not that we don't have time. Everybody has the same twenty-four hours in a day. It's just a matter of how we choose to spend those hours.

The challenge with our children is not just finding a way to throw some spirituality into their lunch box, but how to make it something they're prepared to spend time on. That's the challenge. We know it's valuable, but how can we put that in words that mean something to them? While working with the younger generation, I have found that they frequently say they don't believe in rituals, and that's fine. Don't worry. Don't force them. It's actually our fault; we haven't been able to properly explain why we do them. Just say, "Okay, No problem. God does not need rituals, but that same Divine whom we worship in the ritual exists in everyone and everything." This is something that our younger generation can and does grasp. They are the ones who often come home enraged about discrimination, inequality, violence, and climate change. They *want* to work in the world. Hurt by the lack of equality, the disparity they see, they actually want to do something to bring positive change.

Therefore, to inculcate spiritual values in them, simply say, "You don't have to worship God through rituals. Worship God through everyone you meet. Wherever you go, whomever you meet, whether it's the guy refueling your car, a coworker, a friend, an employee, an employer, a home-less person on the street, see them all as divine and ask yourself how you can help them, even if it's just with a smile or a kind word." What you'll find, as I have, is our children are not only prepared to do that, but they're excited about it too. That's a language that they can speak.

We need to let our children know that according to spirituality, the world is one family. In the Upanishads it is said, "*Vasudhaiva kutum-bakam*," meaning, "The world is one family." This is why we must live in such a way that our brothers and sisters around the world don't suffer. We can explain to our children that this is why we don't eat meat, because the meat industry is an enormous contributor to climate change, world hunger, and water shortages.

If we eat our vegetables and grains—like rice, wheat, soy, and corn as they are, or as bread or pasta, there's more than enough of it grown every year to feed everyone on earth. However, when we take those grains and feed them to livestock, animals whom we later kill for their meat, there's not nearly enough to go around, and tens of thousands of people die of starvation every day, and nearly one billion people go to sleep hungry. Our children may not buy the argument to be vegetarian because the cow is holy or that animals are our sisters and brothers. No problem. Let them be vegetarians because their human sisters and brothers deserve food to eat and air to breathe and water to drink. They may never do what we call puja (religious rites, offerings, and ceremonies), but they will choose careers that are puja. They will live their lives as puja. And ultimately, that's what spirituality is all about.

How do we help kids *be* rather than *do* when there are still chores and responsibilities they need to complete?

We've slipped into an unhealthy pendulum swing, shifting our aim from frenetic *doing* to idle being. We've shifted from having action as the goal to having idleness as the goal. But this is not healthy or beneficial. We were never meant to be idle. In the Bhagavad Gita, Lord Krishna emphasizes that we cannot *not do*. We are always doing—whether with our hands and legs or with our minds. Every moment is action. We can sit down, close our eyes, sit on our hands, plug our ears. But we would still be doing. The mind would continue to think, to fear, to desire, to judge.

Doing is not the problem. The problem is our definition of "being." For too many of us, being means that we stop doing. Being becomes binge-watching Netflix or scrolling social media, which is neither nourishing nor rejuvenating nor uplifting.

The answer to the doing versus being dilemma is not to do less. The key becomes accessing an inner state of peaceful, mindful, grounded "being" even while the hands, legs, and brain are "doing." Spirituality doesn't teach us to ignore our chores or responsibilities. In fact, it's the opposite. One's duty, or dharma, is considered the foundation of spirituality. Knowing our purpose, fulfilling our responsibilities, living our dharma are pillars of the temple of our spiritual life. We have taken human birth on planet earth to fulfill our unique dharma. Human birth is not just a short joy ride where we're just supposed to accrue as much enjoyment and as many pleasures as we can for however many years we have. We are here, intentionally, to work through our karmic package, walk our karmic journey, fulfill our dharma and be instruments in the hands of the Divine, channels for the flow of the Divine here on earth. By actively not doing, we are still doing; we are neglecting our duties, we are abdicating our responsibilities. That still counts as *doing*. Acts of *omission* are just as much *doing* as acts of *commission*.

The key is to *be* while doing, and that's what we need to teach our kids. They need to learn to stay present, grounded, mindful, and connected to themselves while they're doing, and not overidentify as the doer. The easiest way to teach this is when they come home from school with a report card or exam results. Do we respond to them as the taker of the exam or as the divine soul? If they come home with a low grade, are we angry and disappointed, and does our facial expression show withdrawal of love? If so, what they learn is, "I am the taker of the exam. When I do well, I am deserving of love; when I don't do well, I am not. My worthiness as a being, my worthiness to be in Mom's lap, to receive her hugs and kisses and smiles, to be Dad's big boy, is entirely contingent on what this piece of paper says." This is the fastest way to make sure our children identify as the doer, and that they develop compulsive doing and end up as workaholics! They will spend their lives trying to do enough to be worthy of love.

We make this mistake also in sports, art, music, and other activities. If our child is a great athlete and wins the game, we say, "You're the best!"

and we reward that. It's great to support them, of course, but we should really support *who* they are, not how good a test taker or soccer player or singer or dancer they are. Otherwise they will grow up feeling that the love and adoration they receive is due not to them as people but due to the success of their actions. Instead of only celebrating and rewarding what they *do,* why not spontaneously take them out for ice cream to celebrate who they *are*?

Remember to apply the same principle with ourselves too. If our self-talk is always, "Oh my God, I'm so irresponsible; I'm lazy, I'm a bad mom," that's what they learn. Kids learn whatever we do and they absorb it. It doesn't matter how much we try to teach them otherwise. So we need to start living not as the doer, not as a failure or success depending on whether we check everything off our to-do list or not. We need to allow ourselves to simply celebrate who we are, not only on Mother's Day, Father's Day, and birthdays. Let us change the patterns we follow in our families by initiating celebrate-each-other days, just to reward each person for *who* they are. Then our children will learn the beautiful value of who they truly are, which isn't contingent upon their actions.

How do we let go of control over our children as they grow older—say, when they are going off to college?

This is one of the greatest challenges of parenthood—letting go of children as they move on to other phases in life. Similarly, children find it difficult to let go of parents when they pass away, even if they lived a long life. Letting go is always a difficult challenge.

Recognize that your child is being guided and led. There's another beautiful poem by Kahlil Gibran titled "On Children," which speaks so beautifully about how children have come through us, not of us. "They come through you but not from you, And though they are with you yet they belong not to you." We tend to think of our children as extensions of ourselves. The poem reminds us:

You may give them your love but not your thoughts,

For they have their own thoughts.

You may house their bodies but not their souls,

For their souls dwell in the house of tomorrow,

which you cannot visit, not even in your dreams.

You may strive to be like them, but seek not to make them like you.

Time always moves forward. Our children are the ones moving forward with time. He ends the poem by telling us not to worry, because God loves the bow from which the arrow flies as much as God loves the arrow that's flying through the sky. It's a beautiful metaphor. We've been given this sacred opportunity to have them come through us, but they're not of us. They were never ours, but we were given this beautiful opportunity to have them, mold them, and be with them. Now, like the arrow that flies forth from the bow, our child is going off into the world. Also, remember that where that arrow ends up is in large part based on the bow itself. You are the bow your child has been sent from, and the direction that they're going is the direction that you've given them. Have faith and find peace in this knowledge.

It is also important to remember that everyone comes into this world with their own karmic package. If you have an apple seed, you may plant it in the most fertile ground, water it perfectly, and make sure it gets exactly the right amount of sunlight, but if you were hoping for peaches you're going to be disappointed. You can sing it peach songs, do peach dances, read peach books to it, plant it in a grove of peach trees, yell "Peach!" at it all day every day but you'll never get peaches from an apple seed. The best you're going to get is apples. But if you keep yelling "Peach!" at it, you might actually scare the apple tree from growing at all. Then neither will you get peaches, nor will you get apples. So your attachment to your own agenda for what your child becomes and how they live can actually paralyze them and thwart them from reaching their fullest potential.

So remember that you are the bow that has sent your children on their way. The direction is based on what you've taught them and given them. And simultaneously remember your children are also those seeds that have come into this world with their own karmic package, their own dharma. Let go with faith that whatever that seed contains will blossom and give the best fruit it is meant to give.

When I first decided to move to India, I was twenty-five. I had graduated from Stanford and was in the midst of a PhD program when I traveled to India, had this incredible spiritual experience, and stayed on for a few months. Swamiji made me go back to finish my next semester of the PhD program, but I knew I needed to be in India. Everybody told me, "You're making a horrible mistake. You shouldn't go back to India. You should stay here, finish your degree, get yourself established, and then maybe, if you want, you can take off a year or two and go to India. But don't go now. Make sure to get yourself settled and established first." I knew I was meant to go then, not after I had made a name for myself, not after I had taken care of finishing my degree and getting everything established. I knew the call had come and I must answer it.

My mom, of course, was also quite against me going. You can imagine the overprotective, anxious American mother of an only child, who assumed her daughter would live a "normal" life. So she also tried to persuade me not to move to India. I asked my dad how he felt. He is a very calm, deeply thoughtful, and introspective person, and my mom usually dominated in our family discussions. I wanted to know how he really felt about my decision, as I have always trusted him deeply. He said, "In twenty-five years, you've never made a decision that I thought was wrong. I don't understand this decision, but just because I don't understand it, who am I to assume that suddenly you have started making wrong decisions?"

This was amazing for the father of a twenty-five-year-old who had just announced that she was leaving her PhD program and moving to an ashram in India. I share this story because, for me, that's really the most perfect ideal of parenting. It is blue-ribbon parenting of a young adult. "I know you, and I trust you." Parenting our young adult children is not about micromanaging their decisions. It's not about asking every day, "Who are you going out with? Where are you going? What time are you going to be home? Is your homework done?" It's about, "I know you. You're my son. You're my daughter. I trust you, which means that the decisions you make are going to be right for you."

This is really the time to shift from being a father or mother to being a friend. Your child should be able to tell you anything, especially when they move away for school or work. If they fear sharing their dilemmas or troubles with you because they worry about your reaction, they'll keep quiet. You don't want that. You want your children to know that you're always going to love and support them, and they should feel free to tell you anything. So before they go, promise them that you will not judge them for anything they share. Keep the communication pathway open, supportive, and judgment-free.

These days, going off to college or moving away for a career is not even much of a separation anymore, because smartphones keep you in touch constantly. So just keep anchoring deeply in your faith in the direction you've given them, and keep the channels of communication open so the relationship keeps blossoming.

Parents

You've said that our expectations are the cause of our worries and problems. But what about our relationships with our siblings and our parents? Aren't we allowed to expect something from them?

Expectations are not inherently bad. We expect justice in life. Of course we do. We expect that the roof of our house will not fall on us when we're asleep, that the sun will rise in the morning, that when we treat someone with love they will treat us with love. There's nothing wrong with that. We have to have some degree of expectation. If we couldn't expect that the roof won't collapse overnight or that our heater won't catch fire and burn down our house, we could never go to sleep. Expectations are the only way we can move through the world.

Similarly, with our family members we have an expectation that they will love us, love one another, and treat us with respect and care. There is nothing wrong with those expectations. The problem arises, however, when our expectations are not fulfilled. How do we respond then? If you examine your expectations deeply, you will notice that, along with the expectation, is a sense of entitlement to having the expectation fulfilled. If you do not feel entitled to having the universe fulfill your expectations, you will not be disappointed when it doesn't! But look at how we react when our expectations are not fulfilled. Typically not well.

That is the key to frustration or peace. Our own reaction is the only thing we have control over. We hold expectations of our parents, our siblings, God, our elected officials, those dispensing justice in our courts, and we expect that they will do the right thing. In our home, we expect that there will be love, respect, honesty, care, and protection. But, the key to preventing misery in life is to hold those expectations lightly. Hold them with the awareness that our family is made up of fallible human beings who have their own karmic package, their own strengths, weaknesses, fears, unfulfilled expectations, and frustrations. They are moving through the world with their own toolkit. Sometimes, they act in ways that are *not* what we expect.

We have no control over others' words or deeds. When family members and loved ones hurt and betray us, it is due to their lack of mindfulness, their lack of presence, connection, and skill in that moment. The moment may have required patience or compassion and at that moment they didn't have that virtue in their toolbox. Sometimes we expect people to read our minds: "You should have known I wanted that. How did you not know?" *Especially* from our loved ones we frequently expect this. They may ask what's wrong, and we say, "Nothing." And when they move on, we get offended and say, "You should have asked again. You should have known I was upset." This is ridiculous, because they did ask and we said, "Nothing." Our hurt is frequently based on the lack of a proper communication channel, either verbal or nonverbal. Inadvertently we get hurt, the person in front of us has no idea why, we say nothing is wrong, they move on, and then we're more hurt. It's a ridiculous, vicious cycle that plays itself out in homes across the world.

Since we can only control ourselves, the question is, "How can I be in peace and love when my family members are hurting me? How can I know that they love me, that they didn't do this on purpose, that they didn't mean to?"

Our highest expectation should be of ourselves: I *will* stay connected, I *will* stay grounded. As Pujya Swamiji says, others may go up and down but I don't have to go up and down with them. I'm not a puppet. Just because someone is my family member, I don't have to let them pull my strings and make me dance. I'll stay connected and grounded. This way, I become a nexus of love, an energy center of love and peace in the family, and it changes not only me but the whole family.

How can we resolve conflict between our parents?

We are not here to change other people's karmic packages or to judge them as good or bad. For children whose parents are fighting, it's important to remember that their parents came into this world and into this marriage with very specific karma they had to work out, lessons they needed to learn, and experiences they needed to have. Kids frequently find themselves stuck in the middle.

It's important for children to love both parents without letting one use them against the other parent. This is where, as in every circumstance in life, our own internal grounding is so important.

Pujya Swamiji always says that if you are in peace, you will spread peace, but if you are in pieces, you will only spread pieces. If you can experience love, you will manifest love. So if you can experience love and peace with your mom, you'll bring her that. If you can experience love and peace with your dad, you'll bring him that. But never think that you will be able to solve their conflict or bring happiness to their misery or that you are the cause of the conflict or misery. You're neither the cause nor the solution. What you are is just someone who ended up in this situation due to your own karmic journey, and your lesson lies in knowing and accepting that they both love you, and you love them both, even though they don't always get along. It's neither good nor bad, neither right nor wrong. It's just what is. But none of it is your fault, and none of it is yours to solve.

Make sure that you do not internalize the conflict between your parents and re-create it in your life. Do not bring their conflict into your own relationships as a pattern you've learned and internalized.

As parents, if you are fighting with each other, try to avoid fighting in front of your children. It causes them deep anxiety and makes the foundation of stablility in their lives begin to wobble. Children need to feel secure in the home and especially with their parents. If there isn't stability, your children will likely carry these struggles throughout their lives. It doesn't mean that you can never fight with each other or that you have to pretend to agree on everything. It means simply to try to maintain a peaceful, loving, stable environment around your children as much as you can.

Once, a young sister and brother came to see Swamiji. "We want to drop out of school," they said. "We do not see any point in education." Swamiji assured them that education was of the utmost importance and asked why they had lost interest. "Our mother is an MD and our father is a PhD but every day when they come home all they do is fight! What is the point of their degrees if they do nothing but fight?" Not only do our children get deterred from marriage, but they also get deterred from education!

Living Through the Golden Years

What's the best way to live as seniors in the golden years of our lives?

Indian tradition delineates four phases or ashrams, of life, each with its own duties and responsibilities. First, is the stage of childhood and education. That is our *brahmacharya* ashram of life. Our duty is to study, to learn, to imbibe not only knowledge but also wisdom, to dive not only into books but also into the nature of our true selves.

The second phase of life is the *grihasth* ashram, which is the householder phase. In this phase, the primary duty is to establish oneself on a career path and have a family. In this phase we must bring home the bread, take care of our family members, tend our home, earn money, and use that money wisely for ourselves, our communities, and the world.

Then we retire. This is known as the *vanprastha* ashram, and features a slow withdrawal of constant engagement with the outside world. Our children are grown. They are taking care of themselves. We no longer need to put food on the table or a roof over anyone's head. We've earned enough and achieved enough, and now we start to turn more purposely and intentionally to our spiritual practice.

The final phase is the *sanyas* ashram. These are the golden years of sanyas, when we pull away from things of the material world, let go of our attachments to people and possessions, and in preparation for leaving our bodies, connect deeply to the Divine, to our soul, which is eternal and immortal.

By the time we reach our golden years, we've completed our worldly duties. We've finished our education, accumulated money, had our family, raised our children, educated them, watched their careers develop, and seen them married. So it is time to turn to our sanyas, the time of life where we dedicate our attention and focus to God. Otherwise the binding cycle of attachment never ends.

There was once a young disciple living in an ashram with his guru. One day he says to his guru, "You know, I'm living here, but my mind is really on the outer world. I want to know what it's like, what it would be like to have a family and live in that world. So I think, Guruji, maybe I should go for a short while. I just want to experience it once, and then I'm going to come right back. I want my mind to at least know what it's like. Otherwise maybe I'll have regrets my whole life."

So the guru says, "*Chalo*, okay, take ten years, go out, get married, have your family, do your thing. But in ten years' time, come back."

The boy leaves the ashram for the material world, promising to return. Ten years later, he doesn't come back. One day there's a knock at the door of his house. His wife answers and there's an old man on the doorstep asking for her husband. The man sees the visitor, immediately recognizes his guru, and falls at his feet. The guru says, "Okay, now come with me. Your ten years are over."

But the man says, "No, I can't, because you see my children are very young. My poor wife would be all alone. What is she going to do? There are three mouths to feed and the kids are in school. We just got our house. I only need five more years, just to get them settled. Let the kids grow a little more, and then I'll leave my wife some money in the bank."

The guru goes away. He gives him not five years but fifteen years. Fifteen years later, the guru comes back and says to the man, "Okay, now what?"

The man says, "Oh, Guruji, I'd love to come, but now we've got grandkids, and they're babies. They really need me because my son is working and he's out all day long, so they need someone to take care of the grandkids. Just give me a few more years."

Five years later, when the guru returns, he sees that the man is not there, but there's a dog in front of the house. He immediately recognizes that his disciple has reincarnated as a dog. He says to the dog, "Now what?" And the dog says, "Yes, I know. I died. I've reincarnated as this dog to protect them, and I have to stay here another few years because now they're doing very well, but they have so many enemies. Everyone's out to get them, and that's why I'm here as this dog to protect them. Guruji, just give me another couple of years."

So the guru goes away and returns a few years later. This time, two young children answer the door. The guru can instantly see what has transpired since he left. He tells them, "Go upstairs near the family safe. You will find a hole in the wall next to the safe. In that hole is a snake—bring me that snake. Do not kill it, but break its back so it doesn't hurt you."

The children, of course, are very surprised, but they do as this old wise man tells them. They go in, find the snake in the hole in the wall, break its back, and bring it to the guru.

They ask him, "But how did you know there was a snake in the wall? You've never been in our house before." The guru replies, "Do not worry. Just go back inside."

He takes the snake, slings it over his back, and walks away. As he walks, he tells his disciple, now in the form of the snake, "See? There's no end. You came back as a snake to protect the wealth. First it was the wife and the kids, then the grandkids, then you needed to come back as the dog to protect them, now you're a snake to guard the wealth in the safe. There's no end. There's no such thing as just one more time, just another year. You have to draw that line, because attachment doesn't stop."

The same is true of most people's lives. When we reach this phase of sanyas, the teaching of the scriptures is to renounce. But it doesn't mean we abandon what we have spent our life nurturing. This is an important distinction. The sanyas phase of life doesn't mean, "I don't see you, I don't talk to you, I don't care about you, I forget your birthdays."

It doesn't even necessarily mean we must walk away on a physical level. Detachment from the material world and reattachment to the spiritual world must take place at the level of our mind: our intention and attention. Often we may pull away physically. We may leave behind our family and live in an ashram in the mountains. But if our minds are still with the family, if our attachment is still there, then for all practical purposes we are still there, even if our body has moved to an ashram or an isolated mountain cave.

Just because someone is meditating in a cave doesn't necessarily mean they're free from attachment and illusion. There are people living in caves who spend all day checking their WhatsApp and social media. Conversely, there are many people living in families, doing their duties in the world, who are actually more spiritual and more detached on a spiritual level than some of the so-called spiritual people living in isolation. The detachment must be in our mind, in our focus and awareness, not only where our body is sitting.

The sanyas phase of life means that inside I am not stuck. I am not sitting down to meditate but finding myself unable to do so because I'm wondering how my grandson is doing on his math exam today. It's an inner state of renunciation.

Of course, if you can go live in an ashram, that's great. There's nothing like it; it's the ideal situation. You can live out the golden years in sadhana, in seva. You've spent your whole life working for yourself and your family, and now you give your energy, experience, and expertise to the world. Your family expands. When we talk about sanyas being a renunciation of family, it doesn't literally mean that you have no family. It means that the world becomes your family. You've gone from having a family of two or four to having a family comprising all of creation, more than eight billion humans and all the animals and plants on this earth. Sanyas doesn't mean that you don't care about anyone; it means you care about everyone. The scriptures teach us "*Vasudhaiva kutumbakam*"—the world is one family.

Thus, sanyas in the golden years becomes a benefit to your own spiritual growth, to your preparation for that final transformation. You've been a benefit to your family; now you're able to be a benefit to the global family.

However, the teachings of sanyas can apply and benefit you spiritually throughout your entire life, not only in the golden years. There is no phase of life in which you should be attached to the things of this world. Even while doing your duty in the workplace in the householder phase of life, you work for your family members but don't get attached to the fruits of that work or to the people you are working for. The Bhagavad Gita and other scriptures remind us in so many ways that, whatever phase of life we are in, ultimately the highest teaching is to recognize our true self, to not get stuck in maya or illusion, to not be distracted by attachment or desire. This pertains just as much to the householder phase as it does the sanyas phase. The difference is that in the householder phase we are still doing the work, earning money for the family. Our hands are doing work in the world, fulfilling our duty, but our attention and intention should be focused on God.

We perform our duties in all phases of life so that even earning a living or raising a family does not thwart our highest purpose, which is self-realization or God-realization. Our relationships, duty, and actions are a powerful way of expanding our consciousness and walking the path to awakening. But if we get stuck, it thwarts our progress.

Sanyas is a very beautiful and natural stage of preparation for departure from the physical realm. Otherwise, when death comes, if we're still attached to the physical plane of existence, we're not able to let go. This is what creates the bondage of the soul. This is what is meant by the soul being stuck, not being able to go forward, to attain that ultimate union with God, or to go on the next incarnation. So sanyas ashram is a preparatory phase where we say, "God, whether I have two years left or twenty, these are my golden years. At some point I'm going to return to You. My form will change again; it's changed from young boy to young man to old man, then it's going to turn to ashes, and I need to prepare myself for that. I need to stop identifying as the physical body and shift my identification to the soul, the spirit, consciousness, that which doesn't change and that which doesn't die."

There is a beautiful prayer in the Upanishads that says:

Om asato maa sad-gamaya
Tamaso maa jyotir-gamaya
Mrtyor-maa amrtam gamaya
Om shaantih shaantih shaantih

It means, "Oh God lead us from falsehood to truth. Lead us from the darkness of ignorance to the light of wisdom. Lead us from the false identification with the transitory physical body to the true identification with the eternal, immortal soul."

CONCLUSION

Welcome home to yourself. Through these pages you've learned that spirituality is not about becoming something or someone else. It's about becoming *you,* the truth of who *you* are. The power of satsang, the presence of divine truth, is that it opens the space for us to recognize the truth within ourselves. Through the questions and answers in this book, I hope you have had the experience of delving into your own truth and a deeper, fuller, and more spacious experience of your own self.

Now you have the opportunity to hold this truth in your heart and live it. Spirituality is not an academic exercise. The point of embarking on a spiritual journey and walking a spiritual path is not to merely imbibe semantically the wisdom of others. It's not about reading, listening, and then being able to say, "I've read such and such," or "I've learned such and such." Spirituality is not measured by how many authors you can quote or what tips you know. It's measured by how you live. It's measured by the light and peace you experience within yourself and exude in the world.

Through these pages you've read questions that people like you have asked regarding topics and situations that probably apply to your life as well. It may not be an exact match. Someone may have a grudge against a parent and you have a grudge against a sister-in-law or coworker. Or perhaps someone is struggling with her husband and you are struggling with your adult child. The experiences vary from person to person, but the

COME HOME TO YOURSELF

core suffering is the same and therefore the teachings are the same. The truth is the same even when circumstances differ. We must learn to be energetic transmitters of love and peace regardless of whether the negativity in our lives comes from our in-laws, our neighbors, or our colleagues. We must let go, forgive, and unhook our peace from other people's actions, whether they are our spouses, our siblings, or our extended family.

I've written a lot in this book about the power of our own minds to create our destiny. Remember, no one is injecting you with misery or anger, jealousy or resentment. When you feel those emotions or feeling states it is because you have chosen to co-create that reality for yourself. Just as we stay away from food that we know will upset our stomachs, we must avoid engaging in thought patterns or communication patterns that will poison our minds and hearts with misery. Indigestion, vomiting, and diarrhea are not worth it, no matter how appealing the street food may have been. Similarly, inner discontentment, tension, and conflict are not worth it, no matter how irritating or upsetting the circumstances may be. Just as we have the power to say no to unsafe food and choose to eat an apple instead to protect the health of our bodies, we must realize we have the power to say no to thoughts of resentment, jealousy, anger, and greed. We must choose thoughts of love instead, and protect the health of our minds and hearts.

Note that this is not a suggestion to repress or suppress or spiritually bypass. It is not a recommendation to pretend you aren't hurt or angry. That serves no one and ends up causing deeper harm later on. Becoming free is not about hiding your stuckness or ignoring it. Becoming free is about consciously choosing how you will live, how you will think, what you will focus your attention on, and what you will let go of. Ultimately, as you move through the world—regardless of the roles you play—the connection to the truth of *you*, the depth of *you*, the fullness, wholeness, and divinity of *you*, is what will determine whether you live in peace or in pieces, whether you feel whole or full of holes. The boundless, borderless, eternal consciousness that is you is accessible whether you are a stay-at-home parent, a CEO, married or unmarried, twenty or eighty. Each of us has the same purpose in life—to discover and experience the truth of ourselves, the highest, deepest, fullest truth that is one with both the Creator and all of creation, as well as with unmanifest, infinite, pure consciousness. It's never too early or too late. The right time is now.

Take some time and allow yourself to actually implement and live these teachings. Take this book as a course of Peace 101 or Happiness 101 for your life. It's a course to be engaged with. So take these teachings and live them. Begin anywhere. Begin with whichever question or answer touched you the most deeply as you read. Start there and see how you can implement that teaching today. Then tomorrow take another one. If need be, take a week to fully absorb the meaning and depth of each question and answer.

Spirituality is not a race or competition. It's an unfolding. Think of the way rose petals open to the sun—slowly, gracefully, but fully. That is the point. Open fully. Let it be slow if that's what your heart and mind need. But let each petal of you, each aspect of you that causes suffering to yourself or others, each aspect that is rooted in ignorance and illusion, each aspect that is running on autopilot rather than being deeply present, let each aspect open fully to the light of truth. And then, like a rose, share your fragrance with the world. The dharma of a flower is to be fragrant. Give your light like that. Give not for what you'll get in return, but give because it is your nature to share your light, to share your fragrance, to share your love.

And if you have found these teachings inspiring, share them with others. One cannot actually gift wisdom or spirituality to someone else. But we can gift books that impart wisdom and enhance spirituality. That is what most people need, much more than another sweater, picture frame, or handbag. So gift this book to your loved ones and friends. Have a study group where you take one question at a time and discuss how this applies to you in your lives.

And come home to Rishikesh. If, as you read the book, you could feel as though you were sitting on the banks of the Ganga, at Parmarth Niketan ashram, if you could feel the sacred breeze that flows off the tops of the towering Himalayas and across the waters of the rushing Ganga, then my goal has been achieved. But there is something uniquely special about actually being here. So come home. Come and sit in satsang and together let us dive even further into the divine ocean of truth. You are always welcome.

ACKNOWLEDGMENTS

How can I even begin to acknowledge the amazing people whose love, support, guidance, and assistance have gone into this book? First and foremost, of course, is HH Pujya Swami Chidanand Saraswatiji, whose closed-eye, meditative pronouncement of "Sadhviji" nearly twenty years ago catapulted my journey into giving satsang. Rather than simply answer the question he was asked, he used that moment to send me onto a brand-new path in life—a path of leading satsang, a path of allowing me to get my ego-self out of the way so that grace could flow through me. It was the spiritual equivalent of being thrown into the deep end! And yet he knew that I would find my metaphoric fins to swim and also that my life's dharma was to help others across the stormy waters of confusion, despair, hopelessness, frustration, and misery.

My entire family at Parmarth Niketan have supported the evening satsang so beautifully, taking loving care of all those who pour in each night after the sacred Ganga arti (lighting ceremony on the River Ganga) and also curating questions from our online audience. Without you all, there would be no public evening satsang, and thus, no book! Thank you for your dedication and commitment to this daily offering. You are the beautiful, powerful wings on which this wisdom is being carried across the world.

I'm so grateful to the entire team at Mandala Publishing who saw the great value in sharing this wisdom internationally, realizing that truth transcends all borders and boundaries of time, place, race, and religion. If it is true in the Himalayas, it is true in Houston, Honolulu, and the Hudson Valley! If it is true for the person who asked the question, it is true for all of us! The team at Mandala have taken this book from the original Penguin publication in India to a much longer, deeper, more comprehensive, and more cohesive compilation of wisdom on the universal questions that plague our minds and hearts.

And I'm so grateful to you all: those who come personally and sit together in satsang; those who connect online from your rooms, homes, offices, and dorms across the world; and those who are reading this book. Inherent in the word *satsang* is the word *sangha*, or community. Our spiritual community is one of the greatest, strongest pillars of our own growth, development, awakening, and realization. Thank you for being part of our sangha.